Southern Scholars in Goethe's Germany

UNC | COLLEGE OF ARTS AND SCIENCES
Germanic and Slavic Languages and Literatures

From 1949 to 2004, UNC Press and the UNC Department of Germanic & Slavic Languages and Literatures published the UNC Studies in the Germanic Languages and Literatures series. Monographs, anthologies, and critical editions in the series covered an array of topics including medieval and modern literature, theater, linguistics, philology, onomastics, and the history of ideas. Through the generous support of the National Endowment for the Humanities and the Andrew W. Mellon Foundation, books in the series have been reissued in new paperback and open access digital editions. For a complete list of books visit www.uncpress.org.

Southern Scholars in Goethe's Germany

JOHN T. KRUMPELMANN

UNC Studies in the Germanic Languages and Literatures
Number 51

Copyright © 1965

This work is licensed under a Creative Commons CC BY-NC-ND license. To view a copy of the license, visit http://creativecommons.org/licenses.

Suggested citation: Krumpelmann, John T. *Southern Scholars in Goethe's Germany*. Chapel Hill: University of North Carolina Press, 1965. DOI: https://doi.org/10.5149/9781469657684_Krumpelmann

Library of Congress Cataloging-in-Publication Data
Names: Krumpelmann, John T.
Title: Southern scholars in Goethe's Germany / by John T. Krumpelmann.
Other titles: University of North Carolina Studies in the Germanic Languages and Literatures ; no. 51.
Description: Chapel Hill : University of North Carolina Press, [1965] Series: University of North Carolina Studies in the Germanic Languages and Literatures. | Includes bibliographical references.
Identifiers: LCCN 65008919 | ISBN 978-1-4696-5767-7 (pbk: alk. paper) | ISBN 978-1-4696-5768-4 (ebook)
Subjects: Americans — Germany. | Learning and scholarship — Southern States.
Classification: LCC PD25 .N6 NO. 51 | DCC 378/ .430922

To the Memory of my Brother
ERNEST HENRY KRUMPELMANN
NEW ORLEANS
1894-1923

CONTENTS

PREFACE XI
1. INTRODUCTION 1
2. SOUTH CAROLINA – HUGH SWINTON LEGARÉ 6
3. MARYLAND – GEORGE HENRY CALVERT 23
4. VIRGINIA – JESSE BURTON HARRISON 46
5. THOMAS CAUTE REYNOLDS, SOUTH CAROLINA, VIRGINIA MISSOURI 77
6. BASIL LANNEAU GILDERSLEEVE, SOUTH CAROLINA, VIRGINIA, MARYLAND 104
7. JAMES WOODROW, SOUTH CAROLINA 134
8. MATH AND AFTERMATH, SOUTH CAROLINA 149
   a. OSCAR MONTGOMERY LIEBER 149
   b. DAVID RAMSAY 153
   c. THOMAS E. HART 157
9. EPILOGUE 159
10. NOTES 163
11. INDEX 193

PREFACE

The scholarly tradition that prevailed in the aristocratic circles of the old South made formal learning a desirable goal for its post-Revolutionary youth. The fact that German universities then began to attract Southern students away from the previously visited British institutions was due at least in part to the influence which Harvard University and its "Literary Pioneers" exerted both directly and through the founder of the University of Virginia, Thomas Jefferson, on ambitious young intellectuals of the Southern States.

The present volume owes its origin to the study of my late friend and colleague, Professor Orie William Long, *Literary Pioneers. Early American Explorers of European Culture* (Harvard University Press, 1935).

The collecting of material for the present volume was in some cases difficult and laborious due to the dearth of readily available source material in a region ravaged by a long period of martial vicissitudes in which many of the scholars mentioned here were participants and *ipso facto* victims. However extensive research conducted in the libraries and other repositories of manuscript material in the United States and Germany has yielded results which seem to merit publication. The principal fruitful sources have proved to be the holding of the University of South Carolina, the University of Virginia, the Johns Hopkins University, Columbia University, Harvard University, the Huntington Library at San Merino, California, and the Library of Congress. Other prime sources of information were the Archives of the Missouri Historical Society in St. Louis and the collection of the Pennsylvania Historical Society in Philadelphia. In Germany an academic year was spent in an examination of the archives and other records of the universities of Göttingen, Marburg, Bonn, Heidelberg, Munich, Hamburg, and Berlin (Humboldt).

To the officers and members of the staff of each of the above-named institutions, as well as to the staff of the library of Louisiana State University and to other officials and scholars mentioned in the text and notes of the following composition the author herewith wishes to express his sincere gratitude for their kindness and the interest manifested in the labor involved in this undertaking.

To Herren H. Kossach and Ernst Rombeau of the Humboldt University, Berlin, I feel especially indebted for their extraordinary courtesy and cooperation. Nor can I close without acknowledging the obligation and gratitude I feel to the United States Educational Commission in Bad Godesberg (Fulbright Commission) for facilitating my extended visit to Germany.

JOHN T. KRUMPELMANN

Louisiana State University
Baton Rouge, Louisiana
October 1964

INTRODUCTION

The publication by the Harvard University Press in 1935 of Orie William Long's *Literary Pioneers. Early American Explorers of European Culture* was an invitation to extend, both chronologically and geographically, the exploration of the field of German-American cultural relations. Professor Harold S. Jantz's "German Thought and Literature in New England, 1620-1820",[1] is an extension of this research chronologically, whereas the present author's *Bayard Taylor and German Letters* (1959),[2] the outgrowth of a Harvard dissertation "Bayard Taylor as a Literary Mediator between Germany and America" (1924) essays to extend the field both geographically and chronologically.

In the present volume the period investigated extends from that contemporaneous with Professor Long's era to the last quarter of the Nineteenth century and changes the locale from New England to the states south of the Mason and Dixon line. There is no intention to set up a rivalry between the two regions. In fact, of the six "scholars" presented in this study both George Henry Calvert and Jesse Burton Harrison obtained an earned degree from Harvard; a third, James Woodrow, studied in residence there and Basil Lanneau Gildersleeve was awarded an honorary degree by that university. Not only did Hugh Swinton Legaré die in the Boston home of his bosom friend, George Ticknor, but, almost immediately after Legaré's decease, Joseph Story, Associate Justice of the Supreme Court and Dane Professor of Law at Harvard, in eulogizing his fellow-jurist before the members of the Harvard Law School concluded:[3]

> I dismiss the subject with the remark, that the Constitution has lost one of its best friends; the Supreme Court one of its brightest ornaments; the country an inestimable man, whose independence, whose public virtue, whose rare endowments, and whose freedom from all the arts of popularity gave full assurance of a life of the highest value to the State.

Only the ubiquitous Thomas C. Reynolds was without close ties with Harvard University, but Dr. Reynolds' Heidelberg dissertation received generous and favorable notice in *The Law Reporter* (Boston), edited by Peleg W. Chandler.[4]

Furthermore, it will be noted that the representatives of the Southern States present a less homogeneous civilization than that presented by the conservative, Puritan inhabitants of close-knit, Anglo-Saxon, but anti-Anglican, New England. As the very names of the Southern States echo the nomenclature of English royalty, so we find in George Henry Calvert the blood-strains of Lord Baltimore and Peter Paul Rubens. If the French of Acadia are known to New Englanders through the fictional Basil, the Blacksmith, of Longfellow's "Evangeline," this same race is known to the South Carolinians through representatives of the maternal side of the family of Basil Lanneau Gildersleeve. The Gallic element in South Carolina is further represented by Hugh Swinton Legaré of Huguenot ancestry. While Thomas Caute Reynolds was proud of his tidewater Virginian ancestry and boldly proclaimed the vocation of his father as "slave-owner," Jesse Burton Harrison from the Piedmont region of the Old Dominion was of Puritan-Quaker leaning and an early and prime advocate of the abolition of slavery. James Woodrow, a native Scot, came to the South *via* Canada and Ohio and became a most loyal Confederate. Needless to say, he was a Presbyterian, a minister, – the uncle of President Woodrow Wilson.

These "scholars" were, as every true scholar needs must be, pioneers in the truest sense of the word. Not only was a South Carolinian, Philippus Tidyman, the first American to earn a doctor's degree at Göttingen (1800) but T.C. Reynolds and George Guerard, both Charlestonians, were, as far as I have been able to discover, the first Americans to matriculate at the University of Munich and Charles Boehme of Baltimore the first North American to register in Heidelberg (October 29, 1831). And they remained pioneers throughout their careers; witness the fact that of the six principals here discussed not one died in his native land. Legaré, Reynolds and Gildersleeve, all native Charlestonians, deceased in Boston, Saint Louis and Baltimore, respectively. Calvert of Maryland died in Newport, Rhode Island. Harrison of Virginia passed away in New Orleans, and Woodrow, a native Scot, succumbed in South Carolina. Contrast this with Professor Long's "Pioneers," all of whom, with the exception of the two historians, Bancroft and Motley, died in their native Massachusetts.

A word should be said about the connotation "Goethe's Germany." It must not be construed so literally as to mean the period between 1749 and 1832, but it embraces also that Germany in which the spirit of Goethe continued to prevail even after the physical death of the poet. To be sure two of the "scholars" introduced in these pages did visit Johann Wolfgang Goethe in Weimar and tarry there at the Ducal Court perhaps longer than any one of Professor Long's New Englanders would have relished attending the ceremonials and social functions connected with court life. A third Southern scholar, Reynolds, remained in Weimar a month and was introduced to the Court through the good offices of his friend, Ottilie von Goethe, the daughter-in-law of the poet. The others came no nearer to Weimar than did Longfellow. But Legaré, like Longfellow, did visit August Wilhelm Schlegel in Bonn in 1835, but at greater length and with more conviviality. Gildersleeve mourned the passing of Goethe's Germany when Bismarck, the friend of John Lothrop Motley, changed Goethe's Germany into a new Deutsches Reich. James Woodrow's silence about the Sage of Weimar seems significant since German science had led this Presbyterian divine and scientist to become an evolutionist, even as Goethe before him had been led by his own scientific studies to anticipate certain phases of Darwinism. But Woodrow of South Carolina remained a churchman.

It is not the purpose of this study to prove, but merely to present in some systematic sequence a series of facts that have all too long lain undisclosed to critical observation. Not even the South itself has generally realized what attraction German universities and German learning has long possessed for its gifted and privileged youth. In the closing pages of my study "Young Southern Scholars in Goethe's Germany" published in the *Jahrbuch für Amerikastudien* in 1959[5] I made some general remarks concerning the attendance of the youth of the South at German universities and expressed mild skepticism as to the adequacy of the data available at that time. As the validity of the statements there made is confirmed in the subsequent pages of the present study, the following utterance, published in 1835, will suffice to exemplify the opinion of the German university system held in Southern literary circles over a century ago:[6]

> What preserves in its original strength and grandeur the rich and massy arch of German literature? The incomparable exertions of the German student. The student whose mind knows no other commune than the thoughts of the mighty dead. The German student who knows the power and majesty of truth, and thinks no care, nor labor too great to possess it... The universities of Germany are unexcelled in the world. Is it wonderful that its literature is unequalled? ... Let the youthful mind be taught to ascribe as much value, as much greatness, as much immortality, to literary as to political interests. Let this be done and our universities will surpass even those of Germany, will furnish their country, instead of Schillers and Goethes, their prototypes Shakespeares and Miltons.

That fewer of the Southern scholars who studied in German universities have become renowned than have the "Literary Pioneers" of New England, is, in the judgment of the present writer, due to differences in the kinds of social order in which they lived. In composite, ecclesiastical, mercantile New England industry and commerce necessitated the rise of communities which in turn demanded their leaders. Here men of education and erudition achieved for themselves careers in the ministry, in the fields of law and politics, or in the domain of letters, where close-knit society encouraged and made possible the sustentation of journalistic enterprises. Accordingly so many of our New England "Explorers" made for themselves careers in one or more of these quasi-learned fields. In the vast domains of the agrarian South the planter could be a "gentleman", but he was denied the close intellectual contacts afforded by church-meetings and journalistic enterprises. Plantations were too remote from each other to promote a facile exchange of ideas, oral or written, between scholarly neighbors. Ministers were likely to be itinerant and hardly members of a community. Hence the Southerner spoke to rare audiences and became an orator, or he read in his own library and became more learned, whereas the New England scholar became, through intimate contact with neighbors of like erudition, (either oral or written), a professor or author. It was, in short, largely a matter of communication.

Moreover, witness the contrast between the early faculties of Harvard and of the University of Virginia. The former group was composed almost wholly of New Englanders, if not exclusively of former Harvard students. The first faculty of the Virginia university was almost entirely British. Of course one could not expect a Puritan university to staff its faculty with Royalist scholars from England. On the other hand Virginia, especially tidewater Virginia, was Episcopalian. Harvard even sent its own Everett "to travel and study abroad for two years, previous to assuming his duties"[7] as Eliot Professor of Greek Literature in Cambridge. Harvard sent "'little Bancroft' to Germany on a scholarship"[8] and Bowdin offered to reward her Longfellow with "the chair of modern languages,"[9] provided he would go to Europe to prepare for his duties. But the University of Virginia rejected the applications of Jesse Burton Harrison and of Thomas C. Reynolds, both of whom were alumni of Virginia institutions, the former having an additional degree from Harvard, the latter having a doctor's degree from Heidelberg, when the respective applications were made. Each position was given to a foreigner! No provincialism in the Old Dominion!

And, lest we forget, the outbreak of the War between the States wrought havoc in the ranks of those young scholars who had studied in German universities. Not only did most of them rush from the academic halls into the first of the conflict, but many of them did not survive the hostilities. Those who did return found a society so desolated by war and its aftermath as to render the pursuit of scholarly interests either difficult or impossible.

But, despite the differences in their backgrounds, one finds that there was much in common in the reaction of all these American students to German cultural contacts. At the same time, because of the differences in social heritage and environment, already indicated in the preceding pages, one must expect to discover, and does discover, some different results wrought by contacts with German cultural circles and institutions on the American "scholars" from "down South" and on those from "down East."

SOUTH CAROLINA

HUGH SWINTON LEGARÉ

When Hugh Swinton Legaré of Charleston, South Carolina, in his unique position in the Cabinet of President Tyler, holding the portfolios of both the Attorney General and the Acting Secretary of State, while accompanying the president to the unveiling of the Bunker Hill monument, peacefully passed away in the Boston home, nay in the very arms, of his bosom friend, George Ticknor, on July 20, 1843, a strong cultural bond between the North and the South, which had been nurtured largely by a common enthusiasm for the learning and letters of Germany, was tragically sundered.

Daniel B. Shumway's study "The American Students of the University of Göttingen"[1] reveals that between 1830 and 1860 South Carolina sent more of her sons to study in Göttingen than did any other state with the possible exception of Massachusetts. He lists the names of fifteen South Carolinians who attended that university during the period indicated. A subsequent study, "Die ersten amerikanischen Studenten an der Universität Göttingen" (1956) by Hertha Marquardt[2] notes that when Benjamin Franklin visited Göttingen in 1766 he was accompanied by "his friend, the English physician, Dr. Pringle" [Sir John Pringle, 1707-1782]. It is interesting to observe that at the outbreak of our Civil War sons of the Pringle family, long very prominent in affairs of the state of South Carolina, were studying in German universities.[3]

Marquardt further indicates that the first *bona fide* American student at Göttingen was "Philip Tidyman aus Charleston, South Carolina, (geb. 1777), der am 4. Juni 1800 bei der medizinischen Fakultät immatrikuliert wurde." To quote further:

> However, he seemingly did not desire to continue studying in Göttingen, but only to take an examination, for already one week after his matriculation, he announced to the Dean, Prof. Gmelin, that he desired to take an examination. He was examined in June, 1800, by Professors Wrisberg, Richter and Blumenbach. Tidyman has ibeen accordingly the first American to pass a doctoral examination in Göttingen.

His dissertation *De Orysa Sativa*, a fitting subject for a South Carolinian, was submitted "Pro Gradu Doctoris Medicinae et Chirugiae" on July 24, 1800, prefaced with two dedications in Latin, one to his maternal uncle Hugh Rose and the other to his brother-in-law John Drayton (1766-1812), Governor of South Carolina from 1800 to 1802 and from 1808 to 1810. The document conferring the degree sought is dated July 24, 1800, and signed by the renowned "Dr. Jo. Fr. Blumenbach (Decanus)." The dissertation was published in Göttingen in 1800.

When Herzog Bernhard of Saxe-Weimar-Eisenach visited Charleston, December 16-19, 1826, he received a visit from Dr. Tidyman, whom he had known in Philadelphia, who accompanied him when he visited public institutions of Charleston, showed him a rice mill and "honoured me with a dinner, at which I met several of the distinguished inhabitants of the place, as Mr. Lowndes, Major Gardene ... and Mr. J. Allen Smith."[4]

> The Duke also further states of the last named[5]:
> Mr. Joseph Allen Smith, who passed seventeen years of his life in Europe [circa 1791-1808], principally in Russia, and enjoyed the especial favor of the Emperor Alexander. He was present at my brother's marriage and inquired after him in the most ardent manner. This extremely amiable and interesting man had lost the greater part of his property.

When we recall that Bernhard's brother, Herzog Carl Friedrich of Saxe-Weimar-Eisenach (1828-1853), the elder son of Goethe's patron, Karl August, married Marie Paulowna, daughter of Czar Paul of Russia, in St. Petersburg on June 14, 1804, we know how and when Joseph Allen Smith (1796-November 29, 1828), and his friend, Joel Roberts Poinsett (1779-1851), both of Charleston, South Carolina, became so well known in Weimar. When we discover that Poinsett, who had returned to Europe in 1806 to carry out his long-cherished plan of travelling in Russia, "was indebted to his friend Smith for 'his favorable introduction to the Court of St. Petersburg'",[6] and learn that Czar Alexander told him that he "was the second American gentleman who had visited Russia" and "was glad to hear that I was a friend of Mr. Allen Smith who was remembered in Russia with esteem and whose departure was universally regretted",[7] we are able to understand why Aaron Burr, the third Vice-President of the United States, noted, while in Weimar, that these two South Carolinians were, at so early a date, known in the court circles there.[8] Hence we wonder whether they were not the first American "gentlemen" scholars to be known in Goethe's Germany.

According to the list of "Goethe's American Visitors", compiled by Ida G. Everson,[9] and "intended to be complete as far as can be determined from the records in the *Tagebücher*"[10] Aaron Burr was the first (January 4 and 7, 1810) and Jesse Burton Harrison of Virginia and later of New Orleans, Louisiana, (March 25 and 27, 1830) was the twentieth and last American to visit Goethe in Weimar. It is especially intriguing that Burr recorded in his diary: "The Americans known [in Weimar] are Smith and Poinsett, both of South Carolina."[11] It has long been known that the latter was Joel Roberts Poinsett, later United States Minister to Mexico (1825-1829), and subsequently Secretary of War in the Cabinet of President Van Buren. The former, until now not properly indentified,[12] was Poinsett's old "fencing friend", Joseph Allen Smith, mentioned above, who was responsible for Poinsett's favorable introduction to the Imperial Court at St. Petersburg, and who, according to Poinsett, "first established amicable relations which have existed between Russia and this country."[13]

Probably the most distinguished scholar of South Carolina to become sufficiently attracted by the erudition of Germany in the early Nineteenth Century to resolve to study at a German university was the above-mentioned Hugh Swinton Legaré. Representing the fifth American generation of the Huguenot family of Solomon Legaré, who in 1695 or 1696 led a band of his co-religionists, including the ancestors of the aforementioned Joel R. Poinsett, to the vicinity of Charleston, Hugh had enjoyed a sound training in classical studies, as well as learning in the law under his distinguished townsman, Mr. Mitchell King, whose sons were later university students in Germany.[13a] Having graduated from the South Carolina College at Columbia with highest honors in December, 1814, and having qualified for admission to the bar, he felt he must go to Europe to complete his education. Late in May of 1818 he embarked at Charleston for Bordeaux. A month later he writes from France of his intention to "proceed to the University of Göttingen" by the end of September.[14] Concerning this trip his sister informs us:[15]

> One of his chief objects was ... to go to the University of Göttingen – one of the best institutions in Europe. It combined everything. The study of Civil Law was foremost in Legaré's catalogue of studies and in that institution he would have a great advantage of pursuing this study as well in German as in Latin. But when he arrived in Paris he learned that the institution was closed and not likely to be opened during that season. This was due to a fracas, not uncommon to the colleges of Germany, between the students and the citizens (in this case the tradesmen.)[16]

Because of this information Legaré resolved to remain in Paris.

In September (1818) he betook himself to the University of Edinburgh where he devoted the winter to the study of law. There he lived with his companion, William C. Preston, later to become, even as Legaré himself became, one of the most illustrious citizens of South Carolina. Here too began his "life-time intimacy with George Ticknor",[17] who at this time wrote from Scotland that "the general estimate of American character had been raised by the presence in the university of William C. Preston and Hugh S. Legaré."[18] Evidently Legaré's desire to study at a German university was reenkindled by Ticknor who was then fresh from his long study at Göttingen (August 4, 1815 - March 26, 1817), for on the fifteenth of February (1819) Legaré reports from Edinburgh his resolution to travel[19] "through Holland" on his way "to Berlin or some other German university." He adds: "There I shall spend May, June, July and August... By becoming a member of a literary institution in Germany, I shall of course get an insight into the character of that important empire – not to mention that, ... I do not despair of being able to add theirs to the languages I already know. Besides, theirs are the greatest – indeed, ... the only *fit* schools in the branch of education that I am now particularly engaged upon." But again "political disturbances" ["Young Germany"] made it inadvisable for him to go to that country."[20] Late in 1819 he sailed for New York.

After serving in the Lower House of the General Assembly of his native state from 1820 to 1822 and again from 1824 until 1830 he became Attorney General of South Carolina, which position he retained until April, 1832, when he was appointed American Chargé d' Affaires in Brussels by another eminent legal light of Louisiana, the Jacksonian Secretary of State, Mr. Edward Livingstone.[21]

During the latter part of this domestic political interlude Legaré played the leading role in the establishment and sustentation of one of the South's most outstanding literary journals of all times, *The Southern Review* of Charleston (February, 1828 - February, 1832). Since the life-span of this periodical was limited to a period prior to Legaré's acquisition of a working knowledge of the German language, and hence before his direct acquaintance with German literature, his critical discussions in this field of learning are rather limited. Nevertheless some of his extensive contributions do betray his interest in, and some knowledge of, German letters and erudition. His initial essay "Classical Learning"[22] is eloquent in its espousal of the German cause, as indicated by the following excerpt.

> In Germany, however, whose learned men, whatever may be thought of the accuracy or refinement of their scholarship,

> are the most impartial, precisely because they are most conversant with universal literature, and with what has been very expressively called its comparative anatomy... If we were called upon to exemplify the difference between sound criticism and the petulant and presumptuous dogmatism of prejudice and ignorance, we should refer to W. Schlegel's course of dramatic literature for the one, and Voltaire's strictures upon the Greek tragedies, in his various prefaces, commentaries, etc., for the other.

The following lines from his review of the *Travels through North America, during the Years* 1825 *and* 1825[23] "by his Highness, Bernhard, Duke of Saxe-Weimar-Eisenach" manifest the attitude of an American Classical scholar to Goethe's Germany in 1829.

> The Germans are, of all nations that ever existed, the fairest in their criticism upon others. Their studies are too enlarged for bigotry, and excessive nationality has never, we believe, been numbered among their faults. This remark is strikingly exemplified in their literary opinions.

In his essay on "Early Spanish Ballads"[24] the opening sentence deals with German literature's deliverance "from the bondage of French authority." There reference is made to "German critics" in general and to Schlegel in particular; but that is all. The article on "Lord Byron's Character and Works" naturally introduces "Goëthe's [*sic!*] famous drama Faustus."[26] Schiller is called an exemplary man.[27] In speaking of "Byron's Letters and Journals"[28] mention of Schlegel occurs in connection with Winckelmann. Now Legaré, referring to A. W. Schlegel's "valuable Lectures on Dramatic Poetry", quotes from lecture five *in extenso* concerning the "distinction between the 'classical' and 'romantic' styles."[29] In evaluating *Manfred*, Goethe's *Faust, Werther*, and *Kunst und Alterthum* are brought into the discussion.[30]

"The Public Economy of Athens" is a critique of a work, in four books, of the same name "translated from the German of Augustus Boechkh, London, 1828" (*Southern Review*, February, 1832). In Legaré's *Writings*[31] a note is appended: "When I wrote this article I had not read Niebuhr's *prolegomena* of his history, with which my introductory remarks sometimes so strangely coincide. – Brussels, November 10, 1834." This gives us a hint as to Legaré's reading shortly before his visit to Niebuhr's successor in Bonn and is a basis for his inquiry concerning Niebuhr on that occasion. Nevertheless he had written in the opening lines of the original text:

> It is but of late years, and first and principally in the Universities of Germany, that the researches of scholars have been directed by the spirit of a distinguishing and comprehensive philosophy.

During these years as editor, author and critic, Legaré felt most keenly the handicap imposed upon him by the insufficiency of his knowledge of the German language. He clearly expressed himself on this point in a series of letters to his young friend Jesse Burton Harrison which have heretofore remained unpublished.[32] On April 2nd, 1829, he writes:

> I think you will gain beyond all calculation more than you can conceive by a residence of two or three years in some literary institution in Europe, or Germany I should prefer. I should have gone there myself, but the universities were all in a commotion when I was in France and I thought it best to go to Edinboro. The advantages of studying in Germany are manifold, but I will remind you of one – the opportunity of becoming thoroughly versed (which I regret I am not) in their language and literature. Their classical studies too are certainly more thorough ... than at any other European universities.

His next letter to Harrison, dated Charleston, 26th August, 1830, shows his vivid interest in classical and philosophical lore, his continued admiration for German scholarship and his appreciation of recognition in the university circles:

> I owe you a thousand apologies for my long neglect of your very interesting letter from Germany... The Homeric question and the primitive languages are great matters. Whoever shall write a really able and learned book upon those subjects (if material for such a book can – – possibly be scraped together) will do an important service to mankind. The notion of treating the most ancient poetry as allegorical is, as you know, as old as Plato and his different schools, but is not the less plausible on that account! Of one thing I am, at all events, sure is that, if any discoveries are to be made in that department of literature, they will be made in Germany. It is impossible not to be struck with the difference between their manner of treating such subjects and that of the most learned English... I attempted in the course of the last summer to exemplify this in a small way. I read thro' Plato's works in the original, with a paraphrase or commentary of

Tiedeman, a Marburg man.³³ I was very much struck with the *Republic* of which I found that no book I had ever read [gave?] me a just idea. My own opinion was submitted to the public in [the] 27th No. of the Southern Review *à propos* of my Cicero's fragment *de Republica*.³⁴ In the course of the disquisition I ran a parallel between that work and the one just [mentioned]; it is an imitation – in some places a mere translation. I should be glad to send it to you but I not [*sic!*] believe it would cost a great deal more than such a thing is worth. I have understood that Mr. [Edward M.] Michaelowitz,³⁵ a Russian, tutor in Oriental languages in the So. Car., [South Carolina College] translated it into German and sent it across the Atlantic.

By the bye that gentleman has mentioned to me what was so flattering to my self-love, that I can scarecely deem it true – which is, Professor Schütz (is it?) of Heidelberg had done me the honor of alluding to some opinions of mine advanced in an article on "Roman Literature" in the *second no.* of "Southern Review" in very favorable terms. I think there must be some mistake about it, as it exceeds my credulity [that] a German professor of expert (?) learning should see anything to admire in speculations of a young lawyer in So. Carolina.

In a letter of January 24, 1832, in which Legaré expresses his willingness to publish Harrison's article on "English Civilization" in the *Review*, he informs the latter by implication of his expected appointment to a position in Europe.

It is more than probable that I shall visit Europe in a very few months, and if I do, the Low Countries, the Rhineland and other parts of Germany will be among my special objects. I shall probably stay there long enough to get a thro' course of studies, Greek and German literature principally and civil law. If you can by any chance help me to an acquaintance with Schlegel and others of that fani'la [?] I shall thank you to do so.

On March 12, 1832, he writes:

I will order a copy of the review [Vol. 8, Feb., 1832] ... to be forwarded to you. You will see your article on English Civilization and two by me... Your article is excellent – both in style and thought.

In a letter from Charleston, dated April 24, 1832, Legaré confirms the report of a European appointment and restates the purpose of his European mission.

> I received a letter from the Department of State announcing officially my appointment as Minister to Belgium... I shall, on arriving in Belgium ... set to work to acquire German. A. W. Schlegel is at Bonn? If so I shall see him in September or October. German, Greek, Public and Civil Law, History – voilá my studies.

Despite the above resolution it seems that it was May 22, 1833, before our Minister attempted to find a German tutor, and five days later before he "opened a German grammar and got some idea of the pronunciation and characters." It was June 4th before he took his first lesson in that language.[36] His tutor was to visit him every other day. His progress in the study of German is faithfully recorded in his "Diary of Brussels."[37] On the fifth of July he purchased "a German translation of the *Romancero* of the Cid and a history, in German, of the Knights Templars."[38] By July 19th, 1833, he undertakes "to read the preface of Wolf's Lectures on the first four books of the Iliad," in German, and finds it "horribly difficult." On May 2, 1834, he writes to his sister:[39]

> I began, yesterday, (for it is quite an epoch in my life) to read Goëthe's [sic!] Faust in the original, and am happy to find it less difficult than I was led to expect. It is now eleven months since I first began to learn German, – from this must be deducted two months for my visit to Paris.

One year and two weeks later (May 17, 1835), he announces:[40] "I leave Brussels tomorrow or the day after for Cologne and Bonn, perhaps I shall go up the Rhine as far as Heidelberg." He arrived in Bonn (Hotel Stern) on May 22 and on the next morning sent to August Wilhelm Schlegel a letter of introduction which had been given to him by M. Arrivabene. It would seem that since the death of Goethe, the American scholars sought out Schlegel in Bonn as their earlier fellow-Americans had visited Goethe in Weimar, for George Ticknor visited Schlegel there on November 10, 1835 and Henry Wadsworth Longfellow followed in December. Since Legaré's visit antedates both of these, and since he reports at greater length on his association and conversation with Schlegel during this sojourn in Bonn, his comment seems to deserve more detailed reproduction and wider circulation. Legaré records in his "Journal of the Rhine":[41]

[I] am informed by M. Schlegel that he will receive me at any time before 1. At half-past 11, go out to make him a visit ... am admitted at M. Schlegel's. Shown into the apartments on the ground floor, I see, among other things, the *bust* of the master in marble, – a very flattering one, as I found afterwards, though M. Schlegel is rather handsome, in spite of a blink in one of his eyes. His old woman servant presently comes down again and asks me to walk up. After a moment's expectation, an elderly looking gentleman, but still active and fresh enough of [for?] his age, comes in, quite in dishabille, without cravat and in slippers. I soon saw the whole man, and led him on from topic to topic, in order to get as much out of him as possible. Speaking of Pozzo di Borgo, he said he met him once in Vienna in 1808, when he (S.) was travelling with Madame de Stael. The gaieties of that dissipated city were at their height. How is it possible, says Pozzo, that people should enjoy themselves so carelessly, while their country is trampled on as it is. In their joyous *insouciance*, they asked Madame de Stael if she thought the peace would last till *after* the hunting and shooting season: and here a loud laugh – (quite a frequent accompaniment of M.S.'s conversation). Then we talk of the University of Bonn, – of the perfect religious toleration that exists in Prussia, where young men of the Catholic and Protestant communions study together, etc., – English politics, etc. I get up to take my leave until we should meet again at dinner at the Arconati's, but, as I am doing so, here, said he, is something you must see. There is a likeness of Mad. de Stael (under it hung a miniature image of Schlegel himself) taken after her death, but exceedingly resembling her. Corinne is not *so very* ugly in this picture, and has especially pretty, tho' rather shrewish eyes.

. . . .

[Dinner at Arconati's, the evening of the same day.]

After waiting some time for M. Schlegel, his carriage drives in and he soon makes his appearance, "neat, trimly dressed, fresh as a bridegroom." ... At dinner, the conversation was very various and agreeable. We talked of foreign countries, with which M. Schlegel was very familiarly acquainted, – of *races* of men, Negro, quarterons, etc. The latter, he said, always retained the African features, *flat nose*, etc. I told him it was not so *chez nous*, where some of them have the Caucasian face in its perfection and are very handsome. A subject we talked a good deal about was the criminal code and trial by jury. He is evidently full of a reform in the former, which he regretted his friend, Sir James McIntosh, had not lived to accomplish. I ventured to say that I knew no problem more puzzling, and less likely to be soon satisfactorily solved, than what is the best way of disposing of a *felon*, that is, a determined criminal, – and that the question would probably have to be answered differently according to circumstances. *Unanimity* in the jury, which he attacked, I stoutly defended; affirming that, without requiring that, there would be very insufficient examination of cases by these occasional undisciplined judges, and I was not sure whether the institution would be worth fighting for without it. "Nay, but," said he, "even with a majority of only seven to five, *we* are very much attached to the system." A case was mentioned in which a man, having been convicted on very doubtful evidence, of a murder committed seven years before, the king of Prussia, of his absolute power, set aside the sentence, and had the cause re-judged in Silesia, where the accused was acquitted. H.M., in his zeal to do good, violated the forms. Speak of M. De Tocqueville's recent book on the Democracy of the United States. Tell them I had not read it, and so get off without giving a general opinion on the subject. Add, that, from some observations on it in the *Débats*, he seems to have seen things in a truer light than foreigners usually do, – e.g., he dates our republicanism, not as people on this side the Atlantic absurdly imagine, from the Revolution, but from the very foundation of the colonies, which, I explain, adding at the same time, that nothing could be more widely different than such a revolution, and one (like that of '89, for instance) where everything had to be pulled down and set up again; witness the South American abortions.[42]

. . . .

[At coffee in the saloon after dinner]

M.S.'s *libellus* on the Hippolytus of Euripides and the Phaedra of Racine being mentioned, I say that I had read such a *diatribe* over, and considered it as incontrovertibly just and an admirable specimen of comparative criticism... The conversation turns on other kindred topics, – Spanish theater, license of satire, etc...

. . . .

[During a carriage ride with Schlegel alone after coffee.]

I ask M. Schlegel how it happens that, his account of the genius of Sophocles being supposed just, (...) so many ancient critics seem to prefer Euripides.

. . . .

Thence the conversation turns on the picturesque and the beautiful...

. . . .

[Hugo and Savigny] do not seem to stand very well in his estimation... Savigny, he adds, is of what they call the *historical* school...

. . . .

[Then to tea in Schlegel's study.]

The first thing I see is another *bust* of himself, backed by a half-length portrait. Armour propre, it seems, is no *iconoclast*, or rather the contrary. I ask after Niebuhr... Gives me clearly to perceive that he was no friends [*sic!*] with the great historian, whose department (that, I mean, of Roman history) M.S. now actually fills, and some of whose opinions he disputes. ... He says Niebuhr was altogether impatient of contradiction, and has no doubt that his end was hastened by the revolutionary events of 1830, which preyed inconceivably upon his mind. ... The conversation turns afterwards on Oriental literature, to which (Sanscrit, especially) M. Schlegel is now particularly devoted. Presents me with a letter of his to Sir J. McIntosh on that subject, which he sends me the next day with a note.

I left him at half past 9.[43]

On the morning of May 27th Legaré drove to the Drachenfels with the Arconati's and Mr. and Mrs. Sidney Brooks. There they were joined by Schlegel. The next day Legaré was ordered confined to quarters by his physician, M. Nassé [*sic!*]. Illness detained him in Bonn through May 28th, four days longer than he had intended to remain. He complains that this malady "sadly curtailed the pleasures and advantages of my *sejour:* in the first place, I had to renounce a teaparty at M. Schlegel's, though he repeatedly called on me since." On the very last day of the sojourn (May 29th) Schlegel called at the hotel to take leave of him. During the few hours, when he felt it safe to leave his chambers in the "Stern", he visited the *librairie* of M. Weber where he purchased "Schlegel's Dramatic Literature in German and a translation into modern German of the Nibelungenlied."[44]

Thus ends Legaré's account in his Rhine Journal of 1835 of the visit to Schlegel which he had predicted three years earlier in a letter to Burton Harrison dated April 26, 1832: "I shall, on arriving at Brussels set to work to acquire German, and to see W. [*?sic!*] W. Schlegel at Bonn. If so I shall see him in September or October."[45]

It is interesting to compare Legaré's account of Schlegel with that which his friend, George Ticknor, wrote in his own *Journal* at Bonn on November 11, 1835.[46]

> The first evening [November 10] I went to see Schlegel. He is, of course, a good deal changed since I saw him in 1817, for he is now, I suppose, about seventy years old, but he is *fresh and active*.[47] He is much occupied, as he has been the last sixteen or eighteen years, with Sanskrit, about which he has published a good deal and holds the first rank; but he lectures here on two or three subjects each semestre, and in the course of the last year on Homer, on Roman history and on the German language, lecturing on the first two in the Latin language, extemporaneously, which I am told he does very well. He talked to me about his Sanskrit a little more than I cared to have him, but that is the privilege of age; and he still loves to talk politics, as he always did, and show his knowledge in remote departments where you would least claim anything from him. But it is pardonable vanity.

The next day he reports: "Schlegel is very entertaining though very vain."[48]

And now to quote what Orie W. Long designates as Professor Longfellow's "vivid description of his visit" to Schlegel at Bonn early in December, 1835.[49]

> I was *shown up into* a small room furnished with a desk or two, ... a table, sofa and chairs. On one of the desks was a *bust* of Schlegel. The *servant maid* threw a few fagots into the chimney, and kindled the fire. *In a few minutes* enter Schlegel, *an old man*, stooping under the burden of some three-score years. He wore a little, black skull cap, a frilled shirt, *without cravat*, a loose brown or rather clarat [*sic!*] surtout, drab pantaloons and clock [cloth?] *slippers*. His forehead broad and high, eyes large, and the expression of his countenance intellectual and pleasant. He rather lectured than conversed: – so I shall not pretend to record what he said. He was, to tell the truth, rather discursive; and I could not get him upon *topics* of interest to myself. Still I was much gratified to see the translator of Shakespeare. He is very much of a gentleman – and takes snuff from an ornamental box of tortoise shell.

On October 10, 1837, speaking of fellow-members of Congress from South Carolina, John Quincy Adams of Massachusetts said:[50] "Legaré is another, much more polished, better educated, and better disciplined; a fine speaker, a brilliant scholar, but yet a shallow bottom." One wonders what this ex-President of the United States, himself a student of German and the translator of Wieland's *Oberon*, would have said of the depth of Legaré's cranial cavity had he compared the above utterances of his neighbors in "the land of the Bean and the Cod" with those of his fellow-Congressmen from the Palmetto State.

Between April 22 and May 16, 1836, Legaré made another excursion in Germany, *via* Nordhausen, Magdeburg, Potsdam, Berlin, and Leipzic, to Dresden, where he spent several pleasant days with his friend, George Ticknor (May 1-4), and thence by way of Munich and Frankfurt back to Belgium. Although he deplores the physical appearance of the country and the state of the people, e.g.,

Nordhausen, Thursday, 22 April, 1836:[51]
"In short, everything looks poverty-stricken and primitive. This is more strictly true of *Hesse*."

Magdeburg, 23d April:
"Such fare as one gets in an old country house of a decayed gentleman's family. Man very stout and stupid, beasts very spare, but not less dull than the man for all that;"
he is, nevertheless, still mindful of his devotion to German literature. He writes in Potsdam on Sunday, April 24th;

> I put my hands into one of the ponderous gauntlets [of Tilly in Magdeburg], and thought of Wallenstein's Lager.
> Speaking of Schiller reminds me of Goëthe and Faust, and Faust, of the Brockenberg. I ought to have recorded that, as I came rushing down the last of the mountains ... looking to the left, I saw a peak higher than the rest, all covered with snow... This peak was precisely the Brocken, – the seat of Faust's witches.

At Wittenberg Legaré alights "at the London Tavern, near the church in which are the graves and pictures of Luther and Melanchthon."[52] The visit to these shrines of the two great reformers he calls "the most interesting excursion of the sort I ever made", partly because his cicerone was more fluent in Latin, the medium of their conversation, than was Legaré himself, but chiefly because of his respect for the memory of the two great reformers.

Much of the five days spent in Dresden was devoted to the art galleries. Ticknor's presence in the city rendered Legaré's visit much more pleasant and profitable. He made the acquaintance of Retsch, the illustrator of Goethe's *Faust*.[53] He also reports:

Ticknor proposed that I should hear Tieck read a play of Shakespeare. He is, you know, the renowned collaborateur of Schlegel in his translation, and is famous as a reader; but once he begins he must go thro'. This rather alarmed me, yet I consented, but unfortunately he was ill.

At Munich he reports on May 10: "Saw the cathedral, ... with two towers covered with globular roofs, like mustard pots."[54] Although he devoted much time to the art collections in Munich and was entertained at a dinner party by the Papal Nuncio, we find only one reference to literature. He was sadly tempted to buy "the *Carlsruhe* edition of Herder, in forty-four volumes, (unbound) for 39 flor [ins]."[55]

The last entry in the "Journal of the Rhine", dated, Frankfort, May 16, 9 P.M., relates that Legaré passed through "Augsburg, Nuremberg and Bamberg." He calls Nüremberg, "with Wittenberg, the most interesting couple of objects I have seen in Germany", and discourses on the art treasures of the city of Peter Fischer and Albrecht Dürer.[56]

Legaré had invited his fellow Charlestonian, Harry Middleton, then in Belgium, to share his carriage on about April 8th to 12th, 1835 in "taking a *course* in Germany of about four or five weeks."[57] He continues: "My objects are Dresden, (a week); Leipsic, (some days); Munich, (ditto); Berlin, (ditto); and perhaps Vienna, (a week); Nuremberg, (a day or so); Augsburg and Frankfort; perhaps Heidelberg; then down the Rhine and back to Brussels." Both, season of the year and places in this description, fit the above journey. Evidently Middleton did not accept the invitation, but it was not long after Legaré's return to America in August, 1836, that he was instrumental in sending two young representatives of South Carolina to Germany. On December 4, 1838, he wrote from Washington, where he now represented his native state in Congress, to Thomas C. Reynolds[58]: "I send you the passports, and some letters of introduction, for Brussels and Bonn." Reynolds delivered one letter to August Wilhelm Schlegel in Bonn. He kept no copy of it but says[59]: "[it] was written in a style which indicated familiar acquaintance with the person addressed." Judging from one of the letters which Reynolds could not deliver (to Count Arrivabene) the epistles were "pour vous recommender deux jeunes gens de mon pays (Charleston, Caroline du Sud,) qui vont à Bonn, pour faire leurs études universitaires. Ils se nomment Thomas Reynolds et George Guerard."

Immediately, in this initial letter, Legaré imposes a literary trust on his young friend[60]: "There is an edition of Schiller's works, which was coming out at Stuttgard [*sic!*] or Tubingen, (Cotta's,) when I left Europe. There were nine volumes already published, and three still due. I want these three to complete my set." On June 7, 1839, Legaré addresses Reynolds in Berlin[61], evidently at the university, expressing the urgent necessity of obtaining for him M. de Savigny's "Der Beruf unserer Zeit zur Gesetzgebung", or something like that, in which the author develops the doctrines of what is called the 'Historical School' of Germany." He adds: "But there is a work that I must positively have, as soon as I can. It is one of the great critic, M. Bekker, on Demosthenes. The title is 'Demosthenes als Staatsman [sic!] und Redner'." He also wants "the common *octavo school edition* of Bekker's Thucydides." In the same letter he reminds Guerard that he will find in Berlin Huguenots, descendants of the same race of which the South Carolina Guerard's and Legaré's are offsprings.

The following year (April 23, 1840) he writes to Reynolds, now a student at Heidelberg,[62]: "The Thucydides was just what I wanted, and it happened to arrive when I stood most in need of it, for I was writing a paper for the New-York Review, in which I had occasion to be very critical in my notice of the great historian." He adds:

> If you see the New-York Review of July, you will read in it the leading article "on the Constitutional History of Greece" and "the Democracy of Athens", which is by me. I should like to know whether the learned men of Germany think such things worthy of their notice. I published in the 10th No. of the same work an article on Roman Legislation [October, 1839] ... to bring to the notice of our American public some of the learned works of the *actual* school of Germany.

Another lengthy and learned classical treatise "Demosthenes, the Man, the Statesman and the Orator"[63] also appeared in the *New York Review*.[64] It was evidently for the preparation of this article that he needed so urgently "M. Bekker's" book mentioned in his letter to Reynolds (*supra*), for among the works of reference listed at the beginning of the article "Demosthenes als Staatsbürger, Redner und Schriftsteller, von Albert Becker", etc., leads the rest. The second is "Quaestionum Demosthenicarum Particula tertia, (*etc.*) Scripsit Antonius Westermann, *Lipsiae*, MDCCCXXXIV. The third is a British title. This means that practically the whole disquisition is based on German scholarship.

The essay on "The Origin, History and Influence of Roman Legislation" tells the same story. The five reference books were published: 1. In German, Berlin, 1835; 2. in Latin, Berlini, MDCCCXXXII; 3. in Latin, Bonnae, MDCCCXXX; 4. in English, Boston, 1834; 5. in Latin, *Lipsiae*, 1826. Again the German element of the critical apparatus preponderates over that of any other nationality.

The two titles of reference prefixed to the essay on the "Constitutional History of Greece" are translations of a work of a German Classicist, Wilhelm Wachsmuth of Leipzig and of one by Karl Friedrich Hermann of Heidelberg.

As early as July 17, 1832, Alexander H. Everett wrote requesting from Legaré contributions for the *North American Review* during his residence in Europe. On December 18, 1832, Everett expresses his disappointment at not having received any such contribution, saying:[65] "I know no gentleman in the country whose name I should feel so [word illegible] satisfaction in adding to our list of contributors... I am glad to hear you meditate an excursion to Germany. I hope you will collect as much material as you can upon the state of science and letters, and give it to us either for the Review or in some other form." Both Caleb Sprague Henry and Joseph G. Cogswell, as editors of the New York Review, "were eager to have Legaré write for their magazine. They wanted more contributions than he had time for."[66] It may therefore be assumed that such a ready market for his writings was one reason why efforts to persuade Legaré to assist in the resurrection of the *Southern Review* upon his return from Europe in 1836 were of no avail.[67]

After Legaré became Attorney General of the United States (1841) he continued to turn to German authorities. Thus, we are informed that in preparing for his great argument in the Supreme Court of the United States in the case of *Jewell vs. Jewell* (1842) "he sent to Vienna for Eichorn's Kirkenrechts" [*sic!*][68] for purposes of his argument. His term as Secretary of State *ad interim*, from May 8, 1843 until his death on June 19, 1843, was too brief to manifest the secretary's attitude toward Germany. But an excerpt from a dispatch to the Department of State when he was *Chargé d' Affaires* in Brussels discloses his admiration for the German system.[69]

> Specimens of this most beneficent progress in true civilization [increased manufacture due to peace] are the change brought about in the German custom-house system by the King of Prussia, – an immense step to what I have more than once had the honor of calling the attention of the Department, – and the projected construction of a rail-road from Antwerp to Cologne, opening to the whole commerce, fostered by this wise Prussian system, a new and unobstructed outlet by the Scheldt, etc.

The fact that Hugh Swinton Legaré, the scion of a Huguenot pilgrim, who had found refuge in South Carolina, died in the arms of George Ticknor, descendent of an English pilgrim, who had found refuge in New England, symbolizes a community of interest born of an enthusiasm for the German erudition which pervaded the souls of both scholars and caused them to rise above the pettiness of sectionalism.

A most judicious estimate of this illustrious Carolinian is found in the monograph, *Hugh S. Legaré, Late Attorney General of the United States, Eulogy*,[70]

> As a scholar, he stood without rival among the public men of his day.... In the languages and literatures of Modern Europe he was perfectly at home. He not only read, but spoke the languages of France and Germany with the ease and elegance of a native, and was profoundly versed in their history and literature. He had explored, with particular industry, and success, their rich mines of learning, and historical *discovery* (so to speak), which the acute and recondite researches of modern German writers have opened, and enlarged his own accumulated stores by the super-addition of the fruits of their valued labors. With all his affluence of intellectual wealth, he made no ostentatious display of his acquisitions. They were assimilated into the solid nutriment of his own mind, and their effect was seen rather in the enlarged score and vigor of his conceptions, than in any exhibition of mere learning.

MARYLAND

GEORGE HENRY CALVERT
THE SOUTH'S EARLIEST ADVOCATE OF GOETHE

Duke Bernhard of Saxe-Weimar-Eisenach, while visiting in Washington from November 2nd to 15th, 1825, "became acquainted with Mr. Calvert, who told" him that "his son had studied at Göttingen and had some time ago travelled to Weimar, where he was presented at court and very well received."[1] This son was, of course, George Henry Calvert (1803-1889), a descendant of Lord Baltimore, the founder of Maryland, and of the Flemish artist Peter Paul Rubens. When he matriculated as a student of philosophy at the University of Göttingen on February 3rd, 1824, he became the first Marylander to enjoy that privilege.[2] According to Hertha Marquardt[3] the matriculation of Calvert of Maryland, William Emerson of Massachusetts and Noel Clark of Georgia in 1824 renewed the influx of Americans to "Georgia Augusta" which had been without representation from the United States since the departures of Robert Bridges Patton (July, 1820) and George Bancroft. On September 9, 1820, the latter had successfully defended his thesis and thus became the first New Englander to earn, by due process, the doctoral degree in philosophy from that university.

Since Calvert has recorded his youthful European adventures in his *First Years in Europe,* Boston, 1866, and since an excellent account of his life is available in Ida Gertrude Everson's *George Henry Calvert, American Literary Pioneer,*[4] a brief recital of his chief German activities will suffice for the present exposition.

Although young Calvert had attended two academies in the vicinity of Philadelphia, and, at the second, Mount Airy Seminary in Germantown, he records the presence (1814-1819) of "a conscientious assistant" to the principal, "John A. Quitman, son of a clergyman in Duchess County, N.Y.," who was certainly competent to teach German, Calvert evidently absorbed little or no German from the locality or from the teacher. Nor did the fact that he later "had known [Edward] Everett and heard his lectures on Greek orators" at Harvard[6] cause him to acquire a knowledge of the German tongue.

Calvert tells us that "two months after leaving Harvard (1823) in this abrupt manner [He was expelled.], I sailed from New York

[August 9] for England on my way to Göttingen."[7] He explains in the year of 1885:[8]

> I had been sent to Göttingen because young English gentlemen resorted thither; and this had become the fashion in England because the numerous sons of George III had been sent thither. I used to pass daily a large house where they were lodged, thence called *das Prinzenhaus*. Thankful I am (remotely even to the Dukes of York, Cumberland, Kent) that I spent nearly two years within the walls of supreme Göttingen, – supreme in the first quarter of this century among German universities. Hereby the thought, mind, method of mighty Germany were opened to me. Hereby the deep, subtle, clear, creative pages of Goethe became luminous to my eyes.

When, after spending some time in Belgium with the family of his maternal uncle, whose invitation was probably the direct force which brought him to Europe, he entered Germany on January 10, 1824, he was so distressed at his inability to understand the language of a drama that he left the theater in Coblenz before the performance was half completed.[9] He designated his first stay in Frankfurt am Main, January 12th to 19th, 1824, as one of boredom.[10] At a later date (1866) the poet Calvert amplifies the remarks of the student Calvert by stating:

> Goethe was remote and nebulous. The sweet, sightly, succulent ears of his wisdom lay buried in the multiplex husks of German verbs, adjectives, nouns, adverbs.

"It was about nine o'clock in the evening of Wednesday, January 21st, 1824, that the Eilwagen came to a grateful halt" in the university city.[11] The young American, who, "deaf and dumb as to the speech around" him, reports that he "knew not twenty words of German,"[12] took up quarters at the "Crown Inn." On the afternoon of the next day he delivered his letters of introduction and an hour later received from Professor Blumenbach an invitation to a ball for the evening. This diversion took place in the "Hotel zur Krone" just across the corridor from Calvert's temporary lodgings. So, as a real Southerner, he made his "debut at the University of Göttingen very gaily at a dance, given by its most renowned professor."[13] Here he made the acquaintance of "three pleasing, refined daughters" of Herr von Laffert, Supervisor of the University. The eldest daughter, Frau von Vedenmeyer, was the wife of the chief judge of southern Hanover. On that evening began the "friendly attentions" of these two socially important families, which, he tells us, "only ceased on the last hour of my stay in Göttingen, twenty months later."[14]

On the following morning he moved into the Birkenbusch Haus in the famous Weender Strasse, 37.[15] Calvert must now apply himself to acquire a knowledge of the German language. Since "the best teacher," Dr. George Friedrich Benecke, whom Orie Long has rightly titled "the patron of all Americans"[16] "had not an hour disengaged," he was obliged to accept as his tutor "Dr. B.," a Brunswicker of whom he says: "The Doctor was the only ass I ever knew in Göttingen," and "what is rare among teachers of a German university, ignorant as well as dull ... and blessed with patience that went hand in hand with his obtuseness."[17] In spite of the usual difficulties which faced most of our early students at German universities, Calvert was able, in the three months intervening before the start of the Easter semester, by "working hard, that is, seven or eight hours a day," and with assistance from the Laffert sisters, to learn to read Lessing's *Fables*[19] and to understand enough spoken German to follow the lectures in May. Also at the latter time he succeeded in acquiring as his tutor Benecke, with whom he read Lessing's *Nathan* and "first opened the magic book of *Faust*."[20]

On May 4, 1824, Calvert attended his first formal lecture under A. H. L. Heeren in the latter's house in the Pauliner Strasse, 19. Of these lectures in Modern History he reports:[21] "I, who had never heard or seen the name of Thomas Paine uncoupled with derision or scorn, looked up with a sudden surprise into the excited countenance of the professor, as he pronounced *Common Sense* the most important pamphlet in history." In *First Years*[22] he relates how Heeren entered precisely at ten "with a shrinking mien and rapid gait, as a very shy man about to make his maiden effort at public speaking... At ten minutes before eleven Heeren ceased speaking, and hastily gathering up his notes, hurried out of the room in the same crouching way as he had entered."

Among the other prominent professors active during Calvert's first semester he lists Bouterwek, under whom Ticknor had studied in 1815, Eichhorn, Gauss, Langenbeck, Gustav Hugo, and Otfried Müller. He records there were in the summer term, 1825, 1545 students matriculated in the four faculties, 310 in theology, 816 in jurisprudence, 217 in medicine, and 182 in philosophy.[23] Apropos the living expenses of a Göttingen student he informs us:[24]

> For furnished lodgings he pays from two to ten dollars a month, two or three for a single room, four to six for two, and eight to ten for a suite of three. Breakfast is furnished, and also tea ... by the landlord at a stipulated price. For his

> dinner he sends to a *traiteur,* or dines at one of the hotels, the charge varying ... from three to ten dollars a month. Attendance, boots, and washing are cheap...
> The average total annual expenditures of a native student is about three hundred dollars... From experience I should say that his [an Englishman's] estimate supposed a minuteness of thrift inconsistent with the habits of one who indulges in so high a luxury. ["An Englishman ... declared that, for one hundred pounds sterling, a man might live like a gentleman and keep a horse."]

This estimate of the cost of student-living is of special interest in the light of the fact that we possess the figures furnished by Henry Dwight with whom Calvert became acquainted during the New Englander's short stay in Göttingen. Dwight reports:[25]

> Two good rooms, well-furnished, cost twelve Frederick d'ors, or sixty-eight Prussian dollars annually. Each student breakfasts in his room, the family in whose home he resides providing him with what he orders, and charging a very small commission for their trouble. A French breakfast, that is one without a fork, costs about a dime, one with a fork, one and a half or two dimes. The students dine at restauranteurs, at *table d'hotes,* or in their rooms, without wine, at four to eight Spanish dollars per month. Wine costs from one fourth of a dollar to a dollar per bottle.

Recalling his Göttingen associates Calvert writes in 1866.[26] "Of another fellow-countryman, long since deceased, I have a pleasant remembrance, – Henry Dwight, the youngest son of the former eminent President Dwight of Yale College. He came later to Göttingen [September, 1825] and stayed only a few months." Dwight writes in a letter dated Berlin, November 1, 1825:[27]

> I felt not a little reluctant at leaving Göttingen even after my short residence of only three months in that city.
> I felt also very unwilling to exchange my acquaintances here for new ones, and above all to part with a friend to whom I had become strongly attached, whose literary attainments, the brilliancy of whose mind and the minute observations that he had made of various countries of Europe, in which he had resided, made him one of the most interesting of companions.

Whether these words apply to one of his American companions we cannot determine, but it is evident that our young Americans were all enjoying good fellowship in Germany. Typical of this spirit is the mutual admiration that evinces itself between Calvert and William Emerson. In *First Years* Calvert wrote:[28] "I had not been many weeks in Göttingen, when there arrived a fellow-countryman, in whose mind and character I found that support and comfort which ... make a friend so valuable." On April 1, 1824, the youthful theologian wrote to his younger brother, Ralph Waldo:[29] "I can't possibly described the pleasure I felt in finding Calvert here. We were of course immediately well acquainted. He is very much of a gentleman in his manners, and studies with great diligence." In the same letter he reports that Calvert had introduced him to Dr. Hume of Charleston, South Carolina, "an intelligent and cultivated man... who has since gone to Berlin."[30]

Other English-speaking acquaintances of Calvert in the German university circle were "Dr. Pusey, an English celebrity and J. W. Semple, advocate of Edinburgh and translator of Kant and Seth B. Watson.[31] Another fellow-student named William Weir,[32] "a manly Scotsman," who accompanied Calvert as far as Cassel on the night of his final departure from Göttingen, was evidently a wit as was also Calvert himself. Calvert relates how, while speaking of thriftiness, Weir jestingly opined that it takes two Jews to make a Scotchman and the Yale man, Dwight, rejoined that it takes two Scotchmen to make a Connecticut-man.[33]

Calvert has also given us his impressions of a bevy of the professors at the university with whom he came into contact. Blumenbach's lectures were considered in Göttingen as "capital comedy." In "Göttingen in 1824" we read "'If you have no theater, you have a capital comedy.' 'Where?' 'Blumenbach's lectures.'" In a letter of July 1st, 1825, Calvert wrote:[34] "Old Mr. Blumenbach makes the subject of Natural History even more interesting than it is of itself by the relation of amusing anecdotes, which are sometimes more amusing than instructive." Dwight writes on September 25, 1825:[35]

> Blumenbach illustrates all his lectures by anecdotes. With these he keeps his pupils in a continual roar, making his theories and his facts humorously indelible by the power of association. So great is his popularity in Germany, that several deputations have arrived here from other universities to congratulate him; bearing with them plate or other presents among which are several medals, which have been struck off in his praise.

Although he did not attend the lectures of Johann Gottfried Eichhorn on Old Testament exegesis Calvert did make morning calls at his house on Sundays, and was sometimes a guest there for supper.

Nor did he have any interest in the lectures of Georg Sartorius, but was a devotee of the latter's rival, Friedrich Saalfeld, whom he calls "one of the hardest workers in a numerous company of fourteen-hour men."[36] With him he studied three semesters, attending daily his lectures in Politics, the History of Europe since the French Revolution, Law of Nations, Collegium Practicum Diplomaticum, Political Economy and Public Law. Also outside of the lecture halls he associated with Saalfeld. "For some time" they "dined together at the public table of the *Stadt-London* Hotel" and spent many a pleasant evening in Saalfeld's bachelor's quarters.[37]

It was Saalfeld who suggested that Calvert remain a fourth semester at Göttingen and obtain the degree of doctor of philosophy,[38] which, the American tells us, he might have done: "Had there been in the 'Faculty of Philosophy' a genial department, ... so that I could have enjoyed high lessons in criticism on the principles and mysteries of style, in poetry, a new life would have been given to a fourth semester."[39] With Friedrich Bouterwek who taught logic, ethics, aesthetics and literature he had already studied.

Of his old tutor Benecke, professor and librarian, with whom he also read the *Nibelungenlied* and who "was also a master of effective anecdote,"[40] Calvert reports:[41]

> Benecke told me that Coleridge, when in Göttingen towards the end of the last century, was an idler and did not learn the language thoroughly, and that he got a long ode of Klopstock by heart and declaimed without understanding it, playfully mystifying his countrymen with the apparent rapidity of his progress. When the "Opium Eater" appeared, Benecke at once attributed it to Coleridge, from knowing, he said, that Coleridge took opium when at Göttingen.

At the end of his first semester Calvert spent a gay vacation (September-October, 1824) traveling with his uncle and aunt from Belgium, visiting Gotha, Weimar, Leipzig, Dresden and Berlin. Of this first visit to Weimar he writes:[42] "The Diary has no note, nor have I any recollection of what we saw there." He mentions a conversation "sentences of which might have been heard by Goethe, had he been on the alert, for in high talk we passed under his windows on our way back to the hotel."

In Leipzig he visited the university and, after listening to two of the professors of history lecture in the auditorium, he visited each of them in his "sanctum."[43] In the forenoon he heard and visited Professor Wieland "who on that day happened to be biographical and thence more attractive, sketching Frances I, Maria Theresa, Frederick the Great, and Joseph I." In the afternoon he heard Professor Beck lecture on the Seven Years War.

During this same vacation the more serious Emerson hastened to seek an interview with Goethe. To use his own words:[44]

> Nothing but the hope of seeing Goethe would have induced me to take this circular route. I knew that he was very seldom visible to strangers, but I resolved to hazard the attempt. We arrived in the pleasant town of Weimar at noon, and I immediately repaired to his house, and sent up my card, on which I had previously added "Boston, N. America" to my name. He sent me word that he was then surrounded with company, but if I would call at 4, he would see me...

Goethe's *Tagebuch* records on September 19, 1824:[45] "Will. Emerson aus Boston, Nordamerika, in Göttingen studierend protestantischer Theolog. blieb für mich." In a letter home, dated October 10, 1824, Emerson wrote from Göttingen:[46] "He hardly ever admits a stranger, since he is often plagued with requests of that kind; but the words – 'of Boston, N. America' – which I wrote on my card, served as a passport. I was half an hour with him, and it was a half hour I shall not soon forget."

The following spring, probably inspired by Emerson's account of his visit, Calvert betook himself to Weimar. He set out from Göttingen on Saturday, March 19 and, arriving at Gotha on the evening of the same day, he remained there for a week, having been "introduced at a club at which all the Literati, Statesmen, etc., etc. of the *ci-devant* sovereignity of Gotha assemble every evening to play cards and smoke pipes."[47] Seven hours after leaving Gotha he found himself "passing by the ruins of the Theatre of Weimar." Calvert continues "In spite ... of the loss of what was my principal inducement for coming to this place, I have passed 2 weeks very agreably [*sic!*] in it." This time he visited Goethe on March 27th and tarried to enjoy the attractions of life at the Ducal Court. Like Emerson he spent a pleasant half hour with Goethe in his house on the Frauenplan. His *modus operandi* in obtaining admission to the Goethe house seems to have been furnished by Emerson. In his article "Weimar in 1825" he relates:[48]

> Towards four I was again ringing Goethe's bell. The servant asked my name. I gave him my card on which I had written, "aus Washington, America." My home being near the capital, I availed myself of this to couple myself with that sublime name – honored by all the hundred millions in Christendom – the presenting of which to the imagination of a great poet might, I hoped, suddenly kindle an emotion that would plead irresistibly in my behalf. The servant quickly returned and ushered me in.

The conversation began with formal questions and replies: "How long I had been in Europe; the route I had come; the sea-voyage." Goethe then inquired about several of the professors in Göttingen. Since Calvert had been in residence there over a year he was competent to answer intelligently and we may assume that the information was the same as that given us in his essay "Göttingen in 1824."[49]

Describing his feelings in Goethe's presence Calvert wrote some thirty years after the event:[50]

> Seated beside one wiser than the wisest of the seven sages of Greece, in whose single head was more knowledge than in the heads of all the seven together; the wisest man then living, nay, save two or three, the wisest that ever has lived ... in this privileged tete-à-tete, it was not Goethe who taught me, it was I who taught Goethe.

The news of the election of President John Quincy Adams had only recently reached Germany. Therefore it fell to Calvert's lot to explain to the sage of Weimar how the electoral college votes to elect the president of the United States.[51]

Immediately after this interview Calvert sent to Goethe a copy of the *North American Review* of October, 1824,[52] which he had in his hotel room, and which contained an unsigned article on "The Life and Genius of Goethe" by George Bancroft.[53] Goethe's reply was a note inviting Calvert to come to his house on the evening of March 29. Upon entering the drawing-room that evening Calvert was disappointed that Goethe was not present. An entry in Goethe's *Tagebuch* reports: March 29. "Ottilie had a tea party, in the front rooms, the von Froriep family, the North American [Calvert], and a few Englishmen. I busied myself with Helena."[54]

That evening Calvert was charmed by the company and decided he would remain in Weimar and visit the Court. He mentions the[55] "three young Englishmen, acquaintances of Goethe's daughter-in-law, Frau von Goethe," and tells us "Frau von Goethe, sprightly, intelligent, and graceful, did the honors with tact and cordiality. In five minutes I felt myself at home." Then began a round of social functions which included his formal presentation at the Grand Ducal Court. Calvert apprised his uncle on April 11th[56] that he met a student in Weimar he had known in Göttingen who was spending his vacation with relatives in Weimar and through the "politeness" of the latter was at once "introduced to the principal personages of the place." "Like all other strangers (who are treated with particular kindness by the court)" he "was invited on the Sunday following (every Sunday there is a court dinner and strangers are always invited as a matter of course) to dine with the Grand Duchess – the company consisted of the Court Ladies many of the first Dignitaries etc. of the Dukedom, and 8 or 10 Englishmen who like myself enjoy the hospitality of Weimar." The Grand Duke was unwell; hence Calvert did not meet him "on the first day of" his "presentation"[57] at Court. Calvert relates:[58] "At a quarter before three, on Sunday, April 3rd, in the year of 1825, I descended the steps of the Erbprinz [Hotel] to enter the sedan which was to bear me to the palace." During the course of the afternoon the Grand Duchess spoke of her son Bernhard who just seven months later happened to speak with Calvert's father in Washington.

On the occasion of his second formal dinner-visit at Court on Sunday, April 10th, he "had the honor of being in due form presented to[59] Goethe's patron, Grand Duke Karl August." From the manuscript of the "German Diary" of Jesse Burton Harrison, preserved in the Library of the University of Virginia we learn that Dr. Froriep of Weimar "introduced Calvert at Court" and that the "Old Duke concluded from his remarkable quietude, folding of his hands, etc., that he was a Quaker." In spite of this observation Calvert reports to his uncle: "There are [*sic!*] an unusual number of handsome *unmarried* ladies for the size of the place, and from the deficiency of native beaus, foreign ones are received with particular favor." He announces also that we will attend a court Ball on Thursday (April 14th) and "One more Dinner on the Sunday following." Shortly before the end of his stay in Weimar he was a guest at a party given by Countess Julie von Eglofstein and manoeuvered himself into a seat next to her at the table. He departed from Weimar on Monday, April 18, about three weeks later than he had originally intended to remain.[60]

If one is surprised that comparatively little is said about Goethe during and immediately after his long stay in Weimar, Calvert himself has already prepared an explanation.[61]

> But to be frank, I thought very little about Goethe. Here was, indeed, a gigantic example of the wasted opportunities of youth. True, with the most intense will, I could not have had another interview with Goethe. From the illness into which he fell two or three days after my arrival, he did not recover until after I had left Weimar. His daughter-in-law promised me I should see him again; but the day never came.

Then, too, we must recall what he wrote in *First Years in Europe*[62] concerning his first visit to Goethe's Frankfurt, concluding with the words:

> It is a profound virtue of this poet-sage that his meanings reveal themselves but dimly to the young and the unculti-

vated. His pages are to delight and enlarge seasoned, chastened minds.

So too had it been with Calvert's younger contemporary, Bayard Taylor, who, during his youthful residence in Frankfurt (1844-45) was an admirer of Schiller rather than of Frankfurt's great son.[63]

Calvert arrived back at the university on April 21, two weeks before the lectures for his last semester began. He registered for "only two regular courses per day, the one Blumenbach's Natural History, the other the History of the Arts with Professor Miller – besides these I have twice a week the History of German Literature."[64] He continued his private lessons in German with Benecke. On July 1st he writes to his uncle, Mr. Charles Stier in Antwerp:[65] "Mr. Herren I hav'nt [sic!] seen for some time but am expecting an invitation from him soon to a supper party." He adds: "I have made two excursions to the Plesse and the neighboring spring with a party of Ladies (Mr. Laffert's family) and am going tomorrow evening to take tea with them," thus indicating that as a true Southerner he was combining social activity with academic discipline.

At this time he was expecting to depart from Göttingen on September 20th and go via Frankfurt as far as Heidelberg and then down the Rhine to Cologne. But in his letter of August 15 he announces that he would not leave until October 1st. Exactly one month later he set his date of departure as September 22 and his destination as Frankfurt. When he departed from Göttingen late in September he did visit Frankfurt. On October 1st he wrote from Bonn[66] announcing he would remain there three or four days. Here he visited A. W. Schlegel and received a visit from Niebuhr. In *Scenes and Thoughts of Europe* (1846) he reminisces:[67]

> Schlegel kept us waiting some time in a neat drawing-room, where hung a portrait of Madame de Stael. He then came in hurriedly, adjusting the tie of his cravat. He was affable and lively, and in his dress, bearing and conversation, seemed anxious to sink the Professor and appear the man of the world. Niebuhr was out, but came in an hour to the Hotel to see us. He was a tall, striking man and spoke English perfectly. The sight of an American seemed to excite his mind. He plied me with questions about our institutions and customs. Doubtless his thoughts were often busied and puzzled with the new historical phenomenon of the great Republic... But Niebuhr was not the man to seize its significance or embrace its grandeur. His mind was exegetical and critical, rather than constructive and prophetic.

Calvert spent the winter at Edinburgh and returned to America in the spring of 1827.

Summing up the extent of his linguistic attainments before leaving Göttingen at midnight on September 24, 1825, he says that he "gained ... an introduction to the spirit and method, the thoroughness of German mental work." He continues:

> I learned to know ... the wise impartiality, the manly search for truth, the thoughtful grasp wherewith the scholars of Germany handle the great themes of science and study.

and concludes:

> And further I brought away a treasure, the full value whereof I could only learn much later – the German tongue which was later to lay bare to me the thought and beauty and wisdom that lie within the pages of Lessing, and Schiller, and Richter, and Goethe.[68]

It is evident that Calvert's interest in Germany centered in its cultural greatness as did the interest of Basil L. Gildersleeve who followed Calvert to Göttingen a quarter of a century later, who spent the last decades of his life in Calvert's Maryland and who might well agree with the following words of Calvert but who would have insisted, as would also Hugh S. Legaré, that our Marylander should have given more recognition to the supremacy of Classical erudition in Germany. Calvert wrote:[69]

> It is significant that on Germany's roll of power there is a preponderance of men of thought over men of action. In kings and emperors she is weak. Few military and civic leaders has she whose deeds can match the words of her Luthers and Kants and Keplers and Leibnitzes and Lessings and Goethes and Schillers and Hegels and Richters and Humboldts.

After spending his first post-Göttingen winter in Edinburgh, Calvert, on returning to America, established his residence in Baltimore where he began to busy himself with literary activities so many of which mark him not only as an enthusiast for German literature, but as the first protagonist and advocate of Goethe, the *man* and the poet, who hailed from our Southland.

In the fall of 1830 he was appointed to the Chair of Moral and Intellectual Philosophy at the University of Maryland. With one of his colleagues he founded a weekly, the *Chronicle of the Times*, which served as an outlet for their writings. The issue of November 13, 1830, contained his translation of "The Hymn of the Archangels" from the Prologue to Goethe's *Faust* which, according to Everson, "appears to be the first American version of the famous hymn."[70] A revised form of this rendition is contained in his Maryland story, *The Life of Herbert Barclay* (Baltimore, 1833), with a note stating that the translation was "published in this country in the year of 1830."[71] In the second volume of the *Chronicle*, now titled *The Baltimore News*, appeared on October 31, 1831, an unsigned "To Adelaide, in Absence," an imitation of Mathisson's "Adelaide," which Everson assigns, probably rightly, to Calvert, as she does also with "The German Muse From the German of Schiller," which appeared in the same periodical on October 29, 1831.[72]

A Volume from the Life of Herbert Barclay (1833) mentioned above is a skeleton of a story giving the author an opportunity to introduce much German lore and literature. In this respect it reminds the reader of Longfellow's *Hyperion*. In addition to the revised version of the *Archangels' Hymn* from *Faust*, it also contains a translation of the dialogue between Faust and Gretchen from the "Garden Scene" beginning:

Who dare him name? (3432)

and ending:

Why not I in mine? (3465)

which for many reasons invites a comparison with these same lines in Bayard Taylor's translation. The volume also contains an ode "To Goethe" in English verse.

From Calvert's *Autobiographical Study*[73] we learn that one evening Edward Everett brought him a copy of Carlyle's *Life of Schiller* requesting that he write a criticism of it for the *North American Review*. Everett, it seems, had promised the editor of the American edition of the biography that he (Everett) would perform this task. Calvert sent to the editor, Alexander Everett, his critique, which was accepted and published in the July (1834) number.[74] Looking back on this literary effort Calvert opines: "It suited the then state of knowledge – or rather of ignorance – among us on subjects of German literature, and carried some instruction to readers in 1834. I should not care to have it republished in 1882."

The review begins with a lengthy, general, philosophical discourse, outlines the history of German literature from Luther to Schiller, presents a rendition of fourteen verses of *Don Carlos* in English and mentions that drama twice more. Another feature is the introduction of frequent translations from the "Briefwechsel" between Goethe and Schiller. In fact about ten *per centum* of the entire article is devoted to this exchange of epistles. The reason for the prominence of just these two phases soon disclosed itself in Calvert's subsequent publications.

In 1834 he published a translation in blank verse of Schiller's *Don Carlos*, said by Friedrich C. W. Lieder to be "the first translation of a Schiller drama by an American."[75] Harry W. Pfund has given us a precise and adquate evaluation of this rendition as judged in the light of present day criticism.[76] We shall be content to cite what should be good contemporary authority, a review published in that periodical in which appeared the first important article on German literature in an American periodical, Edward Everett's review of *Dichtung und Wahrheit* (January, 1817), and also George Bancroft's article (October, 1824) which Calvert had personally carried to Weimar and presented to Goethe, the *North American Review*.[77] The reviewer says in the number of October, 1836:[78]

> His translation of Schiller's "Don Carlos" shows an accurate knowledge of the German language and an uncommon power of rendering German poetry faithfully into English. In some passages the translation is rather stiff, but it is always true to the original. It sometimes fails of being idiomatic English, but never of giving the sense of the German.

Evidently the mature Calvert realized that his selection of this drama had been a youthful error for he wrote in his *Autobiographical Study* (1885):[79]

> Had I taken in hand Goethe's "Iphigenia" or "Tasso," I should have had a shorter and more difficult, but more profitable task; for "Don Carlos" is rhetorical rather than poetical, and its interest depends more on the story than on the thought. But, to the young, Schiller is more attractive than Goethe, and less simple, less subtle and less true. In acknowledgement of my obligation to Coleridge, I dedicated to him my "Don Carlos" in the following lines:
>
> To S. T. Coleridge
>
> Were that alone thy glory, that thy name
> Is linked to Schiller's, and that worthily
> Thou hast interpreted his gorgeous muse, –
> Deathless thou wert with mighty "Wallenstein," etc.
> Baltimore, April, 1834.

In *The Poets and Poetry of Europe*,[80] Henry W. Longfellow asserts that "Don Carlos" has been translated "by Mr. Calvert with much skill and fidelity."

Edgar Allen Poe wrote from Baltimore on June 12, 1835, to Thomas Willis White, editor of *The Southern Literary Messenger:* "I suppose you have received Mr. Calvert's communication. He will prove a valuable correspondent."[81] Consequently two of Calvert's contributions were published in this periodical within the course of one year, a scene from his *Arnold and André* (June, 1835) and "A Lecture on German Literature" (May, 1836). The lecture, originally delivered before the Athenaeum Society of Baltimore on February 11, 1836, was later published as a pamphlet. Again we must judge the work in the light of the enlightenment of the public for which it was intended. It is a good popular lecture and as such must lose some of its eloquence when reduced to print. Again we shall let the *North American Review* express judgment.[82]

> This Lecture shows a wide acquaintance with German literature, and an enthusiastic love for it... In point of style, this Lecture is liable to objection. The sentences are occasionally long and involved; the constructions are sometimes harsh; and there are many compound words used, which the genius of our language forbids. But with all these drawbacks, the Lecture is highly creditable to the learning and the ability of its author.

In any case one must decry the frequent occurence of the misspellings of German proper names.

In the lecture occurs the sentence: "In the union of learning with genius, Richter surpasses Coleridge." We have just seen evidence of Calvert's admiration for Coleridge. In his treatment of *Wahrheit aus Jean Paul's Leben*[83] which appears in the *New York Review* for October, 1837,[84] we get the results of his lengthy review of the voluminous autobiography of the same Jean Paul Richter toward whom Calvert shows at least an equal degree of sympathy for his eccentric genius. He tells us that "the interesting character of the man, not less than the celebrity of the author induced" him "to make Richter the subject of the first of the papers on German literature" and concludes: "Our strictures ... go no further than to deny to Richter as creative Artist a place by the side of a Schiller or a Goethe."[85] This interest in Richter is corroborated by a passage in his *Autobiographical Study* (p. 249):

> In the alphabetical commonplace book I find ... several [references] to Jean Paul Richter's "Levana" and to his

"Aesthetics" which I brought with me from Göttingen. These volumes of Richter are abundantly scored with pencil marks, showing the profit and enjoyment I reaped from the penetrating insight and humane spirit of this original thinker. So much impressed was I with "Levana" that I began to translate it... Another volume of quite different character... I likewise began to translate – this was "Klueber's Voelkerrecht." [J. L. Klüber, *Europäisches Völkerrecht*].

In 1839 Calvert published in the *American Museum of Literature and the Arts*[86] a review of *Selected Minor Poems Translated from the German of Goethe and Schiller* by John S. Dwight that was so flattering as to merit Dwight's interest in reviewing for *The Harbinger*[87] in 1847 Calvert's volume called *Poems*. Dwight notes that all the poems published in that periodical over the signature "E. Y. T." are Calvert's. Included in *Poems* are, among others, a translation of Goethe's first "Wanderers Nachtlied"[88]

> Thou who dost in heaven bide,
> Every pain and sorrow stillest,
> Him whom twofold woes betide
> With a twofold solace fillest,
> O, this tossing, let it cease!
> What means all this pain, unrest?
>   Soothing peace!
> Come, O, come into my breast.

and "Sweetness of Sorrow" (Goethe's "Wonne der Wehmut"), and a new rendition of the "Hymn of the Archangels" and his long poem "Freiligrath," written in honor of the revolutionary poet Ferdinand Freiligrath whom he had visited in St. Goar a few years earlier and whom he promised to assist by advancing a cash donation and by offering to deliver a benefit lecture on art in Boston, when Longfellow and Carl Beck "were raising a fund to bring the political exile to America."[89] The last stanza of the poem will suffice to show that our democratic aristocrat from America could be almost as vitriolic as a poet as was the author of "The Dead to the Living."

> Woe to the country such must fly!
> Its core is foul with cankering blight;
> Its throne's a gilded, brazen lie.
> The poets are a people's light;
> As were a sunless firmament,
> Is the cursed land whence they are sent.

Already in 1834 Calvert betrayed, in his review of the "Life of Schiller," his interest in the exchange of letters between that poet and Goethe; hence it is not surprising to learn that he published in English in 1845 volume one of the *Correspondence between Schiller and Goethe, from 1794 to 1805*. The translation is good; but it was the preface to the work which attracted the attention of the American public. In the preceding year the Reverend George Putnam in his Harvard Phi Beta Kappa oration had made "a blind and most rude assault on one of the mightiest dead," Goethe (p. V).

In his preface Calvert counterattacks with almost equal vigor. Note these sentences from the preface:

> If of Goethe we knew no more than can be learnt from his works, in them there is that will convert the gall of such abusive generalities into a mere nauseating insipidity. When a bad man's brain shall give birth to an Iphigenia, a Clara, a Mignon, a Macaria, you may pluck pomegranates from Plymouth rock, and reap corn on the sands of Sahara.

Such language, directed by a Goethe scholar from the "Sahara of the Bozart" at a "Back Bay Brahmin" seems to have been too much for even the editor of the *Southern Literary Messenger*, who in reviewing the work in the June, 1845, number of his Baltimore periodical, commends the translation, but, in the closing half of his article, condemns the writer of the Preface, saying:[90]

> Mr. Calvert ... animadverts with some severity upon the view taken of Goethe's character and merits, by Mr. Putnam in his Phi Beta Kappa oration at Cambridge, in 1844. We were not pleased with the tone of Mr. C.'s vindication of his favorite; nor can we admit that its generalities are conclusive.

Calvert, who, in September, 1844, had become a resident of Newport, Rhode Island, was installed as "Democratic" mayor of that town on October 7, 1853. His change of residence brought him into closer contact with the New England admirers of Goethe, especially with Charles Timothy Brooks soon to give to the world (1856) one of the best English translations of *Faust*, and with the *Brook Farm* group, as indicated by his contributions to *The Harbinger* and his friendliness toward John Sullivan Dwight. The publication of his translation of Goethe's "The God and the Bayardere" in *The Harbinger* for 1848 is a further indication of Calvert's reorientation.[91] But in general, his activities in politics seem to have caused a decrease, or at least a temporary abatement, of his display of interest in German literary matters.

The year of 1856 witnessed the appearance in *Putnam's Monthly Magazine* of two articles "Weimar in 1825" and "Göttingen in 1824" [92] which later were to constitute the two most interesting chapters of Calvert's volume *First Years in Europe* (1866). In 1858 the *Newport Mercury* reprinted with some minor revisions some of his translations of Goethean verses which had appeared in *The Harbinger* in 1847, e.g., the "Wanderer's Night Song," "The Lost Found" and "Proverbs." [93] *Joan of Arc, a Poem in Four Books*, privately printed in 1860 and published in 1883, must not be confused with Calvert's drama, *The Maid of Orleans; An Historical Tragedy*, privately printed in 1873 and published in the following year. Of course both titles suggest Schiller, but the poem shows no influence of *Die Jungfrau von Orleans, eine romantische Tragödie*. As Everson has asserted of the drama,[94] "Although he was doubtless led to appreciate the beauty of the theme through reading Schiller's poetic treatment..., Calvert's version shows a difference in approach suggested by the titles themselves."

Undoubtedly Calvert's most widely acclaimed work was his *Goethe – His Life and Works. An Essay*, 1872. This is attested to by the large number of reviews the work enjoyed, by the facts that it apparently was issued also in England and that new American editions appeared in 1875 and 1876. Although this work is justly hailed as the first American biography of Goethe it is not fair to its author to compare it with the much more original and more comprehensive *Life of Goethe* by George Henry Lewes which Calvert had read in the summer of 1870 together with Ellen Frothingham's translation of Goethe's *Hermann and Dorothea*.[95] It must be remembered that Calvert entitled his work "An Essay." To be more precise, it is rather a collection of seven short essays than a connected, methodical presentation of Goethe's career. This small volume is less than one fourth the size of the British work which is the direct source of much of its inspiration and information. There is abundant evidence of Calvert's borrowings, both acknowledged and obvious, from what he calls "Mr. Lewes's full and noble life of Goethe." [96] Nevertheless Calvert's "Essay" has enough merits of its own to deserve all the commendation it has evoked. It demonstrates that the author was truly an "American Literary Pioneer," and that, as such, he was writing both for a smaller audience of intellectuals already interested in Goethe and for a potentially larger audience in whom he hoped to awaken an interest in the poet, who, he quotes Schiller as saying, is [97] "even more loved and admired as a man than [as] an author."

It is evident that it was Calvert's purpose to acquaint the English-speaking readers of his little volume with Goethe as a human being as well as with Goethe, the poet. He proposes to defend Goethe against attacks on his character; hence such chapters as "Friendships," "Loves," "Poetry and Sciences." Perhaps the chapter "Schiller" might also serve as a means to this end, for Schiller was the idol of the populace. In the study *Bayard Taylor and German Letters* the opinion is expressed that "Numerous passages in the two Weimar essays, ["Autumn Days in Weimar" and "Weimar in June"] and in the Cornell lecture make it evident that Taylor would have expressly undertaken to defend the moral character of Goethe and to show the master's love affairs in a better light" in his proposed Goethe-Schiller biography (1870-78).[98] So too is it evident that Calvert has expressly endeavored to accomplish these ends.

In his work Calvert quotes[99] "one of Mr. Bayard Taylor's many valuable elucidative notes to his translation of Faust." Since we know that his friend and neighbor, Charles Timothy Brooks, received in Newport, R.I., in the early spring of 1871 a presentation copy of Taylor's translation of *Faust*,[100] we may assume that these two Newport disciples of Goethe discussed the Pennsylvanian's translation at the time Calvert was composing his *Life of Goethe*. Be that as it may, it is noteworthy that only a few pages after the above-mentioned quote, Calvert, apropos of his translation of a "passage from one of the Scenes of *Faust*," discusses at some length his views on some features of such a translation in which, without mentioning Taylor, he rejects such practices as "feminine or double rhymes" and "Latin-English" (pp. 222-225). When one compares translations in Calvert's chapter on *Faust*, and especially those found on the pages intervening between the mention of Taylor and his criticism of these features of a (Taylor's?) translation, with the same verses in Taylor's rendition, one is quite convinced that Bayard Taylor's performance has occasioned these remarks. There are enough coincidental connections between the German literary interests of these two, evidently personally unacquainted, but contemporary American enthusiasts for German literature and advocates of Goethe, to invite further investigation.

Although Calvert always defends even Goethe's conservatism (p. 166) and his great deference for social rank, he does admit that Goethe "somewhat lacked" "historical sense" (p. 261). He suggests that it was for this reason that Goethe[101] "failed to seize in the political and social conditions of man ... the idea ... of progression through revolt and revolution, as the only means of clearing the atmosphere when the moral and social equilibrium has got to be much and chronically disturbed." "Hence," he continues, "he [Goethe] did not fully prize Luther, or perceive the necessity for the French Revolution." Here speaks Calvert, the sociologist.[102] Nevertheless, he does rescue his hero for the revolutionary cause by pointing out that in[103] "working at his *Theory of Colors* (the very revolutionary enterprise of trying to dethrone Newton)," he was no conservative.

Also *vis à vis Faust II*, Calvert seems to be without enthusiasm for its author. He calls much of the Second Part "wearisome" and adds: "One is irritated with an unending intellectual hunt the slipper" (p. 245). He attributes his own cursory treatment of the Second Part to the fact that [104] "the first and great part has already taken up more space than was apportioned to the two." Commenting on the Second Part he designates the Helena episode as[105] "the best, except the last scenes, after the bodily death of Faust." Yet he refrains from suggesting what constitutes the worth of these final scenes. Being conscious of his preachments against[106] "the blight of the blasphemous theological teaching, that 'Nature is sin, Mind the Devil's self'," against "the pharisaical Christians," "the pew-paying Christians," "the pseudo-Christians," "the Middle and darker Ages," and "the vested interests of Priesthoods," we are inclined to believe that Calvert could hardly have had any enthusiasm for "the best scenes, after the bodily death of Faust" in which "Holy Anchorites" a "Pater Ecstaticus," "Pater Profundus," "Pater Seraphicus," "Pater Marianus," *et al.* play such prominent roles.

At a reception tendered Calvert in the parlors of the Fifth Avenue Hotel by the Goethe Club of the City of New York on January 10, 1877, the president, ex-judge, Dr. Anthony Ruppaner, before introducing the guest of honor to deliver his address on Goethe, announced that the club was now in its second year and had added forty-one members to its active list.[107] This recalls that on August 28, 1875, Bayard Taylor had delivered his "Ode to Goethe" on the occasion of the presentation of the bust of Goethe to be erected in Central Park by the Club of which he, Bryant, the oration of that day, Bancroft, Frederic Henry Hedge, O. W. Holmes, Whittier and Longfellow were honorary members, an honor which was later conferred on Calvert.[108]

When the reporter for the *New York Times* quotes Calvert as stating that: "He [Goethe] was fortunate in the time of his birth, in his parents, in his associates, and in his genius" we hear Calvert the aristocrat and the sociologist speaking. When Calvert continues: "He was an eminently religious man, and breathed his religion into all his writings," we hear the voice of the South's foremost protagonist of Goethe. Significant, not only in connection with the above statement, but also as being characteristic of the general attitude of the Southern Scholars in Goethe's Germany is the following which indicates a deeper interest of the Southerners in Luther than is displayed by the "Literary Pioneers" from Puritan regions. In the opening lines of his address Calvert declares that[109] "the chief glory of Luther is, that he created the conditions, moral and intellectual, that made a Goethe possible." When Calvert asserts what today has become a truism:[110] "Especially were his works the offspring of his love" and "Being a good as well as a great man, and having absolute faith in the 'Almighty Love' his was not a religion of fear," he was challenging the concept of Goethe held by many of his respectable American contemporaries. Calvert had "nothing to say of Goethe's" faults, concluding:[111] "A man's faults ... are mostly perversions of useful qualities, which, under healthiest conditions could not be. In a full, rounded, active nature defects are interwoven with excellences."

Thus again we find a similarity between the Goethe-worship of Calvert and of Bayard Taylor and are reminded of the latter's poem *Goethe* referred to above, especially of the line:

"Dear is the Minstrel, yet the Man is more."

It might also be noted that even as Taylor read his "Ode" at the Goethe Club's commemoration of the one hundred and twenty-sixth anniversary of Goethe's birth and in 1871 introduced his translation of the *Faust* with an ode "An Goethe," so did Calvert, when he published this Goethe lecture in 1880,[112] preface it with a sonnet "To Goethe."[113]

> Teutonic leader, – in the foremost file
> Of that picked corps, whose rapture 't is to feel
> With subtler closer sense all woe and weal,
> And forge the feeling into rhythmic pile
> Of words, so tuned they sing the sigh and smile
> Of all humanity, – meek did'st thou kneel
> At Nature's pious altars, midst the peal
> Of prophet-organs, thy great self the while
> All ear and eye, thou greatest of the band,
> Whose voices waked their brooding Luther-land, –
> At last left lone in Weimar, famed through thee,
> Wearing with stately grace thy triple crown
> Of science, statesmanship, and poesy,
> Enrobed in age and love and rare renown.

In the preface to his volume *Charlotte von Stein: A Memoir*, dated July, 1877, Calvert acknowledges as the sources of the facts and the letters "used therein the three volumes of the Letters of Goethe to Frau von Stein, 1776-1826" published by A. Schoell in 1848-1851 and *Charlotte von Stein, Goethe's Freundin, mit Benutzung der Familienpapiere entworfen von Heinrich Düntzer* (1874). He further admits making "slight use" of "the correspondence of Merck, and the letters of Goethe to Lavater and to the Countess Stolberg." Although this work was probably the first portrayal made available for the

American reader of the woman who exercised a more profound and extended influence on Goethe than any other, we agree with Everson's assertion that the volume "might be considered another chapter of his [Calvert's] *Life of Goethe*.[114] Although Calvert deals with Charlotte, whom he calls "guardian-angel"[115] and "my heroine,"[116] he nevertheless defends Goethe against even this "guardian-angel" and this "heroine" whenever the necessity arises.

The following passages illustrate the almost limitless admiration which Calvert cherished for his hero.[117]

> Goethe was so great and so worthy that he should be permitted to be a law unto himself. – – a man from whom other men can learn the law, and to whom few, very few, of the sons of earth are pure and high enough to teach the higher things, and none pure and high enough to pass judgment on him... Goethe was a great man, a man of truth and heart, a good man, one of the most moral, most religious men that ever lived.

Nevertheless Calvert can at times become mildly critical even of Goethe, as he does when discussing Goethe's early fascination for and later undue deprecation of Lavater[118] whom he and the Duke visited in Zürich.

But, when he is in agreement with Goethe, Calvert is capable of withering invective. Because Goethe wrote of Geneva:[119] "for all the world I would not stay a week in this hole," Calvert calls that city "the ancient citadel of Calvin with its provincialism, its musty odor of theology, its traces of Calvinism, traces uncomfortably recognizable in the pharisaical self-satisfaction which pseudo-Christian dogmatism leaves behind it." Here we recall the Protestant Calvert who chose to neglect the Catholic symbolism in the closing scene of the Second Part of *Faust*.[120]

Among the other merits of the volume is the author's manifestation of a spiritual as well as a physical comprehension of the whole situation in Weimar. To compress the story of Charlotte von Stein contained in his voluminous German sources into such a succinct and vividly interesting story, without distortion and with such a display of masterly selectivity, is the work of a man well-versed in and enamoured of his subject. The American layman would have to seek far and wide to find such an effective and vital exposition of the fate of Weimar during the Napoleonic Wars, such a sympathetic and just evaluation of the virtues and "imperfections of Goethe's 'Freundin'" and such an unabashed defender of Goethe.

The fact that the author was able to introduce as integral parts of his text of the biography two translations of Goethe's lyrics, the

"Wanderer's Night Song" and "Found" which he had published years earlier, reveals that the study was the result of a long period of evolution and not the product of a sudden impulse. That he should have the sensitivity to select for transference to his contemporary world such sententious gems of the genial "aristocrats" of Weimar as that one contained in a letter of the aging Charlotte living in the desolation of a town just pillaged by the enemy, to her son Fritz:[121]

> Poor human nature! but happily richly gifted with levity and short-sightedness.

postulates a trace of consanguinity between the Southern aristocrat and those of Weimar, and goes far to excuse such a Germanic divergence from normal English prose style as is represented by the following clause found in the paragraph immediately preceding the *sententia* just quoted:

After a while were relieved her anxieties about Fritz.

Although Harry Pfund records the volume containing the Goethe lecture as "his last published work on German literature of which we have a record,"[122] we must not disregard Calvert's *Autobiographic Study* (1885) which may be looked upon as his *Dichtung und Wahrheit*[123] for in his endeavor to write his memoirs (1881-1885) the American is mindful of the methods of his mentor, Goethe.

Early in this volume (p. 27) the autobiographer gives us some more of the biography of the supreme autobiographer.

> Goethe, being one of the most illuminated of these interpreters [autobiographers] and having (especially in boyhood and youth) lived through extraordinarily ... prolific experiences, would have particular delight in depicting the career of the man whom he knew so much more intimately than others knew him... Self-love he had, as every man should have, but not more than was wanted for self-protection. He was a prudent man, as it behooved him to be who had so rich and vast and susceptive and various a mental domain to administer; and prudence often makes a man, even a common man, seem more selfish than he is. The fertility and gentility of Goethe's mind, and especially its wide compass, render difficult to most men the putting of themselves in full sympathy with it, and sympathy is a necessary precursor to the right understanding and clear interpretation of a large man of genius. It is unsafe for the onesided to judge a many-

sided man, nor is talent competent to pass final sentence upon genius, and pharisaical decisions are not moral judgements. More than biography, autobiography is liable to be copious with redundance...
(p. 30) Had not the mental endowment of Goethe been uncommonly full, his sensibilities sure and active, his reason so subtle and broad that through his pages there runs an unobtrusive but stringent logic, a magnetic interlacement, that knits sentence to sentence and page to page, into such a sympathetic sequence that the reader's watchfulness never relaxes; and had not, moreover, an almost infallible accuracy of perception been the pinion that steadied and guided his imaginative flights, the reader would not bear with the prolonged details in portions of his autobiography, – details which, without the intimate life-knowledge that pulses through them and the poetical spirit that informs them, would be flat and tiresome. Only a poet could have written "Wahrheit und Dichtung"; and when a man of three-score records his doings and saying of his far-off boyhood and childhood, creative imagination co-works with memory, and if resulting reminiscence be not always absolutely faithful to fact, it is faithful to the truth of nature. Goethe's imaginings are controlled by his deep, sure knowledge of human life, and his knowledge is saturated with poetic light. The title of his autobiography "Truth and Poetry," dictated by his love of truth, is as modest as it is profound.

Thus, having reached the age of four score and two, the venerable defender of Goethe, in his last printed work, continues to extol the sage of Weimar with less vehemence, but with such insight and understanding that no writer of the history of Goethe biographies in America can afford to neglect to examine this "autobiographic study" completed by Calvert only four years before his death. Accordingly it seems quite appropriate to recall here the sentiments of the astute critic and informed scholar, Bliss Perry, expressed in his address "The Road to Weimar," "delivered on the one hundredth anniversary" of the death of Goethe. Speaking of "the group of Americans who during the fifteen years before Goethe's death, and for ten years thereafter, served as pioneers in making Goethe known in the United States," he judiciously states: "Of all that brilliant company, it seems to me that Cogswell and young Calvert, through their qualities of heart, had the truest perception of Goethe's character," and concludes by praising the Marylander's "delightful ... pictures of Weimar," and by conferring on him "the honor of writing the first American book about Goethe."[124]

VIRGINIA

JESSE BURTON HARRISON

Jesse Burton Harrison, of English ancestry and of Episcopal and Quaker affiliations, was born at Lynchburg, Virginia, on April 7, 1805, attended a private school of that city, entered Hampden-Sidney College where he was graduated in 1821 "in one of the most respectable classes that ever graduated" there, receiving the "first honor."[1] Thomas Jefferson, having failed in his endeavor to enlist as a member of the first faculty of the University of Virginia George Ticknor, who had graduated from Dartmouth College and who had subsequently resided at the University of Göttingen for nine months,[2] talked to Jesse Burton Harrison and the latter's father about the "brilliant opportunities" afforded by such an education as Ticknor had acquired. The result was that Jesse Burton resolved to emulate Mr. Ticknor's career.[3] He went to Harvard University to hear Ticknor's lectures and to matriculate in the newly established law school.

On January 7, 1823, he writes a letter from Harvard to Thomas Jefferson[4] in which he calls attention to the superiority of foreign universities to our own. He emphasizes the fact that "the great accumulation of books" and "those large bodies of men who reside in the universities abroad and whose researches and writings constitute the instruction and glory of their respective countries" are non-existent in America, even at Harvard University. Here Harrison is already speaking as a disciple of Ticknor.

He was awarded the degree of Bachelor of Law at Harvard with the class of 1825, but meanwhile had been greatly inspired by Ticknor's lectures in *belles lettres*. The latter wrote of him to Thomas Jefferson:[5] "He will carry home with him a valuable stock of knowledge, particularly in modern literature, to some portion of which he has devoted himself with great zeal."

Having been admitted to the bar of the state of Virginia on March 31, 1825, he practiced his profession in Lynchburg for four years making frequent visits to Monticello as long as the ex-President was alive. There he met Lafayette and Daniel Webster in 1824.

In 1826 Burton Harrison applied for an appointment to the chair of French and Spanish at the University of North Carolina. Although his candidacy was supported by recommendations from Thomas Jefferson and George Ticknor, and his Harvard language instructor, the celebrated Francis Sales, wrote:[6] "In regard to French and Spanish, I can truly and conscientiously recommend you as one of the most attentive, assiduous, and intelligent pupils I ever had; and that you are not only skilled in the understanding of the principal classics of the above-mentioned languages, but possess also a pure and correct pronunciation of them", he was unsuccessful in his endeavor.

After having suffered this initial disappointment in his desire to occupy an academic chair, Harrison attained his first literary reputation by an address "A Discourse on the Prospects of Letters and Taste in Virginia" delivered at his *Alma Mater* in September, 1827, in which he advocated a revival of philosophical studies in his native state. Directly after this display of literary eloquence, having learned that George Long, the original professor of Ancient Languages at Mr. Jefferson's university, was contemplating resigning from his position in order to return to England, Harrison visited Charlottesville in December, 1827, to reconnoitre, and thus became the earliest candidate for the succession. It seems that in an interview Long gave "his approval to Jesse Burton Harrison's candidacy" and "counseled him to pursue a course of philosophical study in Germany." Hence Harrison decided that, should the Board of Visitors appoint him, he would leave Virginia for that country at his own expense and return the following September, "unless Long should find himself in a position to tarry longer at the University or a temporary instructor could be employed, who would assume charge of his classes until the ensuing January."[7]

The following letter dispatched by George Ticknor from Boston on January 20, 1828, to J. Burton Harrison, Esq., New York, indicates that Harrison, accepting Professor Long's counsel, had formed his plans to depart from New York for Germany during the following week (January 24th). Ticknor wrote in part:[8]

> From Harve, I would go by diligence to Brussels, & then strike the Rhine about Cologne. I would make my studies either at Bonne [sic!], at Gotingen [sic!], or at Berlin. Bonn is almost the next town to Cologne – & besides the letter I give, if Prof. Welcker is there, go to him freely in my name – he will receive you kindly. If Götingen [sic!] is your mark, go on to Frankfort on the Maine [sic!] & strike up through Hese [sic!] Casel. If you are for Berlin, go through Frankfort to Leipzig & from there to Berlin. –
> All these are great roads, leading through the finest portions of Germany, and abounding in comfortable and cheap

conveyances. I should prefer Götingen – but you may not, & therefore I send to [?] letters for all. They are such, I believe, as will do for all. The rest you can & will do for yourself, & you will find it easier than you think. Your French will help you along the *great* road everywhere, and when you reach your place of distination you will have no difficulty in settling yourself as you mind. When you go to Götingen, desire somebody to take you, in my name, to Mrs. Sartorius, wife of the Prof. & tell her, I am very sorry want of time prevents me from writing her.
And now I commend you to Heaven and your own good purpose. You will succeed. Your letters are as good as you can have – any one of them is worth all I carried to Germany. Dr. Lieber [Franz Lieber, 1800-1872], who writes some of them, at my request, is a German gentleman & scholar here. Tell his friends, he is much esteemed and valued among us. Present my respects to Niebuhr at Bonne [sic!] to whom you will be introduced by Bergmann. If Cummingham and Amory of Boston are not in Berlin & if you go to Halle, inquire for Robinson of Andover. They are good men & may be useful to you.
– Farewell – let us hear from you soon and often. Send me a line from New York to let me know this has reached you safely with eleven other letters.

Your friend and servant,

Geo. Ticknor –

Dr. Lieber goes to N. York tomorrow – find him out (at Bunker's in Broadway – Thursday or Friday –) an hour or two of conversation and advice from him may be very important to you.
  Once more Adieu –
The letter to Martens [?Martens, G. F. von] in Jena is from Dr. Folen [Karl Follen] who is now a teacher at Cambridge. Say everywhere that Dr. Folen, Dr. Lieber and Dr. Beck, who is at Northampton at Round Hill School, are much respected and valued amongst us. They will be asked after by their friends.

G.T.

But Harrison delayed his departure probably believing that his personal presence might be desirable until the Board of Visitors of the University had rendered some decision. On July 24, 1828, the Board authorized the Rector, Mr. James Madison, "to appoint to the vacancy, during one year, any one of the following persons: Gessner Harrison, M. L. Tracie and R. Reynolds." [9] Still Jesse Burton tarried. Finally Mr. Madison, whose personal support Harrison enjoyed, wrote to him on August 15, 1828, acknowledging the receipt of his letter of July 3, and informed him:[10] "The Board ... adopted the expedient of appointing for one year, one of his [Long's] most advanced Pupils." Gessner Harrison was this "one year" appointee.

Stung by this rebuff, but inclined to consider the setback only temporary, J. B. Harrison still hoped to succeed to the position at the expiration of one year and delayed his departure from America. In a letter of the year of 1828 written from Monticello and signed N.P.T., probably the same "young Louisianian" whom Ticknor had met while visiting Jefferson in 1824,[11] Harrison is informed:[12]

> I have taken several opportunities to enlist him [apparently Dr. Robley Dugilson, professor of Anatomy at the University] against G. H.'s continuance in office. Were he to become satisfied that I am active in your service, he would have grounds to ascribe ill faith to me... But merely keeping G. H. out ... I was not appraised of your intention to visit Germany and had almost dismissed all hope of seeing you elected... Your notions concerning the importance which so naturally attaches to such a personage as a "Germanized littérateur" – particularly an American one – correspond to my own, only they are not near so *pronouncé*... At the age of *thirty* you can return to *America!!* master of Greek, Latin, English, German, French and Spanish and with a mind enlarged to such a degree and so thoroughly disciplined as to insure your success in anything you undertake – not in Louisiana, but in the theatre where powers and acquirements of the higher order are beginning to be appreciated.

In another letter of September 21, 1828, Mr. N. P. Trist continues:

> Ever since that matter has been agitated between us I have been regretting that you had not gone six months ago. I am still more sorry that the delay should be prolonged till the end of October. Will this allow you time to accomplish anything serious, in time to communicate it at the beginning of next July? ... I suppose that anything you may have to lay before the Board ought to be sent from Göttingen by the middle of May, at the latest.

Again on November third, when Harrison was once more planning to leave for Germany, the scholarly editor of the *Southern Review*, Hugh S. Legaré, Charlestonian and agrarian, wrote:[13]

> I rejoice to hear you are going to Germany... Let me exhort you to lay hold of Greek and not to look back until you die. All other literature is wretched in finish and eloquence when compared with the Ionian. It is a hard thing to acquire a competent knowledge of it, but every good thing is hard to be got. The Irvings & Coopers & Percivals *et id omne genus* (of whom, by the bye, you have a higher idea than I have) won't do. The soil must be properly manured & broken up before it will produce a majestic & vigorous growth. I think verry little *entre nous* of those Northern smatterers. Dr. Johnson's notion of the Scotch that everyone had a mouthful and no man a bellyful of knowledge, applies to the trans Potomac people. They have yet to acquire the very rudiments of scholarship. I never met a Northern man, except one or two, that had any idea (& then not until he had been in Europe) what the word scholarship means. You think no doubt very differently. You have, *I judge from your style*, been educated at Cambridge [Harvard]. But you will agree with me when you have lived thirty years or so in the world. The Bostonians, however, are in a fair way to improve, but, as for Philadelphia, New York, etc., 'Souvenirs' [gift-books and annuals] and such stuff will satisfy their tastes and their capacities for some time to come.

On the same day a letter was addressed to him from New York by Matthius Bruen, evidently in reply to a request for information about student life in Germany. The source of the information is Henry E. Dwight of New Haven, a son of the eminent President of Yale University, and a fellow-student of George Henry Calvert at Göttingen in 1825. Bruen writes:[14]

> He says: "it cost me to live in Göttingen, Leipzig, Dresden, Berlin – including travelling expenses for 1,000 miles in Germany – about one thousand dollars a year. I passed seven months in Berlin, which is more expensive than Paris. A young man who is merely a student, one who does not go too much in society, can live in Göttingen, Jena, Heidelberg, Bonn or at any other university which is situated in small towns for $500 per annum – In this sum I do not include books. For rooms you pay at G-n about $45 – Every student in G-n must have two rooms – one room not being considered a respectable residence for anyone but a German sans argent.

The lectures cost a Frederick d'or for each course, that is about 20 francs. Clothes are more expensive than in Paris. I paid at the table d'hote in G-n 8 dollars per month – dining at 1 P.M. – which is the hour for dining in small towns. Your breakfast and tea are provided by the family where you live – they charging you about 25 cents a day for the two meals – If your friend wishes to study law, he should go to Gött-n or Berlin – where are the two great law schools of G-y. If his object is theology, he will find advantages at Halle much greater than in any other university. Leipzig still retains its celebrity for Greek and Roman literature. Herrmann, the greatest Greek of Germany, lectures at Leipzig. If his object is to study German, he will acquire the Hanoverian Pronunciation at Gött-n and pass the rest of his time in Berlin and Saxony, particularly at Dresden, the Athens of Germany. If he wishes to study the essence of despotism, I should advise him to reside 5 months at Vienna.'

H.E.D.[15]

Harrison had evidently turned at this time to his cousin, Henry Clay, then Secretary of State, for assistance. Witness the following communication.[16]

Washington, 6th Nov. 1828.

(Private and Inofficial)
I read your letter of the 2d inst. signifying your intention to go to Europe, and your desire to be entrusted with dispatches. But we have some dispatches for Brussels which may warrant our incurring a moderate expense in conveying them. I will endeavor to accommodate you with confiding them to your care. Call and see me on your arrival here, and if the arrangement be practicable, it will give me great pleasure to make it.

I am faithfully yrs.
H. Clay.

But Harrison seems to have again sought to delay his departure, for on November 24, 1828, Clay addressed to him the following from Washington:[17]

(Private and Inofficial)

Dear Sir:

A delay in the transmission of the dispatches which I intended to commit to your hands can take place until the middle of next week, without prejudice to the public interest. I shall therefore wait that time for you, according to the request contained in your letter of the 20th inst.

> In haste
> Yrs. faithfully
> H. Clay.

Not until the following spring do we learn more of the contemplated departure. On April 2, 1829, Hugh S. Legaré strongly advises the German sojourn and expresses his regret that he himself had been prevented from studying at a German university during his first European residence in 1818.[18]

By a strange coincidence on the same day on which Harrison actually embarked on the packet *Charlemagne* in New York for Harve, well provided with letters of introduction, a document of recommendation signed by the then Secretary of State, Martin Van Buren, and money sent by his father with the admonition "to live like a gentleman but without extravagance,"[19] June 2, 1829, Clay wrote him from Ashland (Kentucky):[20]

> I am sorry that you could not execute the plan of your German residence because I was persuaded that benefit would have accrued from it both to yourself and ultimately to our country.

Before departing from New York for his twenty-seven days at sea he called on the first American visitor to Goethe (1810), Aaron Burr, who showed him extreme courtesy and informed him that "hostility of Mr. Jefferson and the government ... made his travelling in Europe quite uncomfortable... He was watched in every coach, hotel & street where he went; this he did not discover 'til at Weimar, ... where the late Grand-Duchess told him that everything he said & did that evening would be communicated to Paris next morning, and so it turned out as the Duke of Bassano afterwards told him."[21]

Harrison remained in Paris several weeks. There he encountered a number of Virginians, among them Dr. Robert Henry Cabell of Richmond, a relative of his; Mr. James Brown of Louisiana, our retiring Minister to France, another "cousin" through marriage; and General Winfield Scott, whose wife was a sister of Mrs. Cabell. From Paris he journeyed through Holland and Belgium. At Ghent he called on Duke Bernhard of Saxe-Weimar who had made an extensive journey through the United States in 1825-1826, bringing him a letter from a mutual friend in Paris.[22] Since Duke Bernhard counted among his fellow-passengers on his return voyage from America in June, 1826, "a Dr. Cabell of Richmond, Virginia, with his wife, a sister of Mrs. General Scott",[23] we are inclined to conclude that the letter was from Dr. Cabell. But, as both Duke Bernhard and Burton had visited Burr in New York immediately before embarking from that city, in 1826[24] and 1829 respectively, and since Burr was well known in Weimar, it might be that Burr too had directed Harrison to Bernhard in Ghent.

Harrison describes in an unpublished letter of September 27, 1829, (Library of Congress) the hospitable reception he enjoyed during his visit to the Duke in Ghent.

> I walked to his house but was vexed to learn that he was staying in the country.... After breakfast the waiter informed me that Monseigneur, in person, was waiting for me. I stepped down and was announced; he rose with great politeness, shook my hand, made me put on my hat, and desired that I go out with him to dinner. He speaks very good English, loves America of which he knows more than all the Americans I have seen in Europe, remembering the names of towns, petty villages, private individuals, private anecdotes and everything in fact. He is a colossal figure: 'tho not very highly intellectual, he is a judicious, sensible man and greatly respected by everybody in Ghent. He carried me to the University-rooms, a magnificent new establishment on the site, as he exultantly said, of a Jesuit church. He showed me next the house of Mr. Schanip which was the residence of the American ministers...

He drove Harrison out to his country place to have dinner with the ducal family. The tutor of the children is an amiable young man from Göttingen.[25]

Bernhard informed his visitor that Duponceau had sent him his review of the Duke's book published in *The American Quarterly Review*.[26] Before his departure that evening Harrison was supplied by his host "with three letters [of introduction] at his brother's court [in Weimar] to the immortal Goethe & two other distinguished men."[27] Harrison took leave "delighted with my first acquaintance with a man of elevated rank."

After leaving Ghent Harrison "ascended the Rhine to Mayence, the Main to Frankfurt and thence through Hesse-Cassel"[28] to Göttingen, where he arrived on September 20th, just one month after leaving Paris. He rejoiced to see the "single arch of the castle of Rolandseck, consecrated to all posterity by Schiller."[29] Having "a letter to the great Schlegel" in Bonn, he called on him and reports:[30]

> He came to the door of his drawing-room, received my letter, led me in and gave me a kind reception. He is a very

53

amiable, pleasant man, with an eye of unusual richness and softness, his figure is rather below the middle height, round, and not ungraceful or ill-set. He speaks English well, 'tho mixed with foreign idioms such as 'will you take place' for sit down – from the French. I was invited to see him the next afternoon, when I spent an hour with him, and met him again for a few minutes the third morning in the street. His conversation related wholly to the university of Bonn, which he freely told me was better than Göttingen at present, and to the most advisable mode of regulating my studies. I am to pursue several hints he gave me and promised that I would try to return to Bonn after I had learned the language, which he agreed was best learned in Hanover. He desired me to come and introduce myself there to Professor Müller, freely in his name, which I shall not fail to do. His translation of Shakespeare is considered scarcely inferior to the original, and, for this as for his general critical works his name is, at this moment, higher than any living writer except Goethe's.

In the library of the University of Virginia is preserved the "Diary of Jesse Burton Harrison on Germany and Italy", which yields an abundance of details concerning his sojourn in Germany and which seems to have been the source of most of the information which he sent home in his letters to America.[31] Here we learn of his tour in the Niederwald after crossing the Rhine from Bingen to Rüdesheim. The excursion up the Rüdersheimer Hill, in a large company, was made on foot and on the backs of gaily caparisoned donkies about the middle of September.[32] Evidently this trip proved enjoyable.

Since his arrival in Göttingen anticipated by some six weeks the beginning of the Winter Semester of the university, the young American undertook a foot tour to the Harz Mountains. The "Harzreise"[33] began in the first days of October. The entries in the diary indicate that seven days were devoted to the tour. The way was *via* Nordheim, where a human execution was witnessed, through Osterode, where Harrison and his companion received an "indifferent dinner" and spent the night in the "Deutsches Haus." After passing the second night in Clausthal, they visited the silver mines. After being caught in a severe rain storm and spending the night in a mountaineer's cabin, they struck out for the "Rehberger Graben." Then through boggy country to the Brocken and up to the Brockenhaus, where "the clouds flitted dark, windy and threatening over the sun." Only the visitor's album delighted them, from which Harrison copies some pieces, some verses of which seem to have reflected his own mood:

> The Harz is for its mines renowned,
> The Brocken for its view;
> They both have their mint it is true:
> But if both are justly weighed,
> Man will know that their value
>   is not a sou.   Clemson – U.S.A.

Their ᴅescent led through Schierke, Wernigerode and Elbingrode. On the fifth day their route was through Bielshöhle, the Rosstrappe(n) near Blankenberg and the Teufelsmauer. The following day is cheerful with Medoc and mutton at Alexisbad, beer at the Weiß[es] Roß [*sic!*] in Stolberg, and then on to Nordhausen. On the seventh day: "Dashed off at 6. To Mitteldorf, 3 Stunden to breakfast, thro bogs and pig sties to Duderstatt which is an ancient walled town only 5 Stunden from Gött. by 1/2 2. Stopped at Englischer Hof ... I resolved to browse here while Ventz went on."

"Ate a comfortable meal at 5; wrote up my diary."

"Tomorrow I go leisurely on to rejoin those companions true, who study with me at the University of Göttingen."

No mention of his recent predecessor at Göttingen and in the Harz, Heinrich Heine, no poetic verses and but little poetry and brightness in nature elated the American initiate on his "Harzreise."

Not much is known of the method by which Harrison overcame that bugbear which has haunted most of his contemporary Americans who studied in Germany, viz. the acquisition of a practical command of spoken German. Having previously felt himself qualified to occupy a chair of Greek, Latin, French, or Spanish at an American university, and already knowing some Italian, he is said to have come into "possession of a working knowledge of German" by the opening of the Winter Semester.[34] We can only add that the German words which found their way into his "Harzreise" are invariably correctly spelled, that the German passages in his "Diary" and his later letters are so surprisingly correct as to lead us to accept his statement, recorded on March 16, 1830, shortly before his departure for Weimar: "I can understand the spoken German perfectly and may travel with greater advantage."[35]

It would seem that one of the first activities of an American student in Germany was to deliver his letters of introduction to members of the university faculty. In his letters home Harrison gives some interesting accounts of what he encountered on these early visits. Writing to his mother from Göttingen in January, 1830, he says:[36]

> Blumenbach, the renowned professor of comparative anatomy, a name dear to Englishmen and Americans for 50 years,

is now over eighty, has been professor here for 54 years, has been married now 50 years, ... and is, next to a great poet [Goethe] ... the most celebrated man in Germany. I had a letter from Mr. Ticknor to him and called very soon. ... He is to be asked for as Mr. Upper Medicinal Counsellor Blumenbach; (for life and death are not so important matters as titles here) ... I knocked [at the door of his study] and heard a sound audible a hundred yards – 'Herein', opened the door and met him coming towards me with open arms, and overpowering me with a shower of German ... he wore a flat crowned, green velvet cap and a long coarse shaggy surtout. Thro' the conversation ... his voice passed by the most abrupt transitions from low to high, abounding in sudden shouts and shrieks, & in poohs! of the most uncouth sort... Recommending me to keep a good heart about the difficulty of learning German, he said George III had sent the Dukes of Cumberland, Sussex and Cambridge here ... and put them under his care, with orders not to speak a word of English... They learned German perfectly, but forgot their English. He spoke of the Americans who had been here with great affection, told me to come of an evening, he wd. introduce me to his lady & daughter & I might sit at the same tea table where Ticknor & Everett had sat... He is a rare character, very kind, attentive, and polite to young men; his lectures are interspersed with amusing & valuable anecdotes & plentifully dashed with such phrases as 'Thou Lord Jesus', 'Thou warm-hearted God', and poohs unnumbered. His lady, I did not see, 'til I could speak a little German.

The next personage he met was "Mrs. Chancery Directress" Wedemeyer, the wife of the Chief Justice of the Hanover District Court, an elegant and accomplished lady who spoke English very well. He writes:

I have spent many pleasant evenings there, and avow a most favorable opinion of the minds & cultivation of German ladies. At her house I always meet the three Fräuleins von Laffert, daughters of the Government Inspector of the University, agreeable & rather pretty.

Another letter he delivered to Professor Dissen, "a renowned Greek scholar", who "can read Pindar better than any but one man in the world and equal him." Finally he called on the Professor of Politics, Friedrich Saalfeld, "a laughing gay little man, speaking capital English, a great lover of America, a despiser of England and a genuine good-fellow", to whom he delivered a letter from Mr. Amory.[37]

He informs us that the university had at that time eighty professors and 1264 students, matriculated as follows: Philosophy, 138; Law, 513; Medicine, 262; Theology, 351.[38]

The following remarks, in the same letter, concerning the Göttinger student are worthy of preservation.

> A Göttinger student is quite an apparition to American eyes: the late barbarous fashion of long hair to their shoulders, with huge mustachioes and an open neck and breast, is almost extinct. Now they are to be wondered at for their ridiculous little caps, barely covering the scalps of their heads, with a protection of leather over the forehead, or rather the right eye, for it is so worn by the knowing ones – their ample flaming cloaks, with the broadest felt-collars and the most gorgeous lining flashingly exposed to the spectator's eyes – for long-shafted steel spurs clattering on the street and in the lecture room – for their really beautiful, rich, luxurious pipes (always carried in their hands and smoked in the streets) splendidly decorated with silk and silver-braided tassels, having the color of their caps, implicitly all of which is directed by the customs of their particular countrymen – for their ice bread [?] swaggering impudence, beer drinking, loud singing in the streets – and before all, for their genuine learning.

Nor does Harrison fail to give us a word about the living conditions of the lower classes:

> 'Til in Germany I had never a just idea of the misery and filth with which a loutish peasantry (I speak now of the villages) can be content to live on, never advancing one step from generation to generation: the same from carroty-headed youth to blue-shirted old age. The lower towns-people of Göttingen are almost worthy of the same remarks, but in my foot journey into the Harz I passed through scores of hamlets to which no plum [sic!] I can muster would do justice.[39]

He concludes with a remark which must have been intended as an equally devastating indictment: "What I am certain is, that there is the most total absence of religion in Göttingen."

It is only natural that he should have informed his mother about his living conditions in Göttingen.

> We can procure very neat, often splendid rooms: a sofa, large mirrors, a variety of bureau, chairs and tables make our establishment very comfortable. Each apartment varies from 30 to 100 Rix dollars per ann. (75 cents to a dollar of the German Empire) and if a good carpet were furnished... nothing would remain to surround us with satisfaction while retired in our castles. The waiting is included in the price of the room and is done universally by maids always obedient to the ringing of the bell, whose fidelity and devotedness to their business is truly exemplary. They provide your breakfast which consists, if you are a German, of coarse, sour brown bread (not bad) and beer, but if an outlander, very much after your choice, but very rarely with meat or an egg – Your dinner she brings from the cookshop at a rate generally 4 rd. per month, in a wicker basket containing dishes of soup, two sorts of meat and a dessert of some sort. She goes all errands, buys whatever you want and is in short usually a very worthy personage. The warming of the room is after a peculiar fashion: by a stove which has no opening in your room, but is filled with wood from a door opening outside... The Germans are fond of excessive warmth in their rooms... But the sleeping – one is crammed in a high cradle-shaped box, and covered with another [bed] of the same size...
> I forgot to mention supper, for as we dine at 1/2 past 12 at the latest, this is a meal not to be forgotten... Then I eat white bread and butter, or *Zuckerkuchen* (sugared breads). The making of tea, I flatter myself, I have brought to perfection.

On March 16, 1830, he writes home again telling something of the social life he was enjoying in Göttingen:

> Generally a Professor who feels under obligation to invite various persons gives a slight entertainment which the students term a general *abfütterung*, what Mrs. Wash. Cabell used to call a general feeding. I thank my stars that I can go frequently to Blumenbach's, to Mad. Wedemeyer's and to Mr. Laffert's, with which families I presume you feel already well acquainted. *Thé Dansants*, subscription parties, once a week, attended by the most fashionable persons.
> Recently the venerable Blumenbach gave a splendid ball, and because his rooms are too small, it was given in the Crown Hotel.[40] About 1/2 past 11 a profuse supper was served at the close of which three toasts were given, the ladies being still present. The health of Blumenbach, the

ladies, and it being the Governor General of Hanover's birthday, his health, they were all drunk with loud cheers.

Soon after this party, the semester being ended, Harrison left for Weimar. On Sunday, March 21, 1830, he departed for Cassel in a hackney coach, arriving in the afternoon and hearing Mozart's "Die Zauberflöte", conducted by Spohr. The next day he devoted to a visit to Wilhelmshöhe. On Tuesday at five o'clock in the morning Harrison took leave of Bode, Dorr, Haven and Coffin and drove toward Eisenach, where he arrived at half past three, glimpsing the Wartburg to the right "rearwards of the city." "Thro' Gotha and Erfurt to Weimar by daybreak ... I find at this period, just six months after coming to Göttingen, I can perfectly comprehend the spoken German."[41]

He took lodgings at the "Erbprinz", where the following "Epigramme von Goethe", evidently the work of J. D. Gries, caught his eye the morning he arrived:[42]

"Der Berliner Freimüthige enthält Folgendes aus Weimar":

> Seit einigen Jahren schon finden sich viele Engländer, Franzosen, Schweizer, u.s.w. bei uns ein, weil sie endlich erfahren haben, dass vor fünfzig Jahren Weimar das deutsche Athen genannt wurde. Sie glauben daher, unsere Stadt als die wahre Hochschule Deutschlands besuchen zu müssen, um hier am Orte aus der ersten Hand deutsche Literatur schöpfen zu können. Allein die Sache scheint einen umgekehrten Gang zu nehmen, die jungen Gentlemen und Monsieurs dominieren in allen Gesellschaften, ja selbst bei Hofe, wo man es mit ihren Wappen nicht so genau nimmt, so sehr, dass sie überall das Wort führen. Unsere jungen Damen suchen davon zu profitieren, und radebrechen mit ihnen englisch, französisch und italienisch um die Wette.

"Whereupon it is pretended that Herr v. Goethe made the following:

"Goethe in Weimar 1829. Time – December"

1. Brittisch, Gallisch und Italisch,
   Davon scheint es nicht zu fehlen,
   Wüsst' ich etwa Kamtschadalisch,
   Möcht' ich wirksam mich empfehlen.
   Ach! ich freute mich zu Tode,
   Könnt' ich türkisch radebrechen;
   Aber Deutsch ist aus der Mode
   Und ich weiß nur deutsch zu sprechen.

2. Geduld, verlaß dich auf mein Wort:
   Gar viel ändert sich auf Erden
   Und geht es nur so ein Weilchen fort,
   Wird bald das Deutsche hier am Ort
   Als fremde Sprache Mode werden.

3. Von Bäumen fällt das erste Blatt,
   Die Flur deckt hohen Schnees Lage,
   Die Schlitten klingeln durch die Stadt,
   Man sieht sie nah'n, die Weihnachtstage;
   Doch trittst du zu Saloon herein
   Und hör'st bei Thee und süssem Wein
   Zehn Sprachen durch einander schrei'n,
   So zweifelst du nicht im geringsten
   Wenn draussen Weihnacht – hier sei
                 es Pfingsten.

Manches lässt die Zeit uns seh'n,
Was uns sonst gedaucht als Fabel:
Sonst hiess Weimar: Deutsch Athen,
Jetzt heisst 's: das Deutsche Babel

    Harrison at once dispatched his letter from Herzog Bernhard to Goethe entreating leave to call on the following morning. He was invited to present himself precisely at eleven as the Grand Duchess was to call at noon. On the first afternoon he called at the *Industrie Comptoir* to present Bernhard's letter of introduction to "Herr Med. Rath v. Froriep – one of the kindest, most estimable of men." The same evening at six he went to the theater where he saw "two *petites comedies*" very well performed and where he admired the architecture as well as the audience. Mr. Froriep introduced him to Mr. Passy, an Englishman married to a Miss v. Stein. After the plays he was invited to go to Mr. Passy's to a "musical reunion" usually held alternately at this house and that of Herrn Froriep. Here he discovered that French and English were "spoken in every corner – German rather scouted." At this gathering Harrison met Mr. Plunkett, the nephew of the Irish Chancellor; Mr. Chandler, an acquaintance of the Middletons of America; Mr. Meade; Hofrat Soret, "the tutor of the Erbprinz"; and Herr v. Seebach. The journal adds: "Music and Whist: ashamed of myself for winning 8 Thalers."
    Here we are told that Mr. Froriep thinks "Göttingen much behind in respect of the newest literature", an opinion previously expressed by George Henry Calvert and suggested by A. W. Schlegel.[43]
    Immediately after this the journal gives the account of the first visit of the last American to have an audience with Goethe.[44]

Next day at 11 drove to his Excellency v. Göthe's – house rather extensive and pretty fair exterior: 2 stories with comfortable attic, the latter appropriated to Mad. de Göthe's receptions – the house flanked by a *porte-cochère* on each side. Found a little confusion below as I drove up – the bonne being in expectation of the Duchess. Conducted up – passed two bronzes from antiques, besides a bronze greyhound. At threshold of his receiving rooms "Salve" written. He dressed in brown surtout, wrapped around his body – noble presence, rich rather voluptuous, cheerful expression of the eye and in a supreme degree of the mouth 'tho somewhat collapsed. The portrait from Stieler at request of the King of Bavaria, who visited him on his birthday in 1828, representing him holding a letter in his hand signed "Ludwig", of which a facsimile hangs in Mad. de Göthe's rooms, is altogether perfect. The room was crowded with bits of reliefs, medals, etc., showing the direction towards art which his mind has for some years taken. His *eigentliches arbeitszimmer*, as Miss Froriep tells me, no foreigner is allowed to see, from a just dread of indecent exposure to the travel-reading public. He saluted me unexpectedly in French, asked pertinent and shrewd questions about Virginia evidently determined to make me the talker; seemed well acquainted with the general plan of Mr. Jefferson's university. I explained to him its connection with the State.[45] Asked where I was educated. Harvard – praised Everett "une bonne tête", had read many of his productions: seemed however to confound the two brothers. If young men from America any longer went to Eng[land] for their education. – Spoke of Duke B's enthusiastic attachment to America. Made a hasty adieu – exceedingly soft hand, wished me success in life. I agree with other strangers that his manner is not free from a slight embarrassment; he is evidently not quite easy in his French.

Subsequently Harrison relates of Goethe's meeting with and marriage to Christine Vulpius, of their son August, "an employe[e] in public affairs – a huge beefeating [?] clown – often too drunk to hold his glass." August's wife, Ottilie, he calls "the cleverest woman, patroness of foreign merit", who "has travelled in England, corresponds with many English and is termed 'the English Consul'."[46]

Harrison's special friend seems to have been Dr. Friedrich Ludwig Froriep whose house he was invited to visit on many evenings in succession. One Sunday morning, while they were walking in the park together, Froriep introduced the American to an English proverb, – "a curse" – "May your soul have no more rest than a German hat!"

He proudly relates that when he dined at Froriep's house he was seated next to Madame General Superintendant Referendar Conta and that Prof. Riemer addressed him as "Herr Doktor." It was Froriep who presented him to "Frau Oberhofmarschallin von Spiegel," an "excellent maternally kind lady", this being "the road to presentation at Court." He relates:

> Next morning I expected to be invited to dine, being now equipped with breeches, sword and chapeau. A *fourrier* was accordingly sent in the morning to beg, I would not take it ill that I could not be received for two days to come as a courier had arrived to announce the death of the Grand Duke of Baden. On Sunday however I was bidden to dinner at 3 o'clock. Went in *porte chaise:* ushered into a room where several persons are already assembled in their uniforms, but all with the same badge of mourning for the late Duchess Amalie [† February 14, 1830]. Froriep presented me to Bielke, the Kammerherr of the Grossfürstin and to Beulwitz, adjutant to the Duke. I had previously sent cards to them and to certain Hofdamen and others. Presently, preceded by an officer of the household, the royal [*sic!*] couple entered, arm in arm; we arranged ourselves in a circle. They spoke to each person in the order he or she stood in. As the Grossfürstin approached me Bielke advanced and presented me. Her appearance is the most decidedly authoritative and commanding – showing high birth and habits of undoubted deference united with great simplicity and modesty, – that I have ever seen. [*sic!*] The spirit of all the Empresses seems to be lodged [?] in her. She speaks French by preference and is slightly deaf; her voice is suppressed, level and sweet; her face altogether tranquil thro' the conversation. She was in deep mourning except for a plain white frill, as were all the ladies. One addresses her with "votre altesse Imperial[e]." Says she understood English, but did not speak it. Mentioned the Duke B., by whom I was recommended to Weimar – his passion for America. I said he had made the name of Weimar very dear to American hearts. Enquired about Göttingen and about American universities. You have also a Cambridge in America? What our plan was? I should say [?] more like the Scotch than any other, but of late we were abandoning British models to adopt German methods. She said that Germany had much that was good for imitation, but there was no longer freedom in German universities. I said we learned not so much by the way of lectures in America, as by the study of authors and by frequent examinations. She

passed on graciously wishing to see me often while I remained in Weimar. Next came the Grand Duke to me – presented by Beulwitz: the truest model of bonhommie: dressed like a General officer in jack boots and white breeches with a cocked hat and cock's feathers. Spoke of Bernhard – had kept notes on his journey – they would make him print it. [! Published in 1828?] ... His French was ... of the rapidest. Passed on with a civil word. When dinner was ready he gave her his arm: we followed without form and sat down as chance regulated. I sat with F. on my right and the Gräfin von Egloffstein on my left... Sat about 2 hours. Out into saloon – coffee and away without taking leave. To come back to tea and cards. At night returned: found numerous society-ladies looking like nuns.

One bows to the two personages before they sit to cards. Then when the parties are formed ... one must advance and make his compliments at the table where each [i.e. the Duke and the Duchess] sits, pass on and then be free for the evening. Mad. Spiegel ... introduced me to the Gräfin Fritsch ... Introduced to Comte Santi, Russian chargé d' affaires and his wife the prettiest woman in Weimar.

. . . .
At 1/2 past 10 or 11 they retire.

The meeting with Sir James Lawrence of Jamaica, Knight of Malta, that evening caused reminiscences of Aaron Burr's visit to Weimar in 1810, who later called on Lawrence in London and proposed that the latter come to America and found on the Mississippi a republic such as is described in his Utopian novel "The Empire of the Nairs", a state without marriage.[47] Also von Gersdorff recalled seeing Burr in Weimar and "setting him down at his lodgings in his carriage."

On Easter Sunday, April 11th, Harrison was again invited to Court where he had a long talk with von Gersdorff about German politics and also "conversed with Miss Pappenheim ... her English is perfect." A few days later (April 16th) he was invited to tea and cards at the home of Mad. de Spiegel who told him she had written to Duke Bernhard informing him of Harrison's arrival and presentation at Court. On Sunday, April 18th (Greek Easter) he was invited to dinner at three o'clock to meet the Grand Duke of Oldenburg at the castle. At 6:30 they returned for tea and cards.

At this time Harrison was a frequent visitor at the Weimar theater. He informs he heard "Oberon", "The Vampire", "The Muette", and witnessed "Hermann and Dorothea" as a drama and "Wallenstein's Lager" on one evening and "Wallenstein's Tod" on another.

63

An "Excursion to Jena" was made on Thursday, the 22nd of April with Froriep in the latter's carriage. They called on Professor Luden. The American was received with great cordiality when he presented his "letter from Prince Bernhard." Luden declared himself to be "a passionate admirer of America" and "anti-English." The professor of history said however that "our system was too beautiful to last", that "we should split, have wars, generals, military rank, and then settled monarchies." This from a scholar who asserted that "a historian was an 'umgekehrter Prophet'" and who had been delivering a course of two lectures weekly for a semester on the history of America based on Ramsay's history.[48]

Luden also informed the Göttingen student that there was nothing in Göttingen "by universal acknowledgement but the Bibliothek; all the Professors old and sour." He amused the young Virginian with "most brilliant conversation, with rich and apt quotations of Latin and brilliant sallies of wit." On this occasion he expressed his unfavorable opinion of the work of John Russell, who had, he opines, misrepresented conditions in Weimar.[49] He asserted Russell was a *Racker*, acknowledged that was a strong word and defined it as a *knave in potentia*.

While in Jena Harrison made his "debut in walzing and in the gallopade at a Ressource Ball in the Stadt Haus." Although he enjoyed this short visit he was not willing to yield to Luden's urging that he remain in Jena.

Since the following seems to be the sole evidence of Harrison's second visit to Goethe in Weimar, I shall quote *in extenso* from his "Diary."

> Two or three days before the time set for my departure, Göthe sent to me and Plunkett, who was also on the wing, desiring to see us at 11 in the morning. We repaired thither – found him in other rooms, very tastefully furnished, with specimens of art – some very good frescoes, torsos, etc. He again addressed us in French but we continued to shift to German which it was my greatest desire to hear from his lips. That we should have succeeded in getting from him something, more than the commonplace incident to the reception of strangers or the good sense of a common man of intelligence, was much to be hoped, when in rushed a Russian countess who, seating herself by him, poured in on him a volley of French on the Russian poet who had defaced all the splendor of all the Anacreons, Byrons, Homers, etc., which lasted for an hour and a half. We stayed 'til the end to take leave. Duchess said to speak English pretty well – Irish accent.

During the month spent in the court circle the youthful American naturally picked up much gossip which borders on the scandalous. Some of this he recorded in his diary and reported, in part at least, in his letters to his relatives in America. Thus, after one of the Court parties he reports:[50]

> Told by Mad. M. of the old Duke's passion for Mad. Jagemann of the theatre: on the birth of Bernard physicians declare that another parturition would inevitably kill the Duchess Luise. She thereupon bade the Duke seek out with her full consent another woman for the necessary gratification of nature. He chose the actress – cohabited with her, the Duchess sanctioning it, interchanging civilities with her and getting angry with people of the court who had not attended the theatre when Jagemann was to play. Duke gave her a letter of nobility, calling her Frau v. Haygendorff [Heygendorff] and had three, perhaps four children, 2 sons and 2 daughters, one of the latter pretended to be daughter of a Polish lady by another father and left young with the Hugendorf [sic!]. The inheritance of one daughter is to be Spiegel's house. Among other lands the Duke gave Heigendorf a garden beyond the Stern, near Goethe's cottage with one adjoining it to Stromeyer, an actor, favorite of Heigendorf and perhaps joint father of some of the children. She is not received however by the present [Ducal] family.

Another morsel of scandalous gossip learned from another lady at the Court was the story of "Madamoiselle Vulpius", the birth of August and the subsequent marriage of Goethe to Christine. At a party at Mad. de Goethe's [Ottilie's] Harrison was presented to Minister and Ministerin v. Gersdorf. He writes: "She is very pretty still, said to have been the reigning favorite of Jerome at Cassel – daughter, Miss Pappenheim, fruit of their love. Daughter pretty – perfect English and decided talent."[51]

Perhaps not scandalous but rather candid is the reported statement of Professor Luden in Jena about the traveller and author, John Russell[52] who is said to have told of "as existing, things which were the wonders of former times and never times." However it is evident that in spite of such remarks Harrison used Russell's work as a sort of guide book.[53] His journal contains many notes excerpted from that volume, and, even though he demonstrates the fallibility of the text, he states as his final judgement in a letter from Berlin on August 3rd, 1830, that "Russell's Tour ... is the only good book on Germany."[54]

After March 30th Harrison engaged lodgings for the month of

April at an English pension called "Salve." Next to him lodged Lord Henry Beauclere, brother of the Duke of Wellington. Plunkett was his fellow lodger. Toward the end of the month Harrison, preparing for his departure from Weimar, reports:

> To take leave at Court, one sends a notice to the Oberhofmarschall the day before. In most cases one is invited to dine; but I, having set Thursday [the 29th] for my Congé-day, was invited to come in the afternoon to tea and cards, there being no dinner on that day. Warner and Beach were also to take leave. We found a small company. The Duchess came around and spoke very familiarly with each, with me more than ten minutes. She said her family were almost all extinct in Russia, else she would give me a letter to her mother. Spoke of having received Dwight's book[55] from Froriep. Said they were naturally anxious to see what impression Germany made on America. I mentioned my desire to study the *servage* in Russia with a hope of drawing profitable instruction with reference to slavery in America. She spoke at length of Russian sentiments on the subject with good sense. Passed on saying she had to *"causer"* with some others. Her last impression is more and more noble and imperial. Her beauty must have been distinguished in her youth; besides the decided charm of her countenance, she showed, on one of the Easter evenings *in gala*, the finest pair of shoulders that I have ever seen. Duke very kind in his hurry-scurry way – dropped his plumes, returned a thousand thanks to those who picked them up. The evening was passed in examining prints – among them Milbert's *Hudson Views*. Duchess did not play, but went around talking thro' the evening.

On May 1st "after more than five weeks residence in Weimar", Harrison departed by extra post with an English gentleman, Reverend J. Lee Warner, for Leipzig, where they arrived by nightfall. On the following day, Sunday: "We first sought out *Auerbach's Keller*, renowned for the revel of the Devil and Dr. Faustus."[56] It was in Leipzig that Harrison saw "Der Freischütz" for the first time. On Monday Froriep called at his hotel. They strolled on the promenade and dined at the "Hotel de Saxe."

On New Year Day, 1830, Harrison had written from Göttingen to his mother.[57] "I shall prefer to go through the borders of Saxony to Berlin in the Spring, there to reside thro' the summer semester." From Berlin he wrote on June 15th, 1830:[58] "I am to spend the summer here, in the middle of August I shall go to ... Carlsbad in Bohemia, where I shall pass a few days, thence to Munich and out thro' Switzerland over the Alps.[59]

It will be noted that his statements concerning his residence in Berlin are rather general and sometimes vague. There is no evidence either in his own records or in the "Verzeichnissen der Königlichen Universität" that he ever registered there. It is however possible, or even probable, that he visited the Humboldt university and attended lectures there as a "Gasthörer" during the Spring which he spent in the Prussian capital.

From an unpublished letter sent from Berlin on July 27th we learn that the many letters of introduction he had brought with him "procured several very gratifying acquaintances. The most worthy of being named is Baron and Minister William Humboldt ... much more distinguished in the estimation of the whole continent" than his brother Alexander. He sent his letter of introduction and in a day or two Humboldt called having sent in advance an invitation to dine at his country seat at Tegel. There Harrison spent a very agreeable day with a select party and found "an infinite deal to admire in his rich collection of ancient and modern art."

He was intrigued to report that Humboldt's special interest in America, even in the United States, was for the Indian languages. He reports:

> A friend of mine has just received from Boston for him a file of Cherokee gazettes [and] he [Humboldt] is searching in this barbarous maze for traces of affinity of the Indian tribes to any European or Asiatic race. He is at present occupied with the composition of a dictionary of the old Mexican language.

We are told that while in Berlin Harrison made, at the request of Henry Clay, "some economic investigations" concerning the handicaps suffered by Germany due to its political disunity.[60] Evidence of this one of Harrison's activities is offered by the discovery in his "Diary" of ten pages of notes on the "Prussian Tarif" levied on textiles, leather, cotton, silk, wool and diamonds copied from Schmidt's "Unterricht der Besteuerung in Preussischen Staaten." Regard for Clay's admonition that information as to the status of Russian serfs might be helpful in connection with our slave problem has already been noted in Harrison's reference to *"servage"* in his conversation with Maria Paulowna in Weimar.[61]

This repeated concern displayed in the slavery question (serfage) in Europe is based on the lively interest he had manifested, before his departure for Europe, in the "American Colonization Society" at home. Not only did he deliver a discourse "The Colonization Society Vindicated in Virginia" at the annual meeting of the Lynchburg Colonization Society in July, 1827, but he was a delegate of the Lynchburg group to the eleventh annual meeting of the national society held in Washington the following December, when Chief Justice John Marshall was a delegate from Richmond. Harrison's remarks on this occasion are preserved in the official report of that meeting in the *Repository and Colonial Journal*, as is also the full text of his Lynchburg discourse.[62]

It is therefore no surprise to find in Walsh's *American Quarterly Review* for December, 1832,[63] Harrison's lengthy and learned article "The Slavery Question in Virginia", occasioned by *The Speech of Thomas Marshall in the House of Delegates of Virginia on the Abolition of Slavery, Delivered, Friday, January* 20, 1832.[64] Although this article does not abound in a display of knowledge acquired during the author's residence in Europe, it does manifest his good opinion of the "Germans, who are perhaps the most valuable of the emigrants to America" (p. 347). He declares: "We have ourselves the very best reason to know that extreme interest is expressed in this project [i.e., the founding of Liberia by the American Colonization Society] by learned Professors and Ministers of State in Germany."[65] This latter statement must indicate that the youthful advocate of the colonization of American "free blacks" in Africa had discussed this question in the learned and ruling university and court circles of Germany. The extension of this statement:

> The Bulletins of the Geographical Society of Paris have often heralded the rising greatness of our little African republic and paid some of the advocates of the Society the flattering compliment of translating large tracts of their speeches.

suggests that Harrison's speeches experienced such treatment, for in a letter from Paris on August 11th, 1829,[66] he had written: "Inform Mr. Cabell and Fletcher that I cut some figure in the Bulletin of the Geographical Society of this month, in my character of philanthropist: it was an account of the Colony of Liberia." An examination of the *Bulletin de La Société de Géographie* discloses a "Notice sur la colonie américaine de Liberia, établie sur la côte d'Afrique" which contains the following:[67]

> M. Harrison, de Virginie, dans son interessant discourse, dit; il y a maintenant onze ans que la société a été fondée. Le rapport d' aujourd'hui ne permet pas de doubter du succes complet qu'elle obtiendra, si le peuple des États Unis lui continue sa protection. Déjà nous pouvons considérer l'Afrique comme regenerée par ses fils revenus dans son sein et l'association de Liberia comme une souche fertile qui reportera dans l'intérieur de l'Afrique les sentiments d'humanité et la civilization.

Whatever may have been his attitude toward formal university training during his short semester in Berlin, Harrison did display some interest in the arts. In a letter from Potsdam he wrote on August 3rd:

> The German theater can hardly be said to be rich in original pieces – half a dozen masterpieces of Schiller and a few of Müllner's and Kotzebue's productions stand at the head; yet the host of translations out of other languages composes the main body of the stock-plays... That the German admirers of Shakespeare have a taste more Shakespearean than the English I had suspected... That the Germans sometimes find reason and nature in Shakespeare where neither exists is perhaps very true. "The Spy", after Cooper, I saw admirably played... The piece is very popular.

Since he wrote in the last page of his "Diary" about the white marble bust of Prince Hardenberg "in the church in Mittelstraße" (Berlin) we may wonder whether his curiosity to see the birthplace and childhood haunts of Francis Lieber, from whom he received through Ticknor letters of introduction to prominent Germans, and whose American-born son, Oscar Montgomery, was later to fight in this same street, did not cause the young Virginian to be in this vicinity.[68] He also tells us that in a conversation with Professor Rauch he was advised to see a certain statue at *Sans Souci*.

The letter from Potsdam also contains the statement: "I shall hardly ever be a German enthusiast." In this connection we must recall his words of June 15, written from Berlin: "Before leaving America I had fairly lost all desire to lead a University life, if anything since has been wanting to decide me, it was found in observing the moderate estimation which Classical Professors enjoy, even when most eminent, in countries where these studies are pursued." Nor must we neglect the statement made in the printed biography of Jesse Burton Harrison (p. 118) "Life in Weimar enamoured Thackery [who was received by Goethe just three months after Harrison had been received] of literature and persuaded him to abandon his purpose of being called to the bar." Nor must we forget that on July 15, 1829, the one-year appointment of Jesse Burton's rival, Gessner Harrison, having expired, the latter was elected permanent professor of ancient languages of the University of Virginia.[69]

On August 3rd, 1830, Jesse Burton left Potsdam on the post coach for Wittenberg.[70] At Dresden he met James Fenimore Cooper, whom he discribes as "a most loquacious [word illegible], what else? – very clever, 'tho not agreeable man."[71] In a letter to Dr. Froriep from America, dated September 1, 1831, Harrison says:[72]

Cooper passed through Weimar and when I met him afterwards in Paris he ridiculed the town: we waged war about it.

On August 10th he left Dresden for Carlsbad in a *Lohnkutsche* with a painter, Professor Hartmann, where his waltzing won from the ladies the compliment that he "danced like a native *Deutscher*." From Geneva he wrote: "I have made on foot about 100 leagues in the last fortnight from Constance to Schaffhausen, Zurich, Zug, Altdorf, St. Gothard, Berne to this point."[73] By September 22, 1830, he had arrived in Venice.

Just two years after departure Harrison was home again in June, 1831, and was fully convinced that he could no longer tolerate living in the small, intolerant town of Lynchburg, where he finds a "'Schwärmerey' which leaves the English Evangelicans a thousand leagues behind."[74] Already at this time he expressed his intention to settle in Baltimore or New Orleans. In closing the letter to Froriep he desires to be remembered to Madame and Miss Froriep, to her Imperial Highness, to Mad. de Spiegel and to Professor Luden.

Henry Clay, himself an emigré to the West, advised Harrison from Ashland (in Kentucky) to move to New Orleans, where there was a good demand for legal talent, and where "your French and Spanish would be of great advantage to you."[75] In December (1831) Harrison was a delegate from Virginia to the Baltimore Convention which founded the National Republican party and nominated his cousin, Henry Clay, as a candidate for the Presidency of the United States. At the same time he declined a very flattering offer made by the family of Thomas Jefferson that he "write a philosophical 'Life'"[76] of Jefferson. Again, after the appearance in Hugh S. Legaré's *Southern Review* for February, 1832,[77] of Harrison's essay on "English Civilization," this request was renewed by his friend N. P. Trist on behalf of the family.

This essay termed by his biographers "the first fruit of his foreign education"[78] sets up the thesis that "in literature and in manners the people of the United States cannot find in England as wholesome influence as on the Continent" and "that in England only the actual is approved, while in France and Germany, as in America, the desirable is the universal quest."[79] Although there are frequent references to German learning, arts and letters – Goethe, Schiller, Schlegel, Heeren, Niebuhr,[80] – there is only one citation in German, that from *Faust*, which Harrison translates:[81]

> Laws and Rights do but inherit themselves, onward, like an eternal disease; wo [*sic!*] to thee, that thou art born a grandchild! Of the Right that is connate with us, of that alas! not once the question is,

used to chide the English who "rarely do more than trace the genealogy of freedom." He goes on to say (324) that "even in that branch of metaphysics, wherein she [England] allows her talents full scope, the science of the moral and intellectual function of the mind, ... she will not bear a very favorable comparison with the Germans."

"German classical criticism surpasses that of England," "their German translations are not the ripest," "Lessing, Goethe, Schlegel, Tieck and Coleridge (... *plus Allemand* que les Allemands) have raised the English Poet to an eminence which no one of the editors of the Variorum Shakespeare had dared to claim for him."[82] Hence we must not be satisfied to get our knowledge of foreign literatures and foreign history "through the hands of England," since "our country is already possessed of those who are competent ... to furnish us proper information on the novelties of letters and science with which France, Italy and Germany are daily adorning the world."

The whole essay serves as a good example of that growth of admiration for the German achievements in the fields of letters and learning that tended to divert Anglo-Saxon America from the sphere of its English heritage and made the Nineteenth Century the German Century in the fields of American Culture and Civilization.

Immediately after the Baltimore Convention (December, 1831) Harrison went to New Orleans, stopping *en route* at Cincinnati where began his friendship with Salmon P. Chase (1805-1873) of that city, later (1864) Chief Justice of the Supreme Court of the United States. Chase wrote Harrison a letter of introduction to the Honorable Edward D. White, M.C. at New Orleans, whose son Edward Douglas White (1845-1921) became Chief Justice of the same court in 1910. After the appearance of Harrison's article "The Slavery Question in Virginia" in the *American Quarterly Review*[83] Chase, himself an anti-slavery man, wrote on April 3rd, 1832, inviting Harrison to contribute articles to and solicit subscriptions for a new periodical to be established by Chase, Dr. Peabody, and Mr. Timothy Walker, to which William Wirt, Daniel Webster and the Everett brothers were also to be contributors.[84]

On January 6, 1832, Harrison was admitted to the bar of the State of Louisiana. The first summer of his citizenship of Louisiana he spent at Saratoga Springs, New York, which visit must have aroused reminiscences of his visit to Karlsbad in the summer of 1830. On his return journey he sojourned in New England and renewed his acquaintance with George Ticknor and Edward Everett. Alexander H. Everett, Edward's elder brother, he now met for the first time. This acquaintance was destined to grow during the next few years.

When he returned to New Orleans he participated in manifold professional and cultural activities. He served as secretary at the meetings of the bar and made strenuous and extensive efforts to earn a reputation in the legal field. In advising Harrison to settle in New Orleans, Clay stated:[85]

> N. Orleans has the air, manners, language and factions of a European Continental City. Society upon the whole is very good, and you may have any sort, gay or grave, American, Creole, or Foreign, learned or unlearned, commercial or professional, black, white, yellow or red.

But he also pointed out that French and Spanish "are almost indispensable." Hence it is not surprising to learn that Harrison "laid the foundation of his strictly professional reputation by editing,"[86] in four huge volumes constituting 3,300 pages, the *Reports of Cases in the Superior Court of the Territory of Orleans and the Supreme Court of Louisiana*, "containing the Decisions of those Courts from the Autumn Term, 1809, to the March Term, 1830, and which are embraced in the Twenty Volumes of Fr. Xavier Martin's Reports, with Notes of Louisiana Cases, wherein the doctrines are affirmed, contradicted and extended, and of subsequent Legislation."[87] The work is dedicated to the Honorable Alexander Porter, later one of the Judges of the Supreme Court of Louisiana, at whose suggestion Harrison had undertaken this arduous task.

The following excerpt from Harrison's preface to the work makes clear the nature of the undertaking.

> Cases determined in Louisiana from 1809 to 1830, a period comprising the sway of the Spanish Law, its modifications by the two (more or less) French systems of 1808 and 1825, and its total repeal in 1828, through which period the foundations of our law were thoroughly explored and established.

The further utility of his knowledge of Spanish is indicated by the fact that it resulted in several business trips to Cuba, where he was able to renew his lifelong friendship with Nicholas P. Trist, then United States Consul in Havana. On August 1, 1839, Trist wrote to him from Havana:[88]

> You have not been a stranger to my thoughts. On the contrary I have become Germanized (not in the language unhappily, but in Carlyle's English). It has been natural for me to think of Goethe – and then of your New Orleans office, and Goethe's picture there and of your Germany trip, etc. Sartor Resartus you have read of course.

J. Burton Harrison was one of the leading spirits in organizing the original "Historical Society of Louisiana" which was formed on May 9, 1835, in the Supreme Court Room in New Orleans. Henry Adams Bullard presided and Harrison was appointed secretary of the meeting. The committee appointed to draw up the consitution was composed of Bullard, Harrison and Alexander Porter. "After arranging for the secretary (Harrison) to correspond with various literary men of the State"[89], the meeting adjourned until the second Monday of January, 1836, at which gathering Bullard delivered a lengthy address which was commented on in *The North American Review* of which Alexander H. Everett was editor (1835-1843).[90] On January 15th Bullard formally became president and Harrison, corresponding secretary. That the secretary did not confine his correspondence to the local scholars is testified to by a number of letters found in the Library of Congress. In reply to such a communication addressed to him by Harrison on September 10, 1835, A. H. Everett declared:[91]

> The establishment of the Historical Society of Louisiana will be ... an event of importance to the historical literature of our country... I shall be ... happy individually and as a member of the Historical Society of Massachusetts to cooperate with you to the extent of my feeble ability.

Exactly one year later Caleb Cushing of Newburyport acknowledged the receipt of an invitation "to cooperate with you in an enterprise interesting to the whole country" and disclosed his "great satisfaction to perceive that intelligent inhabitants of Louisiana were turning their attention to their own local history, and preparing ... to rescue its documents and traditions from decay and oblivion."[92]

On May 4th, 1836, the *New Orleans Bee* announced that Mr. J. B. Harrison was to deliver a discourse at a meeting of the Society "on the third Monday of this month [May 16th]." No one has ever been able to ascertain whether this discourse was ever delivered. It seems certain that the following remarks contained in a letter of September 18, 1837, to the Honorable Henry A. Bullard from Mr. John Gorham Palfrey, the owner and later editor of the *North American Review*, have reference to the first address of the president of the Historical Society and the one that was promised by the secretary, Mr. Harrison:

> When do you mean to let me have your article on the History of Louisiana? My readers and their purveyors are longing for it...

> I wish you would find time to waylay Mr. Harrison in the street for me. I pray him to gratify the hope he allowed me to indulge of having something from his pen.[93]

Since Jesse Burton Harrison had been in his youth almost a member of the Jefferson household at Monticello and a frequent and close visitor of his friend and patron James Monroe at Montepelier, it might be said with justice that he was a politician throughout his entire life, but it was in New Orleans in 1836 that he entered the lists actively and in earnest. At the suggestion of another of his mentors, his cousin, Henry Clay, he then accepted the editorship of the *Louisiana Advertiser* (1820-1840), a newspaper already in 1827 hailed by C. Sidons (Karl Postl, Charles Sealsfield), the great German-American traveller and author, as "die beste" among the newspapers of New Orleans, "ein besonders in kommerzieller Hinsicht vortrefflich redigiertes Blatt."[94] The *Advertiser* was, under Harrison's editorship, the Whig organ in New Orleans for the presidential campaign.

We are told that Harrison brought to this position "a most efficient literary equipment and the enthusiasm of political conviction."[95] He was fortified by his personal reminiscence of at least two former presidents of the country and by acute observation of political conditions in other lands, especially in Germany. He made use of his classical education to embellish his columns in the *Advertiser* with references to and excerpts from the literature of classical antiquity.[96] The following parody called "Terence's Portrait of Martin Van Buren", and based on the *Eunuchs* (Act II, 2, 20), is not only an example of the editor's sense of humor but is a possible suggestion of his acquaintance with the comedy of Ludwig Tieck:

> Does Jackson call black white? I'll swear
>   't is true,
> Then should he eat his words I'll bolt
>   mine too;
> A point asserts, tomorrow contradicts it?
> Behold me, faithful slave of *Ipse dixit*!
> This thrifty craft may rule a great
>   event;
> Perchance may Puss in boots make
>   President![97]

As history records, Van Buren was elected president and, although Henry Clay and Harrison and the *Louisiana Advertiser* met defeat, the closeness of the contest in Louisiana was encouraging for the prospects of the defeated editor. As agreed in advance, Harrison was relieved of the burden of editorship after the close of the campaign in the Fall [1836]. But, when in the Winter of 1836-1837 he was a candidate for a seat on the bench, Governor Edward D. White told one of Harrison's advocates:[98] "If you will say that Mr. Harrison was not the author of a certain stinging article concerning me which appeared in the *Advertiser*, I will appoint him successor to Canonage, for I know he is qualified for the office." However Harrison had been responsible for the said article.

With the cooperation of Judge Alex Porter, United State Senator from Louisiana, an uncle of his wife, Harrison was planning to run for senator as soon as the Whigs would control the state. Evidently he turned for advice concerning the advisability of standing for election to Congress to Christian Roselius, then probably the most eminent legal light of German nativity in New Orleans, as the following communication from Roselius indicates:[99]

> New Orleans, September 10th, 1839.
>
> My own opinion is that it would be imprudent for you to run in opposition to Mr. Preston – if there are two *American* candidates, the Creoles and French will surely start one of their own men, in which case, the American vote being split, defeat would be the inevitable result... If Preston determines not to run for the Senate, I think your chances are very fair.
>
> J. B. Harrison Truly yours
> Pass Christian C. Roselius

During his residence in New Orleans Harrison occasionally lectured at Jefferson College in St. James Parish. He refused the offer of a chair in the faculty of that institution, but was undoubtedly instrumental in bringing to its faculty his friend and admirer, Alexander H. Everett. We are told that Everett came to New Orleans in 1840 "to take the chair at Jefferson College which Burton Harrison had refused."[100] We know that Everett "on assuming the office of president"[101] of that college delivered his inaugural address on June 30, 1841.

The article "Do you pass the Summer in Town?" which Harrison's biographers reprint from one of his editorials in the *Advertiser*[102] is not only a literary gem descriptive of the life and spirit of New Orleans in the heated period, when the fear of yellow fever caused many of the inhabitants to abandon the city for safer climes, but seems to be otherwise prophetically inspired, for the editor wrote:

> or whether the yellow fever shall sap the fortress of life of more than one who was born to be loved by the world, but

whose manly heart burst at the end of an unfinished career, with the thought that the world had not yet yielded him what it owed him!

Even so was the active and promising career of Jesse Burton Harrison cut short when on January 8, 1841, he died in his thirty-sixth year as the results of an attack of yellow fever. On Saturday, January 9, 1841, the following announcement appeared in the New Orleans *Daily Picayune:*

> The friends and acquaintances of Jesse Burton Harrison, Esq., are invited to attend his funeral at 9 o'clock this morning, from the residence of William Brand, Esq., Magazine Street.

Thus was prematurely dissolved the only direct personal bond that ever connected the city of New Orleans with the Sage of Weimar.

THOMAS CAUTE REYNOLDS

SOUTH CAROLINA, VIRGINIA, MISSOURI

The career of the ubiquitous Thomas Caute Reynolds is difficult to follow.[1] Although he was born on October 11, 1821, at Charleston, South Carolina, he moved to his ancestral state, Virginia, while yet a boy. His pride of ancestry is evident from his words written a generation later: "I will state that my ancestor contemporary with General Washington was his second cousin, each being a grandchild of the coheiresses of Mr. Augustine Warner of Warner Hall, President of the Council of Virginia under Charles 2nd, and General Washington's brother having married a sister of my grandmother."[2] Young Reynolds attended the University of Virginia and was graduated at the age of sixteen (1838). On December 4, 1838 Hugh S. Legaré, who at that time represented South Carolina in Congress, sent from Washington to Thomas C. Reynolds, Esq., passports for himself and George Guerard, both native Charlestonians, and also several letters of introduction to prominent personalities in Europe among whom were the Honorable Henry Wheaton, American Minister in Berlin, Professor A. W. Schlegel at Bonn, Virgil Maxcy, American Chargé at Brussels and M. le Comte Arrivabene, likewise in the Belgian capital.[3] Reynolds tells us that he delivered the letters addressed to Mr. Wheaton and "M. de Schlegel." We have in print the epistle to M. Arrivabene which he was not able to deliver. This letter discloses that the two Charlestonians "vont á Bonn, pour y faire leurs études universitaires."[4]

On June 7, 1839 Legaré addressed another letter to Reynolds, now a student in Berlin, where he probably delivered his letter of introduction to Mr. Wheaton. Legaré hopes that the American students have become acquainted "with the most distinguished men of the University, especially with M. de Savigny" and adds: "Pray make my compliments to your fellow-traveller, Mr. Guerard. He, like myself, is a descendant of the Hugenots, and will find many of the same race at Berlin. M. Savigny, I believe, is one of them."[5]

On April 23, 1840, Mr. Legaré writes to Reynolds at Heidelberg indicating that a move from Munich has been accomplished:

I dare say you find [i.e., have found] Munich an agreeable

residence. Poor Drayton Grimké [† 1838] and McMillan King [both of Charleston] seemed very much pleased with society and other advantages of that city.

He further advises Reynolds what to study and how to do it. Once more he wants to be remembered "to your compagnon de voyage."[6]

On February 6, 1841, Legaré acknowledges the receipt of a very interesting letter from Heidelberg. He advises Reynolds against a too protracted residence in Europe. Speaking from his own personal experience he warns:

> I have found my *studies* in *Europe* impede me at every step of my progress. ...Our people have a fixed aversion to everything that looks like foreign education... Nothing is more *perilous*, in America, than to be too long *learning*, and to get the name of bookish. Stay in Europe long enough to lay the ground-work of professional eminence, by pursuing the branches of knowledge most instrumental in advancing it. Let me, therefore, advise you to come home and study a profession.[7]

Again Legaré praises the intelligence displayed in Reynolds' letters from Europe. Unfortunately these letters have never been published, but the philosophy contained in the last letter from Legaré made a deep and lasting impression on the young Heidelberg doctor-to-be. Nevertheless he heeded the counsel of his mentor only in part for he did continue his studies in Germany until he obtained the doctor's degree in law at Heidelberg University on August 11, 1842.[8] The dissertation *De Vera Judicii Juratorum Origine, Nature et Indole. Dissertatio inauguralis quam illustri jurisconsultorum ordine in alma literarum Universitate Ruperto Carola Heidelbergensi ad Gradum Doctoris summos in Jure Civili et Canonico honores rite obtinendos submisit Auctor* Thomas Caute Reynolds, *Carolina – Americanus*. Heidelbergae, 1842, pp. 90.[9]

On May 31, 1843, Reynolds wrote to Francis Lieber, L.L.D., at South Carolina College thanking him for his interest in the thesis[10], informing he "had already sent a copy of that document to Judge Story (along with a letter from M. [Jean Jacques] Foelix)," and saying that Professor Mittermaier "had requested thirty copies to distribute among his friends in Italy & Hungary."[11] He also discloses here that the notice of his dissertation which appeared in *The Law Reporter*[12] was written by another of Lieber's friends who had recently returned from Heidelberg, Mr. (later Senator) Charles Sumner.[13]

The July number of the *Southern Literary Messenger* for 1843 brings a review of the dissertation. After observing that the May number of the "Law Journal" states "that the dissertation ... bears most gratifying testimony to the learning and talents of the author" and adding several complimentary observations about Reynolds having sought "in the fountains of ancient learning, the true origin of an institution which is justly said 'to be more instinct with the spirit of freedom than anything which has proceeded from the Campus Martius or the banks of the Tiber' ",[14] the editor concludes: "We are gratified to learn that Mr. Reynolds has it in contemplation to make this metropolis ... [Richmond] his permanent abode."[15]

Shortly thereafter Reynolds began to contribute to the columns of the *Southern Literary Messenger*. The September (1843) issue[16] contains his article "H. S. Legaré, Late Attorney General of the United States" in which he pays tribute to his old friend and mentor:

> In the languages and literature of Modern Europe he was perfectly at home. He not only read, but wrote the languages of France and Germany with the ease and elegance of a native, and was profoundly versed in their history and literature. He had explored, with particular industry and success, the rich mines of learning and historical *discovery* (so to speak), which the acute and recondite researches of modern German writers have opened, and enlarged his own accumulated stores by the super-addition of the fruits of their valuable labors.

Waxing eloquent in his praise of Legaré he adds:

> To the question, was he an *eminent lawyer*, Judge Story, in his beautiful and touching address to the Law School at Harvard ... answered emphatically and unhesitatingly – "*No man was more so.*"

In the October number of the same year,[17] submitting a contribution, "A Foreign Muse," he says in a letter to the editor:

> I ... send you a few gems which I know you and your readers will prize. They are some original verses by Mrs. Mary Howitt. I became acquainted with that gifted lady while pursuing my studies at the University of Heidelberg, the romantic neighborhood of which ancient seat of learning has been her residence for about three years past. On bidding her adieu, she did me the honor of adding to my collection of autographs, some pages from the manuscripts of her own

original works, and enriched it with these original verses, to be retained as a *souvenir* on this side of the water...

           Yours
           T.C.R.
    Laurel Grove, Henrico, August, 1843.

Then follow the verses:[18]

> Where'er a human being hath once drawn vital breath,
> Hath hoped, feared, loved, and suffered, or bowed
>   himself to death,
> There doth my spirit warmer glow,
> There, there a quicker pulse my heart doth know!
> . . . .
>
>   Paradise
> How goodly is the earth!
> Yet, if this earth be made
> So goodly, wherein all
> That is shall droop and fade;
> Wherein the glorious light
> Hath still its fellow, shade; –
> So goodly, where is strife
> Ever 'twixt death and life;
> Where trouble dims the eye;
> Where sin hath mastery;
> How much more bright and fair,
> Will be the region, where
> The saints of God shall rest
> Rejoicing with the blessed: –
> Where pain is not, nor death, –
> The Paradise of God!

In the next issue of the same magazine (November, 1843) is found an article entitled "A Visit to the Graves of Luther and Melanchthon" by "T. C. Reynolds, L.L.D., Heidelbergensis."[19] Since the author informs us:[20] "'Twas in the month of June, in 1839, that I had started on this pilgrimage. I had been passing a day or two at Potsdam, visiting the haunts of Frederic the Great and Voltaire", we are inclined to believe that this pilgrimage to Wittenberg was made on his way to Munich where he spent the following winter.

It is interesting to compare this article with the remarks recorded by Legaré when the latter visited the same shrines in Wittenberg in April, 1836. The diction of both descriptions is strikingly similar. Evidently the German guide was the same, but, in the case of

Legaré, the medium of communication between the German guide and the Carolina scholar had been Latin.[21]

In the following month (December, 1843) the same periodical carried Reynolds' second Wittenburg article, "A Visit to Luther's Cell."[22] This essay seems to indicate that the author was still on his pilgrimage southward for he informs us that "John Siegling, Esq., of Charleston ... resided, during his absence abroad, for some time in Erfurt,"[23] and suggests that he, on this pilgrimage, also visited the shrine of Goethe at Weimar. As his Southern predecessors had done in Weimar, he also shows a prime interest in the ladies and confesses that a lady in that town offered him a thread or ravelling of a piece she had cut from a gown of Luther, but that he had refused it.[24] Although he does not disclose the identity of the lady, we know the name of one lady who knew him well enough to offer him a token of friendship. It has long been known that: "He once sent to his friend, Baroness Goethe, daughter-in-law of the poet, a copy of Simms' *Yemassee*."[25]

The recent publication of the volume *Ottilie von Goethe Tagebücher, 1839-1841, Weimar, Wien, Weimar*, occasioned by the discovery in the Newberry Library in Chicago[26] by Heinz Bluhm of manuscript material of the daughter-in-law of Goethe, now reveals that Thomas C. Reynolds and his travelling-companion George Guerard were in Weimar from June 2-3 until July 4, 1839, for in her second June entry Ottilie records:[27] "Den Morgen brachten mir zwei Amerikaner Mr. Reynolds und Mr. Guerar [*sic!*] einen Brief von Mrs. Robinson." On June 5th Ottilie received a note from Reynolds expressing his desire to be presented at court, as his fellow-Southerners, G.H. Calvert and Jesse B. Harrison, had been during Goethe's lifetime. Accordingly Ottilie on the same day wrote to Freiherr von Spiegel, Oberhofmarschall in Weimar, and also accompanied the two Americans to Herr Froriep, the gentleman who had introduced both Calvert and Harrison to the Ducal Court. On the evening of the ninth of June she was visited by Froriep, his daughter Emma and Mr. Reynolds.

An entry in the Tagebuch on June 13th records: "Nachmittag mit den Amerikanern visiten [*sic!*] gemacht." The following day she met the two Americans at "Mittag bei Bertha." Reynolds is again mentioned on June 17th, and two days later Ottilie wrote to Mrs. Robinson. On the twenty-second Reynolds joined other visitors at Ottilie's after the theater performance. He was also among Ottilie's visitors on the evening of the twenty-seventh. On July 3, 1839, Ottilie wrote for the two Charlestonians an "Empfehlungsbrief an Martius in München."[28] The following day Guerard and Reynolds called to bid farewell to Ottilie and were on the way to Munich[29] after having spent exactly one month in Weimar.

A diary entry of January 11, 1840, indicates that Ottilie had been sent "une Broschure von Channing" by "Rainolds."[30] Since the "Namenregister" of the Bluhm volume (p. v) enters "Channing, William, Amerikanischer Schriftsteller, Geistlicher," there can be no doubt that the sender of the volume was our Reynolds.[31] On January 18, 1840, Ottilie reports that she had read "Channing über die Sclaverei".[32] Two weeks after her arrival in Vienna she wrote, on February 22, to "Mr. Reynolds nach München." On Monday, April 13th she received a "Brief von Mr. Reynolds aus München." The following day she writes to her son, Wolfgang, then studying in Bonn, who had informed her on April 9th that he was not coming to Vienna as she had hoped he would.[33] This Reynolds letter proves that he had remained in Munich until after the end of the winter semester of 1839-1840. It also poses the conjecture whether he had not visited, or planned to visit, Ottilie in "gay" Vienna between the dates of their exchange of letters, i.e., during the "Ferien" between the two semesters and thereby to cause Ottilie's son Wolfgang Maximilian to accompany him to Heidelberg where they both matriculated as students of law the following May; Reynolds (age 18) on May 9th as registrant number 134, and Goethe (age 19-1/2) on May 13th, as number 168.[34]

In the *Southern Literary Messenger* for December, 1843, Reynolds published "Mr. Simms a Political Writer",[35] a laudatory comment on an address, "The Social Principle: The True Source of National Permanence," delivered by William G. Simms at the University of Alabama. Here again Reynolds finds occasion to eulogize "that gifted scholar and great lawyer, the late Attorney General of the United States," H. S. Legaré. On January 26, 1844, Mr. Simms wrote to Reynolds:[36] "I am obliged to you for the two essays in pamphlet form, on Luther and Melanchthon ... they are truly excellent performances... Take up your topic for critical analysis, and go to work *a la Luther* himself. Try the experiment." Also in this letter, having learned of Reynolds' personal acquaintance with the Howitt's, Simms suggests a review of William Howitt's *Student Life in Germany*.

In the year of 1844 Reynolds was admitted to the Bar and began to practice law in Virginia.[37] On July 15 of that year Simms urged him:[38] "Send me your paper [i.e., newspaper] whenever you publish anything literary. Do not forget the cause of letters," and assured him: "You have my most cordial wishes for your success in your new undertaking." In this connection the editors of Simms' *Letters* inform us: "Reynolds was editor of the Republican (Petersburg, Va.)"; evidently a true statement but one whose verification has proved quite difficult.[39]

In *The Charleston Book, A Miscellany in Prose and Verse* (Charleston, 1845) the local exponents of German erudition are strongly represented. H. S. Legaré presents "The Study of the Classics" and "The Greek Language;" Mitchell King, "The Resolve;" Joel R. Poinsett, "Literature and the Fine Arts," in which he comments on the influence of music "over the moral and social conditions of society;" T. C. Reynolds, "German Graves" and "The Pilgrimage." Each of these last two sketches is reminiscent of scenes Reynolds had witnessed in Germany, and strangely enough, each, in part or in whole, reports the celebration of a holiday of the Roman Catholic Church, the former, All Saints' Day, the latter, St. Wenceslaus' Day in Prague (September 28th, 1841).

But the young Doctor of Laws was not satisfied with the editorship of a small, weak country newspaper. The existence of a vacancy in the department of Foreign Languages at the University of Virginia attracted him as a similar vacancy there had attracted Jesse Burton Harrison some twenty years earlier. Strange that these two young Virginians, the first of whom, after graduating with "first honors" from Hampden Sidney College, had obtained a degree in law at Harvard, and the second, an alumnus of the University of Virginia, who subsequently had earned the degree of doctor of laws at Heidelberg, should have come unto their own, in search of a scholarly position, and that their own received them not! Documents among the "Reynolds' Papers" in the archives of the Missouri Historical Society in St. Louis reveal that T. C. Reynolds wrote on July 29, 1844, from Petersburg, Virginia, to Colonel Willis H. Woodley at Castle Hill, and on August 5th from Richmond to the Honorable W. C. Rives, setting forth his qualifications for the vacant chair and beseeching assistance in obtaining the position. In the University of Virginia Collection of manuscripts there is a document (XII, 55), dated September 10 [no year], recommending to the Board of Visitors the appointment of "Mr. Reynolds [no more definite name given] as professor of Modern Languages."

Since the contents of the two letters just mentioned above are basically the same, we shall present, despite its length, but because of the abundant information it discloses, *in extenso* the epistle written to Mr. Rives.

> Dear Sir:
>
> You will receive, along with this a copy of my dissertation printed by authority of the University of Heidelberg on the occasion of my receiving from its Law Faculty the degree of Doctor of Civil & Canon Law accompanied by the distinction, (the highest The University can confer) of having inserted in my diploma the declaration that it was granted to me "examine rigoroso sumã cum laude superato." I hoped to

have had the honor of seeing you in Petersburg & there soliciting in person its acceptance by you, instead of the copy which I was either falsely under the impression that I had sent you in May last, or which has been sent by me and never received. I hope you will do me the honor of placing it in your library: I will not ask you to wade through it, but you will find in the July No. of the Southern Review, a succinct account of its positions and contents, given by a German scholar intimately acquainted with the Civil & Cannon Law, as well as German and Anglo-Saxon antiquities.

I have deemed it perhaps not altogether unnecessary to accompany it with a statement, fuller than I was able to give in the personal interview which I had the honor of having in Richmond, of my qualifications for the vacant Professorship in the University of Virginia, which you are so kind as to take an interest in my obtaining. I have resided nearly four years in Germany & about half a year in Paris. That I am intimately and accurately acquainted with the German Language, Literature, History, Polity, manners, customs etc. my long residence is, I suppose, ample security. The French language I first studied under a Parisian emigré who is Tutor of French to His Bavarian Majesty's daughters & I took great pains to acquire from him an accurate pronunciation. This was in 1839: afterwards I have had frequent opportunities, in mingling with the society of Munich & Berlin (to the best of which the kindness of my friend and correspondent, the Baroness de Goethe, & of Mr. Wheaton gave me admission,) of practicing myself in conversation in French & of accustoming my ear to the correct pronunciation. I flatter myself that I have in a great measure succeeded in obtaining it: for I have had it tested by Frenchmen when in Germany & have had no fault found with it in Paris. Since my return to this country (last year), I have had little opportunity in *conversing* in French, but I have read a good many books in that language & have had, in carrying on my European correspondence, occasionally to write in it. At the same time that I claim an accurate knowledge of the language, I must candidly admit that I have, in some degree, lost *fluency* in conversing in it. But this fluency could soon be reacquired and I would, if chosen, take immediately especial pains to regain it, as far as practicable, before entering on the duties of the department. And, in all events, one vacation spent entirely in the practice of French conversation with a Parisian or other good French teacher, would enable me completely to regain it. Of course a residence of such length in Paris, or in the adjoining country of the Rhine, has made me familiar with the habits, manners, customs etc. of France &, to her history & literature I have paid special attention. In this connection I will mention that, at a time when it was thought that the post of Secretary of Legation to Mr. Wheaton would become vacant, that gentleman gave me (though not 21 at the time), a letter (never delivered) to the Secretary of State, requesting my appointment to the place & endorsing me as "peculiarly fitted" for it. The character of that gentleman is a sufficient guarantee that he would not have preferred me for such a post, near his own person, if he had not been entirely satisfied not only of my character as a gentleman, of my prudence and discretion, but also of my accurate knowledge of French. He himself has written several works in French & had ample opportunities of judging my character & qualifications, as I passed, in all, two years in the same city with him and was frequently in his company. He has also since honored me with his regular correspondence. If Judge Story, Mr. Sumner of Boston or Mr. Sedgwick of New York would mention the terms in which M. Foelix, the Editor of the Revue Étrangère etc. (Paris), spoke of me in his letters introducing me to them, I am sure it would not be to my disadvantage. M. de Billé, the Danish Chargé at Washington, & Baron de Rönne, the late Russian Minister, could also speak of the terms in which I was introduced to them in letters from their European friends & the constant friendship since shown me by these noblemen is to me a proof of their kind feelings to me.

The Spanish language I acquired before leaving this country (as early as 1835). I am accurately acquainted with Spanish history & somewhat so with Spanish Literature. Though I do not pretend to as accurate a knowledge of the language as I have of German and French, yet I feel myself perfectly competent to give full & complete instruction in it.

Italian I did not commence the study of until the fall of 1842 in Paris. I had one of the best teachers of that city, and, as I do in studying every language which I set about to acquire, took especial pains to secure, first of all, an accurate and pure pronunciation. I have since paid particular attention to this language, devoting, indeed, a considerable portion of my leisure time to it, as it completed the cyclus of my knowledge of the chief European languages. Italian history I am very well acquainted with. Upon the whole I would not hesitate to undertake the giving of full and complete instruction in this department of the School.

In connection with the subject of my qualifications for the Professorship, it is perhaps not inappropriate to mention that a knowledge of Civil & Canon Law & of French & German Law (which I possess) is of great use in studying the history of all the continental nations, & particularly of Italy & the Empire. In addition, during my residence in Munich, Dresden, Berlin, Paris etc., I took great care in & devoted much time to the study of Art in the galleries of those cities.

A perusal of my Dissertatio Inauguralis will, I trust, afford ample evidence of my acquaintance, as well with Anglo-Saxon & Anglo-Norman history, antiquities, laws, manners, customs, etc. I was and am much addicted to Antiquarian Studies & pursuits &, in their course, I have been necessitated to acquire a knowledge more or less complete of several languages which do not enter into the course at the University, but even the practicability of acquiring which by the students may add somewhat to the standing of the Professor & some little eclât to the University. I have made myself acquainted with Gothic, Icelandic, Norman French (as contained in the Coutumier de Normandie & in the Anglo-Norman laws), & somewhat with Basque. The early dialects of German (the Saxon & Frisian) & the Teutonico-Latin & Franco-Latin of the age of Charlemagne I acquired a knowledge of by having, in my antiquarian studies, had frequent occasion to refer to in the ancient chronicles & laws written in them. My Dissertatio contains quotations & references in evidence of it.

I took advantage of my acquaintance with a Danish nobleman in Berlin & a young lawyer of Copenhagen in Heidelberg to acquire a tolerable acquaintance with Danish and Swedish (in which they were kind enough to give me instructions in return for my instructing them in English). A Dutch friend of mine in Heidelberg also set me so far on my way in his native tongue that I can read it & pronounce it tolerably well. These three languages (Dutch, Swedish & Danish, which last is also the language of Norway), I feel myself competent to give such instruction in as will enable the student to pursue them, unaided, himself. With the literature of those countries I must candidly confess myself very little acquainted. Their history I know with some accuracy, as it was included in my general (& extensive) course of European history, The Norse Mythology etc., I have, in my Antiquarian studies, had occasion to acquire a tolerable knowledge of. In my Dissertatio &, more particularly in the Conjecturae appended to it, you will find evidence of it.

I have had no experience in teaching any of the foreign languages which I have mentioned to persons speaking my own language. But I had frequently to explain difficulties in them to such persons, &, as I have mentioned, have aided several foreigners in acquiring my own. I feel however, personally, no difficulty on this score. I am sure I can lead any one over the difficulties of a foreign tongue by the same paths which I followed myself, and I have always found that, where I could acquire as good a pronunciation as from a native of the country, the language of which I was learning, the *difficulties* of the language could be more readily, easily & completely removed for me by one whose native tongue was the same as mine & who had had to encounter & overcome the same difficulties himself.

I confess myself ignorant of the whole family of Slavonic languages (Russian etc.).

With regard to my personal character, I shall say nothing. What it was when I was at the University in 1837-8 is known to the authorities of the University. What it was in Europe the letters which I have from Mr. Legaré & Mr. Wheaton can testify: these letters I shall show to Mr. Johnson, & if you think it expedient & will advise me to that effect, I will transmit them to you to be laid before the Board of Visitors. What character I bear in Richmond, where I have resided since my return to this country, is known to some of the members of the Board from personal observation.

You will, I hope, not deem it indelicate in me to remind you how signally fortunate the University of Virginia has been when it has selected its Alumni to fill its Professorships & how signally unfortunate it has been in the selection of foreigners to (?) the very chair of which I am writing.[41] As a member of the Faculty an Alumnus has great advantages. He has worn the shoe of college life and knows where it pinches. He is intimately acquainted with the usages and habits of the students & the traditionary customs which each University has. He may be able, as I am proud to be, to point to his own college life, to show those, whom he now has to guide & often chasten, that it is possible for a student to pass his time profitably at college without ever disobeying the laws on the one hand, or acquiring unpopularity among his fellow-students by improper subserviency to the authorities on the other. An alumnus also necessarily feels a greater interest in the prosperity of the University and as best proof of that which I feel in the welfare of my alma mater, I beg that if any of the Board are disposed to favor my election to the vacant Professorship, they will not, for a moment hesitate from kind feeling towards myself, to give preference to any other person, if they have any *doubts* of my being as well qualified for the station.

As the History of the countries, the languages of which are taught in the School, should form an important department of it, it is perhaps an advantage on the side of the native, that his feelings & principles will cause him, consciously or unconsciously, to take an American view of it (which a foreigner is incapable of doing): while his acquaintance with foreign literature will enable him to point out to the student the sources whence he can obtain a knowledge of the views taken on the same subject, by the nation itself or by others.

I explained to you in Richmond why my present situation precludes my making a formal application to the Board of Visitors for the vacant Professorship. But I renew to you my assurance that if elected I will accept it, & I request you also to do me the honor & favor of communicating to the Board, should you deem it expedient to place my name before it, the contents of this letter. I have written also to Col. Woodley & I would be under great obligation to you if you could find time to communicate to me, when he returns and reports the qualifications of the persons who are candidates for the Professorship, what you think are the chances of my receiving the appointment. . . . .
. . . .

Your obedient servant,
T. C. Reynolds

The letter to Colonel Woodley contains, in addition to much that appears in the one to Rives, the statement: "I have just taken charge of the Petersburg Republican. It has suffered much from the frequent change of Editors." This probably establishes the reason why Reynolds stated to Rives that his "present situation precluded" his "making formal application to the Board of Visitors" for the vacant professorship, and further confirms the statement that he was then an editor.

When, on September 23, 1844, Schele De Vere, recommended by Longfellow, Josiah Quincy and Abbott Lawrence, was elected Professor of Modern Languages the Richmond *Whig* complained about "Mr. Maximilian Rudolph Schele de Vere, of Prussia, who had been chosen in preference to a distinguished American."

On March 12, 1846, Reynolds wrote to the Honorable Mr. A. J. Donelson, Envoy Extraordinary and Minister Plenipotentiary, Court of Berlin, applying for a position as of Secretary of Legation at Berlin.[42] On May 5th he wrote to "His Excellency Romulus M. Saunders"[43] who was soon to be his superior officer, for on May 13, 1846, Thomas C. Reynolds became Secretary of Legation of the United States in Madrid, in which office he continued until June 22, 1848, at which time his "services terminated."[44] Shortly after his return from his residence in Spain his friend W. G. Simms wrote him on February 27, 1849:[45]

> Having consented to take the Editorial Chair of the Southern Quarterly Review, I am anxious to enrol you among the contributors to that work. I trust you will have the leisure to give us some of the fruits of your recent experience abroad. A paper on Spanish Literature of the present day would be particularly acceptable – another on the Domestic Politics of Spain – ...

On March 1st Reynolds replied and evidently expressed his interest in cooperating, for Simms' letter of March 5th indicates that Reynolds had suggested topics on which he was prepared to write, a "paper on the Jews in Spain," another "upon the newly discovered work of Cervantes."[46] In the same letter, reverting to a suggestion previously made on January 26, 1844, the editor writes:[47] "There is yet another subject which, it appears to me, would be particularly available in your hands – a review of Howitt's Student Life in Germany." On November 5, 1849 Simms writes:[48] "I still wish we could get a good & thorough article on *present* Spanish Literature. The work in press of a Boston writer, whose name I forget, might furnish a good text for such a paper."

It seems that Reynolds never condescended to review the Howitt volume for the *Southern Quarterly Review* because his friendly relations with the Howitts, illustrated by the remarks he made when he published the verses of Mrs. Howitt in the *Southern Litrary Messenger* (1843), would hardly permit him to attack this volume, which Simms had designated "a poor book," by indulging in an "argumentative," "provocative" style and by going "to work *a la Luther*," as Simms had advised him when he first suggested "Howitt's 'Student Life' ".[49] But he did furnish Simms' *Review* two articles on Spain which demonstrated his ability as an advocate to indulge in the kind of style Simms seemed to be looking for. The first article, entitled "The Relations between England and Spain",[50] is political, provocative, and deals with the present, viz:
1. *Papers relative to the Affairs of Spain, and Correspondence between Sir Henry Bulwer and the Duke of Sotomayor*, London, 1848.
2. *The Times*, London: 1848.
3. *El Heraldo*, Madrid, 1848.

In his exposition of this conflict between the governments of England and of Spain the young American writes in a manner befitting a *doctor juris* and a diplomatist. As a "rebel" he seems to favor the Iberian country, but he judiciously concludes: "England may have the best of the technical argument, but Spain has won the battle in a just cause, the assertion of her independence of foreign influence in any and every shape."

The second article,[51] *History of Spanish Literature*, a direct answer to Simms' request of the preceding November, is a lengthy comparative evaluation of the:

1. *History of Spanish Literature;* by George Ticknor, New York, 1849.
2. *Historical Views of the Literature of the South of Europe;* by J.C.L. Simonde de Sismondi, translated by Thomas Roscoe, 2nd edition, London, 1846.
3. *History of Spanish Literature;* by Frederick Bouterwek, translated from the original German by Thomasine Ross, London, 1847.

Naturally the work of our New Englander occupies our reviewer's chief attention. The facts that Ticknor's work has long held a prominent place in its field, that the reviewer, like the author, was an American who had also studied in Germany, that both author and reviewer were very competent in Spanish, and that Ticknor had been a student of Bouterwek in Göttingen, lend added interest to the discussion.

It is astonishing that the youthful lawyer is so forthright, so positive and so scholarly in his criticism. One senses throughout a tendency to seek out the shortcomings of the American author and to attribute them to a lack of catholicity in the attitude of the New Englander, saying "the New England mind [is] akin in many qualities to the German" (p. 95). Nevertheless Reynolds agrees with Bouterwek when he disagrees with Ticknor (e.g., p. 101). He is in accord with both Bouterwek and August Wilhelm Schlegel, as opposed to Ticknor in "their respective remarks on the *Numantia* [*Numancia*] of Cervantes" (pp. 273-276), and adds: "Mr. Ticknor is far behind Bouterwek and Sismondi in his treatment of the subject." He concludes that: "In comparison with them he [Ticknor] is cold, dry and often fatiguing" (294).

In his extended discussion of "the authenticity of the Buscapie" (p. 297ff)[52] Mr. Reynolds discloses himself as a well-read and competent student of the literature of Spain. In the rhetorical conclusion of his critique we are disturbed to detect what seems to be an unfortunate display of sectionalism directed at one who had been a close, warm and affectionate personal friend of such Southerners as Thomas Jefferson, Hugh S. Legaré and Jesse Burton Harrison (p. 312). After asserting:

> We hope that Mr. Ticknor, like the best of the New England writers is imbued with a catholic spirit foreign to the narrow Puritan-like provincialism, which taints the ethics, corrupts the taste, narrows the patriotism, and warps, in all things, the judgment of so large a portion of the Boston public,

the reviewer implies he has little faith in the verity of his hope.

Immediately after the receipt of the complete manuscript of these two articles, W.G. Simms, whose tie with Reynolds was "a love of German and Spanish literature,"[53] wrote on June 6, 1850, expressing his fervent admiration. He assures the author:[54]

> Your general criticism meets my full concurrence. I found Ticknor, as you say, singularly dry costive – cold and tame... A cold blooded, formal, literary puritan – an industrious worker, – shrewd and captious rather than profound and discriminating, – etc.

By contrast he lauds Reynolds:

> Your present article per se is capital, and will do you credit, as a student, thoughtful & earnest, and familiar with your subject, – of considerable acumen as a critic, and a clear, graceful & impressive writer. Your style is very correct and free from excesses of any kind.

Now, when it seemed as if Reynolds might become a literary critic of merit, he changed his place of abode to Missouri and his activities to law, politics, business and war. On February 4, 1849, he wrote from Havana to G.W. Goode, Esq., a native of Henrico County, Virginia, who later took up residence in St. Louis:[55]

> In 1845 you advised me to remove to St. Louis, as a city offering me, on account of my knowledge of German, a better prospect of professional success than any on the Atlantic; ... As Secretary of Legation in Madrid, ... I have improved my opportunities to acquire a more perfect knowledge of French and Spanish, and to some extent of such of the Spanish laws and institutions as I thought might throw some light on Spanish land grants & disputable land titles in Upper Louisiana.

On the 13th of November he writes to Mrs. Horatio Sprague, whose daughter, Heloise Marie, he had married in Gibraltar on March 15, 1848,[56] urging his mother-in-law to allow his wife's income from the estate of her recently deceased father to be sent to America. He says:[57] "To get at once into the practice [of law] I should have to accept the offer made me in New Orleans. As far as I am individually concerned, I should have preferred to go there;" but he concludes that, out of consideration of his wife's physical well-being, they "determined to settle in St. Louis." At Richmond, on February 27, 1850, he wrote to Captain R. M. Nimmo, Commanding the Richmond Fayette Artillery:[58]

> As I am about to move from this Commonwealth, it becomes my duty to resign into your hands the office I have the honor to hold of Engineer to the Richmond Fayette Artillery. . . . .
> When in May 1846 the news reached Richmond that actual hostilities had broken out on the Rio Grande, I had just received the announcement that I would immediately be appointed Secretary of Legation at Madrid.

His actual residence in Missouri began in March, 1850.[59] During his early days of residence there he was attorney for the "Iron Mountain Railroad". The arrival in Saint Louis on March 20, 1852, of the Hungarian revolutionist Louis Kossuth afforded our newcomer from Virginia an opportunity to advance his political career in the German-populated state of Missouri. Gustav Koerner (1809-1896) of Illinois reports:[60]

> In the evening, my St. Louis friend, Thomas Reynolds, a member of the reception committee, a prominent lawyer and politician, who had studied law at German universities and had been ... secretary of the United States Legation in Madrid, took me to see Kossuth, introducing me by anticipation as the future Lieutenant Governor of Illinois ... and, as Reynolds also understood German, we fell to speaking German.

From 1853 to 1857 he served as United States District Attorney for the district of St. Louis. Reynolds, being a pro-slavery Democrat, became a candidate for Congress on the anti-Benton ticket in 1856. Although he made speeches in German, translated articles into German for the *Anzeiger* (p. 41), wounded in a duel Mr. B. Gratz Brown, the editor of the *Missouri Democrat*, the organ of the opposition faction,[61] and was associated with Henry Börnstein,[62] the German "boss", and a writer of German dramas, he was defeated at the polls for the Congressional term of 1857-1859 by Francis Preston Blair, Jr., who had served two terms in the Missouri

Legislature (1852-1856). The nature of the campaign is illustrated by the following excerpts from contemporary journals:
"The barrister ... [Reynolds] steps from the library, the studio, the sanctum of lore and science into the *beer vats* of the Salvator (our Saviour's) brewery."
"Boernstein and Reynolds are partners in brewing mischief as well as beer."[63] In a signed article to *The Pilot* of July 28, 1956, Reynolds felt called upon to defend himself by stating: "The charge that, in a German speech to Germans, I have placed Germans and Irish on a level with negroes, I have only to pronounce it an unmitigated LIE."
On the occasion of the Centennial Ceremonies held in St. Louis on November 10, 1859, commemorating the birth of the German poet Schiller, Reynolds' name appeared twice in the program printed in the *Westliche Post* on November 3rd; first: "Englische Festrede gehalten von Mr. Th. C. Reynolds" and finally as the receiver of the report of the committee. On the twelfth of the same month the *Westliche Post* reports:

> Wenige Amerikaner werden den Geist und die Bedentung der Werke des großen Toten so gründlich zu besprechen im Stande sein wie Herr Reynolds, der durch Vortrag einiger Strophen bewies, daß er der deutschen Sprache vollkommen mächtig ist. Die Rede riß oft stürmischen Beifall.

To support these claims of the capabilities of our academic politician the evidence of his earlier political ally and later political enemy, the already mentioned Heinrich Börnstein, himself a writer of German dramas, may be apropos:[64]

> Ich weiß nur soviel, daß Reynolds gut und flüssig deutsch sprach, wenn auch mit etwas angelsächischem Accent; ferner daß er europäische Bildung erhalten hatte, in der deutschen Literatur gut zu Hause war und seiner eigenen Erzählung nach in Heidelberg studiert hatte.

Reynolds' next political campaign was more successful. He won the nomination for Lieutenant Governor on the regular (Douglas) Democratic ticket and was elected in 1860, polling the largest number of votes obtained by any candidate on either ticket. His vote, 74, 549, surpassed that of his running mate, Governor Claiborne Jackson, by over one hundred ballots and was "a clear majority over all opposing candidates."[65] In presiding over the Senate in 1861, he strongly protested against attempted Federal coercion of the sovereign state of Missouri and planned with Governor Jackson the secession of his adopted state from the Union.[66]

Before the end of the year of 1861 Reynolds, "along with others of the pro-Southern government of the state, was declared out of office"[67] by a state political convention. After the death of Governor Jackson in 1862 Reynolds hastened back to the West from South Carolina, where he had spent most of the year of 1861, assumed the Confederate Governorship of Missouri and continued, in exile, his efforts to align that state more closely with the Confederacy. At a conference of the governors of the Confederate States which lie west of the Mississippi, held on August 13th through August 18th, 1863, Reynolds was named Chairman of the Committee of Public Safety, making him, next to General Smith, the most important official in the Trans-Mississippi Department. At about the same time there was a proposal that the Confederacy name a Plenipotentiary Head of the Department of War West of the Mississippi. General Smith agreed with this move in principle but suggested that Governor Reynolds was the "only man to whom [President Jefferson] Davis would be willing to delegate such powers."[68] Throughout the entire period of the Civil War Reynolds maintained his authority as chief executive of the state and asserted this authority on every possible occasion. In December of 1864 he clearly stated his position from Marshall, Texas, one of the many capitals-in-exile of the Confederate government of Missouri. The *Texas Republican* of Marshall (Texas) then carried a statement which says in conclusion:[69] "Events have made my official station one of oppressive responsibility. Elected in time of peace, in a poll of over one hundred and fifty-four thousand Missouri voters, I am, of all the officers now recognized by either party to this war, the only one whose authority is both derived under her ancient constitution and based on a direct vote of her whole, undivided people." It is signed "Thomas C. Reynolds, Governor of Missouri."

General Smith surrendered his command in May, 1865, his being the last organized troops to lay down their arms. After the capitulation Reynolds, in company with a number of Confederate troops and leaders, crossed the border into Mexico.[70] Early in June "Governor Henry W. Allen and Governor Thomas O. Moore, both of Louisiana; Governor Thomas C. Reynolds of Missouri ... William Preston of Kentucky, and Generals Kirby Smith and John Bankhead Magruder were among the Confederates who stopped at San Antonio en route to Mexico." "They reached Eagle Pass on June 26."[71] It seems that Reynolds from the first had a quite clear conception of the nature of his Mexican exile. As early as May 10, 1866, he wrote from Mexico City to Lt. General J. A. Early, C.S.A.,[72] that he still considers himself a citizen and resident of Missouri, and expects to return to it, as one of the ruling class. On September, 30, 1868, he wrote to Jefferson Davis in Liverpool, England:[73]

> My wife – my sole family – taking refuge with her relatives, I came to Mexico *not* as an emigrant, but as an exile and trusting in my knowledge of languages to aid me in some way to get a living.

Accompanied by Generals Smith and Wilcox, Reynolds left Monterrey on July 5th and arrived in the City of Mexico on July 16th.[74] A month later General Kirby-Smith and Reynolds were in Havana,[75] but it was only for a short visit for Reynolds returned to Mexico to "see the issue of affairs" there. This was reported in March, 1867.[76] However Reynolds had good reasons for remaining: first, he was attached to Emperor Maximilian by ties of sympathy and humanity, and secondly, he held an important position in a British-owned railroad. In his letter to Jefferson Davis, quoted above, he records on September 30, 1868:

> This ["my knowledge of languages"] enabled me to make $50 a month as an amanuensis in Magruder's department of Maury's absurd colonization bureau...

Later, in November, 1867, he received an "unsolicited offer of the General Superintendency of the (English) Railway, from this city [Vera Cruz] to Paso del Macho at $5,000 a year. I accepted, and still hold it." Not until January 9, 1869, did Reynolds indite his resignation of this position as General Superintendent of the Vera Cruz Section of the Mexican Railway, giving three months notice, according to contract, and stating that he was contemplating his return to his native land.[77]

It should be no surprise that Governor Reynolds, who, as a student at the Universities of Heidelberg and Berlin, designated his father's vocation as "Sklavenbesitzer," who visited Ottilie von Goethe in Weimar and corresponded with her when she was in Vienna, whose son Wolfgang Maximilian von Goethe, also a student of jurisprudence, seems to have followed closely on Reynolds' heels to Heidelberg and then to the University of Berlin where they were "Kommilitionen",[78] who spent several years in Germany and who spoke German, Spanish and French fluently, should have become a friend, counselor and defender of Maximilian of Hapsburg, Emperor of Mexico, during his sojourn in that country. It would seem that his knowledge of languages made him the translator and interpreter for his Confederate followers from almost the very beginning of their trek to the capital of Mexico. Already at Monterrey, in early July, 1865, Reynolds wrote "in excellent French" to the French General Jeanningros, who entertained General Shelby's officers at a banquet, a petition from the Confederate visitors "seeking service in the country held by His Imperial Majesty, the Emperor Maximilian."[79] It was Reynolds, probably due to his linguistic ability, on whom was imposed the duty of making arrangements for a duel (which never took place) between Shelby and Depreuil.[80] On February 24, 1866, Reynolds wrote to the Emperor, in Spanish, a petition for a colony and port in the Bay of Banderes in Jalisco.[81]

According to the account of Major John N. Edwards, found in his volume *Shelby's Expedition to Mexico, an Unwritten Leaf of the War* (1872):[82]

> During his stay at Orizava [Autumn, 1866] his Majesty had a long and confidential interview with Governor Thomas C. Reynolds. He had been in the habit of consulting him upon various occasions, and had in more than one instance followed the advice given him by the remarkable, clearheaded and conscientious man. To Reynolds he unbosomed himself fully and without reserve. He dwelt upon the condition of the country and the apparent helplessness of the effort he was making to maintain himself. He complained that he had no advisers who understood the nature of the surroundings, and who could give a sensible and patriotic reason for anything. He wanted sympathy really as much as he did advice, and Reynolds gave him both. He urged upon him the necessity of remaining in Mexico and dying, if needs be, for his kingdom and his crown. Reynolds also recalled briefly the history of his ancestors, the names, great among the greatest of his race, and reminded him as delicately as possible, yet very firmly, that, Hapsburg as he was, he had need of but two things – to perish or succeed. There was a sacred duty he owed, first to his name, and then to those other young and dauntless spirits who had followed him across the ocean and could not be abandoned to be destroyed. Men of the Hapsburg race either conquered destiny or were conquered by it in war harness and in front of the fight. Standing or falling, he should head his armies and trust himself, as his ancestors had done before him, to the God of battles and the sword.

But, Reynolds in a letter to his friend Edwards, on April 30, 1874, complimented him warmly for "having composed an historical romance of such thrilling interest," and objected to some of the author's fictional statements:[83]

> I was not at Orizava when the Emperor Maximilian was there. I had at the City of Mexico, with him and with Gen.

Vidaurri, his counsellor, conversations somewhat like those you relate as had at Orizava.

I remain with great regard
Your friend and comrade,
Thomas C. Reynolds

To demonstrate further Reynolds' regard for Emperor Maximilian attention is directed to two letters written by him to the "Hon. Wm. H. Corwin, Lebanon, Ohio, from the City of Mexico" and marked "Strictly Confidential" ("25th Aug. 1866") and "Confidential" ("27th Dec. 1866") respectively, and now found in the Manuscript Division of the Library of Congress.[84] The first missive says in part:

Call attention to Mr. Seward to the atrocities the liberal forces, availing themselves of the moral support of the United State, were perpetrating . . . .
His Majesty with characteristic frankness. . . . .
The Empress has, in pleasantry, remarked to him that he "was quite a Yankee" [because of his pro-Monroe-doctrine views].

I said to his Majesty that no one could doubt the correctness of his views: that they belonged to his station as an independent sovereign, and that no one would credit that a Hapsburg could condescend to be merely the Head of a French colony.

His Majesty also remarked, with visible earnestness: "I perfectly comprehend my position. I have no children, no desire to found a dynasty, and no personal ambition beyond that of doing good to the country, in which I take the greatest interest. Except in the names, my government is thoroughly republican, and I am only a President for life. I am not understood in the United States. It is as if there were a curtain between the President and me, that needs only to be drawn aside in order to let us fully understand each other, and remove the prepossessions which exist against me, and the orders of things I aim to establish here. I sometimes think, why cannot a personal interview between the President or Mr. Seward, or both, and myself, take place, at which we could interchange views frankly, and possibly come to some understanding. I would readily go to Havana, or New Orleans, to meet them for such a purpose. Such interviews are common in Europe, and produce much good and why cannot we have them on this continent . . . ."

My own opinions on the Mexican question are well known to you – during the last 15 months.

In the second letter Reynolds refers to the "intention of Messrs. Campbell and Sherman to visit Vera Cruz." He offers to these gentlemen his "services in the case" and adds: "I am confident that only good and perhaps decisive results, would have come of the course suggested by the Consul." He concludes: "Let me beg you to urge that Gen. Sherman, if sent back to Mexico, be instructed to confer with the Emperor. Not to do so is a piece of international madness, a *manque de savoir faire*, unworthy of a great nation."

This should suffice to demonstrate that our ubiquitous Dr. Reynolds personally knew and genuinely sympathized with the Austrian prince. We suggest that the Virginian's German background and facile use of the German language contributed to the establishment and confirmation of this relationship.

After his resignation as superintendent of the Mexican Railway had been accepted, Reynolds sailed *via* Havana (April, 1869) to New York where he arrived on April 14th.[85] Having then returned to St. Louis, he resumed the practice of law in the month of May.[86] His civil rights were restored to him in a movement led by B. Gratz Brown whom Reynolds had wounded in a duel in 1856.[87] On May 26, 1869, Reynolds returned the Great Seal of the State, which he had possessed since he became governor in 1863, to the newly elected governor of Missouri, Joseph W. McClurg.[88]

Now that he was again at home, at peace, and accepted, he once more turned his attention to academic, literary and political affairs by renewing his acquaintance with Francis Lieber, whom he had known when the latter was a member of the faculty of South Carolina College at Columbia, to whom he had sent copies of his printed dissertation upon his return from Heidelberg, and who, at the outbreak of the Civil War had, with his entire family, except one son, Oscar Montgomery Lieber, actively and ardently espoused the cause of the Union.[89] On September 4, 1871, he requested permission to publish Lieber's "Erguß" on Washington's sword.[90] Lieber replied from New York on September 7, 1871:[91]

> Washington's Schwert? Ich hatte zuerst nicht die geringste Erinnerung, und jetzt ist die Sache mir nicht klar.
> Certainly, my dear Sir, it has never been published. If it is worth publishing, I should like to see it in print, but it ought to be said, when I made it; that recently it was found in a letter to a gentleman who thought it ought not to be lost, etc. Where will you print it? In a German paper? Look out that no erratum mars it still further. Misprints in poetry are apt to turn a thing into a ridicule, as a little ink-spot on the nose of Apollo Bellvidere would make even 'the man who never laugheth', laugh, could he forget the ruin of the master's work.

You must send me a few copies.

Do not say it is printed with my permission; for that would look as if I recollected what it was. Nothing need be said about that.

From *Ein Erguss*, I conclude it is an unrestricted dactyllic much as Goethe has given several times. . . . .

You mention my present position. Besides being Professor in the Law School of Columbia College, I am – as long as it lasts – umpire in the international claims commission of the United States and Mexico. . . . .

. . . .

I have written all this on the supposition that you are the brother of my former colleague, from whom I have never heard since the beginning of the Civil War, and that you took the degree '*Dr. utrique juris*' in Heidelberg. Your Latin dissertation was connected, in some way, with my Pol. Ethics. Am I right?

. . . .

In his next letter, September 19th, Lieber writes: "I am curious to see my own Effusion, and judge whether it deserves publication. I wish, however, you would say in what year it was made. Is it long or short?"

Evidently Reynolds sent Lieber in his letter of September 25 a copy of the latter's long-forgotten poem "Washingtons Arbeitsschwert" for in his reply of September 28th the poet says: "I have never been more astonished for although I recognize all my own thoughts – that stella duplex [92] of the historical firmament – yet had not the least recollection of the Effusion . . . .

. . . .

You ought to get this thing translated. Stop. I'll send a copy to Longfellow. I desire to have sent 12 copies, and I'll return the price. . . . .

It ought to have been that I *ergoss* the lines in S. Carolina."[93]

It is recorded in the documents in the Library of Congress that the poem was published in *Mississippi Blaetter*, the Sunday edition of the *Westliche Post* of St. Louis on October 1st, 1871, but I have not succeeded in finding a copy of that issue. However, Lieber wrote again from New York on October 16, 1871: "I have received the copies of my Erguss which you have had the goodness of sending me by express. Accept my best thanks. If the Blätter could send me 4 more copies of the Erguss I would like to have them," . . . .

. . . .

"Longfellow wrote me a nice letter about the Erguss, but I suppose he does not think of transl[ating] it."

The following summer Reynolds and Lieber were again busy with plans to publish more of the latter's poetry as is shown by their correspondence. Lieber wrote on July 6th proposing to pay for the printing of his verses and on July 12 about the printing of his poems. On July 24 Reynolds sent to him and to Longfellow a "specimen, just received from the printer, of the reprint of his Erguss," together with "corrected proof sheets of his poetry and directions to the printer." On August 3, 1872 Reynolds wrote:

"I have just received the first copies of the 'Erguss,' etc? and hasten to mail one to you ... I also mail one to Mr. Longfellow." Longfellow's remarks apropos this poem: "Held aloft by the right hand of Governor Reynolds 'Excalibur' flashes again above the waters," was probably occasioned by the receipt of this copy.[94] Reynolds' letter continues: "On Monday I shall send you a package of 300 by express."[95]

Reynolds' reply to Lieber's reaction on the receipt of this dispatch reveals so well the versatility of this scholar-politician, become publisher, that it deserves quotation at length:[96]

> I am much pleased to find that you consider the poems "neatly printed." The ability to judge of poetry in another than one's native tongue is a very rare gift, and I may not be competent to form a just opinion of German versification. In all candor I form my estimate of all poetry, even in English, by the sentiments rather than by the prosody: from this point of view I see true poetry in your lines, and they also sound to my ears like good *verses*. But should they, in this very prosaic land, fail to receive immediate appreciation, your most recent prose has had a very different fortune. Your letter of the 3d inst. on Grant & Greeley was sent by special telegram, and in full to the Republican organ here, (Mo. Democrat) and attracted much attention. I happened to meet Mr. Pulitzer (the locum tenens of that vast humbug, Schurz, in his paper here, during his almost constant "carpetbagger" absence, and the "Joe" of the firm of "Bill [Grosvenor] and Joe [Pulitzer]" of the Cincinnati Convention,) shortly after it appeared, and he pronounced it the ablest and most "dangerous" letter which had yet appeared for Grant: that compliment suffices. I am glad I am out of public life: but I am too rigid a disciplinarian to refuse to support, in a quiet way, my party's nominees. . . . .
> . . . .
> Secondly, you showed me many kindnesses and courtesies in my younger days, and your mention of me aided in my

somewhat successful career in life. . . . .
. . . .
If the old friends, who are constantly writing and sending messages to me on the subject, succeed in their (at present somewhat secret) plan to send me next Spring to Washington to succeed that precious political weather-cock, Frank Blair, in the U.S. Senate, I shall get even with you anyhow by dropping over to New York and taking a "pot-luck" dinner with you.

On August 21, 1872, Lieber informed Reynolds that he had sent to Daniel Beal, President of the Missouri University at Columbia, a letter recommending J.L. Reynolds for a Professorship at that university. This person was evidently James Lawrence Reynolds (1814-1877), a brother of his correspondent.[97]

When Francis Lieber died on October 2, 1872, Reynolds in a letter of condolence to Mrs. Lieber wrote on the following day:[98] "I had anticipated both pleasure and instruction from a renewal this winter of our literary correspondence." In a letter dated March 4, 1879, he sent to Mrs. Lieber thirteen letters of her husband (1871-1872 and a few notes of 1843), the former property of his late brother.

The dairy of Judge William B. Napton, under the date of January, 1872, suggests that Reynolds was then engaged in quasi-literary activities. We read:[99] "He [Reynolds] is now, I expect, writing all the Sunday articles in the Republican relative to Mexican affairs with which he is quite familiar." Even though this suspicion cannot be authenticated, there are grounds for suspecting that Reynolds was the author of certain of these articles. Not only was he then corresponding with Lieber who was at that time an "umpire in the claims commission of the United States and Mexico,"[101] but the article of Sunday, January 7, "The Last Duel fought in Missouri," suggests Reynolds' duel with B. Gratz Brown. The following Sunday appeared the "Defeat of Dias in Mexico." And the third, and last, the "Annexation of Mexico," should have been of especial interest to Reynolds since he became embroiled in an ardent dispute concerning the possible annexation of Cuba when he was serving in our Legation in Madrid in 1846. Nevertheless, there is insufficient evidence to justify the surmise put forth by Judge Napton.

Meanwhile Reynolds was not unmindful of his political obligations. He was a Counsellor of St. Louis County from 1872-1876. On the occasion of the founding of the St. Louis University Club in January, 1872, Reynolds was elected Vice President. There were only two other members on the roster who had degrees from German universities, the Reverend Solomon H. Sonnenschein, Heidelberg, 1863, and James Taussig, Prague, 1846.[102] In 1874 he was elected to the legislature of the state of Missouri and consequently represented St. Louis in the General Assembly of the state through 1875-1876. He also served as master of Chancery. When, in December, 1875, a committee of the Board of Administrators of the University of Missouri, endeavoring to find a candidate to fill the office of President of the University, recommended a list of eight "names most prominently mentioned" ex-Governor Thomas Reynolds was one of the number.[103]

In July, 1884, President Chester A. Arthur appointed Reynolds a member of a commission to study the condition of the commercial relations existing between the United States and the states of Central and South America. Reynolds sent his acceptance of this appointment to the Secretary of State on July 16 and on the 28th of that month wrote to the Honorable Mr. Frederick T. Frelinghuysen to acknowledge the receipt of a letter of the 23rd inst. containing the document of appointment.[104] His ability to use several foreign languages with facility made him on frequent occasions the spokesman for his group. We are told that "he would speak first in the language of the country ... then translate his address into other languages until everybody present understood him."[105] There is a record in the Reynolds Papers in the Jefferson Memorial at St. Louis that he was in Guatemala on March 21, 1885, and was preparing the Commission's report [in Washington] on May 28th, on which date he informs Thomas F. Bayard, Cleveland's Secretary of State: "In preparing my report ... on Nicaragua, I have embodied in it considerable information about the projected interoceanic canal."[106] He formally submitted his report on June 29, 1885. Another item, evidently a clipping from an obituary notice, dated March 28, 1887, states that "the commission was in South America over a year."[107]

Having three times been employed in Spanish-speaking countries Reynolds was seeking once more an opportunity to return to Spain, This time he desired to be appointed Minister of our Legation in Madrid, where he had served as Secretary of Legation four decades earlier.[108] In a clipping entitled "Governor Reynolds' Remains" and dated April, 1887, (Jefferson Memorial) we read:

> It has been known to some of his friends that his failure to receive the appointment as minister to Spain was to a very great extent due to intimations given to Secretary Bayard and President Cleveland that his mind had shown signs of giving way [sic!]... He [the President] had already given the Missouri senators and other friends of Gov. Reynolds unmistakable assurance of his favorable opinion of Gov. Reynolds.

Sad as the connection may seem, the reports to President Cleveland may have been based on fact, for when the corpse of Thomas Caute Reynolds was found at the base of an elevator shaft in the Federal Building at St. Louis on March 30, 1887, under circumstances which suggested suicide, it was learned that he had left behind a letter in which he said:[109] "My mind is beginning to wander. I have hallucinations and even visions when I am awake," etc.

Thus ended the kaleidoscopic career of the ubiquitous Mr. Reynolds, scholar, jurist, diplomat, duellist, politician, statesman, governor, Imperial counsellor, gentleman; of whom Daniel M. Grissom has written:[110]

> Thomas C. Reynolds was a lawyer of unusual skill and ability, having a recognized position as one of the foremost members of the St. Louis bar. He was a man of great learning, of wide and accurate information, an accomplished linguist and diplomat, a capable legislator and always a most entertaining companion. His temper was kindly, his manner courteous, and in all his relations, public and private, with friends and foes, he was truthful and sincere.

BASIL LANNEAU GILDERSLEEVE
CLASSICIST AND GERMANIST

SOUTH CAROLINA, VIRGINIA, MARYLAND

Although it is universally acknowledged that Basil Lanneau Gildersleeve was America's greatest classical scholar,[1] too little attention has been devoted to his intimate knowledge of German literature and his devotion to the cult of Goethe. Born in Charleston, South Carolina on October 23, 1831, he was a freshman at the College of Charleston, the oldest municipal college in the United States, in 1845 after which time his father took him to live in Richmond, Virginia. In 1846 he was a student at Jefferson College (now Washington and Jefferson) at Cannonsburg, Pennsylvania, the first college to be established west of the Alleghenies. The following year he transferred to Princeton University where he began to study German "in good earnest."[2] Here he was graduated in 1849. In the autumn of that year, while teaching in a private school in Richmond, he became passionately fond of Goethe, to whose works he had been introduced by reading Carlyle, and whom he designated as "the most important of all the teachers I ever had."[3] In his column, called "Brief Mention," in the *American Journal of Philology*, a periodical which Gildersleeve founded in 1880 and whose editor he remained until 1920, he writes in 1902:[4]

> My acquaintance with Goethe goes back to the beginning of my Teutonomaniac period in 1847, and I doubt whether any boy of my age ever devoured so much of Goethe in so short a time. There was not much that I left unread form Goetz von Berlichingen to the Second Part of Faust. His lyrics were my delight and I learned many of his "Sprüche" by heart. But while I enjoyed the light and warmth of my luminary, I did not inquire too curiously in what sign of the zodiac my sun was standing, or whose star, not to say petticoat, was in the ascendant, Friederike's, Frau von Stein's or Ulrike von Levetzow's. Since that far-off time every recess of Goethe's life has been explored and every sinuosity of his long career has been lighted up.

Commending Professor Goebel's assumption that "a knowledge of Goethe's biography is a prerequisite for the study of Goethe's poems,[5] he admits that he did not possess that accomplishment in 1847, and philosophically concludes by consoling himself with a couplet from Goethe's "Lebensregel":

> Willst du dir ein hübsch Leben zimmern,
> Musst ums Vergangene dich nicht bekümmern;[6]

Elsewhere he writes of this early period:[7]

> Goethe's aphorisms were my daily food. I committed my favorite passages to memory. I repeated them over and over to myself in my long solitary rambles, and Goethe was my mainstay at a time when my faith had suffered an eclipse. This was the epoch of my Teutonomania, the time when I read German, wrote German, listened to German, and even talked German – to myself if I could not find any long-suffering German to submit to my experiments.

In the summer of 1850 Gildersleeve sailed on a tobacco ship from Richmond to Bremen. He spent three continuous years in study and travel, mostly in Germany, first at Berlin (one semester, October, 1850, to March, 1851), then at Göttingen (Easter, 1851, to Easter, 1852), finally at Bonn (April, 1852, to March, 1853).[8] Having applied on March 1st for his doctoral examination at Göttingen, he left Bonn a week later. The examination was scheduled for March 15th. His committee was composed of Professors Christoph Wilhelm Mitscherlich, C. Fr. Gauss, Georg Heinrich August Ewald (one of the Göttinger Seven), J. Fr. L. Hausmann, Karl Heinrich Hoeck, Georg W. Waitz and Georg Weber. On the Ides of March he defended his dissertation *De Porphyii Studiis Capitum Homericis Trias*, swore his oath and received his diploma which reads:

> Virum. Praenobilissimum, et docentissimum
> Basilum Lannavium Gildersleeve Americanum
> Propter, egregiam, scientiam dissertatione et examine
>   adprobatum
> Die XV M. Martii A. MDCCCLIII
> Philosophae Doctorem et Artium liberalum Magistrum
> Rite, ac legitime creavi et renuntiavi
> Huius Rei has literas, testis
> Signallo. ordinis Philosophorum muniri feci
>
>   Ritter h.t. decanus ord. phil.

Concerning his scholarly background before his matriculation at the University of Berlin, Gildersleeve wrote in 1893:[9] "Of my special preparation for philological work the less said the better... But I had enough German to understand the lectures and that was something." Hence we hear nothing of German tutors and a struggle to acquire a working knowledge of the vernacular such as seems to have been the *bête noire* of most of our American students who attended German universities during the first half of the nineteenth century. This lack of evidence of such a struggle could be due to lack of availability of contemporary personal correspondence and diaries, but what evidence we do possess indicates absence of the linguistic barrier. His industry, as well as his linguistic ability, is demonstrated by his notebooks preserved in the Hopkins Collection. They are a series of uniform (12" x 9"), bound blank-books to the spine of some of which the printed labels indicating the course of study still adhere. Broken places in the binding disclose that German newspapers were utilized by the bookbinder to strengthen the spine. These books are all filled with closely written lecture notes supplemented by reading notes, all in German. Most of these books stem from his West-German semesters, the earliest, entitled "Hoeck, Kaisergeschichte v. Hadrian bis Constantin," 76 pp., Winter semester, 1851-1852, being from Göttingen. Also to that university belong: "F. W. Schneidewin, Gk. poet., 1. Epos. 2 Lyrik, 3 Dramatik, end 13. März, p. 159"; "Leutsch, Metrik ... Schlusz März 13, 1852." Of another notebook "Geschichte der lateinischen Litteratur mitgeschrieben nach dem Vortrage des Herrn Prof. C. F. Hermann" the first eighty-four pages are inscribed in perfect German script, unmarred by any error, blemish or erasure. It would seem that this first part of the copy was made by a professional amanuensis. The remainder of the volume of three hundred and forty-three pages is written in the sort of German that might be expected of a normal student. Gildersleeve also gives us a "Tabellisch Uebersicht" of the lecture notebooks for the "Sommer Semester, 1852" [Bonn] thus:[10]

```
*Welcker, Gr. Kunstgeschichte          107S.

*Ritter, lat. littg, 187S; Horaz 59S.   246S.

*Ritschl, Krit. u. Herm[eneutik] 59S.
            Aristot. 64 S., Kom.
            32S.                        156S.
   Aschbach – alte Gesch.               186S.
*Schmidt, Gk. Magiker 39-Bernays 57S.    96S.
                                        ─────
                                        788S.
```

There are no notebooks preserved from the Berlin semester. It is further worthy of note that Gildersleeve wrote in 1901[11]: "Of my German fellow-students during my one semester in Berlin (1850-1851) I saw little and remember less." This seems to indicate that either devotion to study or incompatibility with the vastness of the Prussian capital made something of a recluse of this Calvinist scholar from our agrarian South. Continuing the above remarks he adds: "But my Göttingen contemporaries, Baumeister and Wölfflin ... stand out distinctly in my memory and of the Ritschelians, next to my nearest friend, Emil Hübner, the figure of Vahlen ... is at present in my mind's eye."

When in 1915 Gildersleeve writes:[12] "In the years of my Teutonomia we American students used to join our German fellow-students in singing 'Schleswig-Holstein meerumschlungen' but there was yet another song,

> Wir wollen keine Dänen sein,
> Wir wollen Deutsche bleiben, ..."

we must recall David Ramsay, whom Gildersleeve loved, not only as a fellow-Charlestonian and fellow-student at Göttingen, but as a fellow-wit and a fellow-martyr-to-be in the cause of our Confederacy, who had likewise been eloquent in behalf of Schleswig-Holstein when they were both at Göttingen.[13]

After returning from Germany young Dr. Gildersleeve served as Professor of Greek, and, during the war years (1861-1866), also as Professor of Latin, at the University of Virginia, from 1856 to 1876. His was the first official appointment to be made on the faculty of the new Johns Hopkins University, January 3, 1876. In the history of that institution, he is recorded as "the chief humanist of the first faculty" who "spent his energies in making his seminary and his learned journal dominant forces for American scholarship rather than in concentration on one monumental *arbeit* or shelf of texts."[14] When we read in the same history that "a group of fellows and students began as early as the fall of 1876 to meet on Saturday evenings in a Baltimore version of a German student *kneipe*" because several of the members had studied in Germany and "desired to keep up their command of German," we see again the influence of Gildersleeve implanting the German spirit in the first American graduate school to adopt the university methods of Germany.[15]

When we learn that "in the Faculty" President Daniel Coit Gilman "particularly relied on the judgment of Gildersleeve and Remsen,"[16] we realize that it was to his two German-trained scholars that the chief executive turned for counsel in shaping this new departure in American university history.

First to Gildersleeve Gilman disclosed his intention to retire, saying in a letter of May 1, 1900: "You have been such a constant, such a wise, such a helpful adviser and so dear a friend that I take you first into my confidence." In an epistle dated June 16, 1901, he informs Gildersleeve: "I lay down my office with the constant remembrance that you and Remsen have been my chief counsellors – the one in all that pertains to science, the other in all that pertains to letters. My hands have been strengthened by such strong, wise, independent and experienced counsellors."[17]

Since Gildersleeve eventually became the Nestor of American professors of classical philology and was called by Charles W. Eliot, President Emeritus of Harvard University, "the most distinguished classical scholar and teacher that America has produced ... the most eminent man in the group of interesting men who constituted the first faculty of the Johns Hopkins University in 1876,"[18] it should be interesting to learn how Gildersleeve appraised his professors at the German universities. In a document marked "Yale lecture" found in the Hopkins Collection we are informed: "All the lecturers were not equally inspiring; all had not the serene wisdom of Boeckh, the vehement affluence of Karl Friedrich Hermann, the rapt vision of Welcker, the inspired swing of Ritschl."[19] In his Fakultätenschau, "Professional Types", he portrays some of his mentors.

> The illustrious Boeckh[20] ... was then sixty-five years old, and the yellow pages from which he read his lectures seemed to be almost as old as the lecturer. There was no attempt at oratory. He sat quietly in his chair, put his nose into his manuscript, fished out what he wanted to say and then said it deliberately, looking out serenely towards Unter den Linden, and nursing his leg from time to time... He said 'In der Dad' instead of 'In der That', and had serious weaknesses in the way of jokes, but he was a great man."

From his *Hellas and Hesperia* (1909)[21] we learn more of this "quiet old Privy Councillor" who introduced the young American to "that mistress of mine [who] bore a lumbering name – Altertumswissenschaft," and whose "teaching made a passionate classicist out of an amateurish student of literature." He was "bent with what is called the scholar's stoop ... a man of shuffling gait, of slow and deliberate utterance, who read his lectures from a yellow 'heft' to which were attached supplementary slips of paper." Gildersleeve concludes: "Boeckh was a great master, the greatest living master of Hellenic studies, and if I became after a fashion a Hellenist, it was due not merely to the catalytic effect of his presence, but to the orbed completeness of the ideal he evoked."

From the same volume[22] we learn that Johannes Franz, whose *Schola Graeca,* of which Gildersleeve was a member in the winter semester of 1850-1851, was conducted in the Greek tongue, that he was first "real teacher of Greek"; and that, although the *Schola* was "not a brilliant success," it influenced this scholar's "whole life" and his "whole teaching." "Professional Types" discloses how Gildersleeve came under the tutelage of Franz:

> Lachmann ... died shortly after I went to Berlin, and I never heard him lecture. Franz, his sworn enemy, planted his lectures on Lachmann's hours, and as Franz's lectures fitted my scheme of studies better than did Lachmann's, I gave up the great critic for the practical teacher. He [Franz] was a believer in writing and speaking Greek... He called himself Pharasicles, and gave a Greek name to each of his pupils, mine being Chrysobrachion, which he developed in the twinkling of an eye from the analogy of Stytobrachion.
> Immanuel Bekker ... was the type of teacher who abhors teaching and did his utmost to deter students from following his courses ... I soon dropped.
> Stahl, one of the law professors, a politician and publicist of the reactionary school, was a star actor, and held forth to crowded audiences.
> Carl Ritter ... had a lordly port and impressive delivery... Ranke, the historian, was the despair of foreigners, a sputterer and contortionist, whom the German students found it hard to follow... In my happy year at Göttingen I had the good fortune to be brought into close relations with one of my professors, Schneidewin ... who was a personal friend, though perhaps none of my professors was more typically German than he. He was a man of prodigious memory and knew his Homer and Sophocles by heart...
> Karl Friedrich Hermann, the most eminent of the classical philologians in Göttingen ... it seemed perfectly natural that he should hump himself over his reading desk, bury his face in his manuscript, spout forth long sentences with immense force and with perpetual gyrations of one of his fat hands.
> Ritter, the historian of philosophy, ... was the textbook type of lecturer.
> Von Leutsch, the most diverting of all the academical oddities I have ever known.
> At Bonn, my chief masters were Welcker, Ritschl and Bernays. It seemed impossible that anyone could have studied under Ritschl without catching something of his fire, something of his spirit.

Friedrich G. Welcker (1784-1868) at the age of sixty-eight (1852) impressed our "lad of not yet twenty-one" as "an ancient of days."

> His bearing was that of an old, old man. He spoke slowly, deliberately ... he had a far-off look characteristic of the blind... He was gentleness, benignity itself whenever he was consulted by a young foreigner. A great celebrity, he was sought by visitors to Bonn, and I shall never forget how one sunny day as I was taking my usual walk in the Poppelsdorfer Allee, I was accosted by a young Englishman, who addressed me in a German not to be reproduced phonetically: "Kunnen sie mir ouohl saaggen, ouo dur Hur Professor Welcker bleibt?"[23]

Also in Bonn in 1852-1853 Gildersleeve "followed Bernays' lectures on Thukydides' speeches and Aristotle's Poetics." He asserts: "Though he was at the beginning of his career as a teacher, he influenced me more profoundly than did some of my older and more distinguished professors." He continues:

> I never think of Bernays without gratitude because it was he who led me into the study that resulted in my doctoral dissertation... But in my talks with Bernays we never chanced upon Euripides, and for many years I was under the domination of Schlegel, and followed the trend of aesthetic criticism that swayed the Germany of my time. The average Teutonic Hellenist of that day was a 'Euripidesfresser' as Menzel was a 'Franzosenfresser', and it is not surprising that a youthful Teutonomaniac should have been caught by what was really a national movement.

This "Fakultätenschau" will enable us to appreciate the kind of men who gave to America its greatest classical philologist, for Gildersleeve himself informs us in 1916:[24] "What I have done in my long life as a teacher, as a grammarian, is due in large measure to the example and inspiration of Boeckh, of C. F. Hermann, of Schneidewin, of Ritschl, of Welcker, of Bernays." Of Ritschl he had related in 1884:[25] " Such was his loving interest in all his pupils that he remembered me through the lapse of years, welcomed me to the hospitality of his charming home when I returned to Bonn in 1860; wrote me once a long letter in his superb hand; and on my recent visit to Germany, I found that, as a pupil of his, I was received as a friend of long standing by those who were nearest to him."

In 1899, discoursing on superannuated professors, Gildersleeve recalls with pleasure[26] that one day in the summer semester of 1852 he "dropped in to hear Ernst Moritz Arndt talk of 'Vergleichende

Völkergeschichte'." He continues: "He was then eighty-three years old, and it was not until the next semester that we were told 'venerabilem senectutem excusans a scholiis habendis vacabit'," and concludes: "To stop is to invite death."

The year of 1903 marked the customary renewal of the degree on the semicentennial anniversary of its bestowal, but even in the sad year of 1917, when his own country was at war with the land in which he had, over three-score years earlier, enjoyed five semesters of academic inspiration, he writes:[27] "But as I read, my mind went back to Bonn and I sat once more in Ernst Moritz Arndt's lecture-room and heard him repeat with unction: 'Ich bin ein Mädchen von Flandern, Und springe von einem zum andern.'"

To be convinced of the verity of Gildersleeve's claim that he had read many of Goethe's works one needs but peruse the record of his scholarly life in the volumes of the *American Journal of Philology*, in his *Essays and Studies* and other volumes. After *Faust*, the "Zahme Xenien" and other sententious passages seem to have made the most enduring impression upon him, as did also the concept of "das Ewig-Weibliche," but he also manifests an extensive knowledge and a keen appreciation of Goethe's lyrics.

Early in the first volume of the *American Journal of Philology*, of which he was the founder and the editor for its first forty years, he quotes: "Das Ewig-Weibliche zieht uns hinan" (p. 74). Again in the eighteenth volume (1897, p. 124) he tells us Pindar's "Ninth Olympian Ode is given up to the Eternal Feminine." Ten years later the aged classical philologian makes the sage observation in speaking of Odysseus: "[one has] measured his voyages by his loves as one measures the voyage of Goethe's life by the incarnations of the Eternal Feminine that marked his career, if they did not make it."[28] Even two years later he wrote:[29] "It is fairly safe to say that there is no great genius of modern times whose career is so well known as Goethe's, and the Eternal Feminine stands at every sinuousity of his path."

In the same year he notes that the second strophe of Pindar's First Nemean ode[30] "begins with a memorable picture that always recalls to my mind Goethe's 'Sänger',

Was hör' ich draussen vor dem Thor?

In fact Goethe's opening may have been suggested by this famous passage."

An editorial in the *New York Times* (January 11, 1924) declares that Gildersleeve "was a gallant soldier who was not less courageous for carrying his Iliad in his pocket," but the following anecdote, reported by Gildersleeve himself, indicates that he carried Goethe's *Faust* in his heart.[31] Riding into battle during his brief combat service in the Confederate Army he reports: "Our talk fell on Goethe and on Faust, and of all the passages the soldiers' song came up to my lips, – the song of soldiers of fortune, not the chant of men whose business it was to defend their country. Two lines, however, were significant:

>'Kühn ist das Mühen,
>Herrlich der Lohn.'

Not too long before the appearance of this editorial Gildersleeve had recalled that, as "Goethe tells us that he rode into the zone of the great guns in order to find out for himself what is meant by 'cannon fever'," he too, mindful of Goethe's example, had "tried to analyze" his "own feelings under similar circumstances."[32]

Although no single monument is found in any one of Gildersleeve's works which marks him as a disciple of Goethe, whom he called[33] "the guide of my youth," there was never a time from his first acquaintance with Goethe to his extreme old age when he failed to commend the wisdom of Goethe's philosophy of life and to resort to Goethe's works for encouragement and support, and, in his old age, for solace. His early study "Lucian" (1859)[34] has frequent references which manifest a broad acquaintance with Goethe's life and works ("Der Zauberlehrling," "Westöstliche Divan," "Faust"), whereas the earlier "The Emperor Julian" (1857)[35] had mentioned Goethe but once. "Classics and Colleges" (1878) is liberal with its references to Goethe ("Märchen," "History of Science," "Iphigenie," "Zahme Xenien") but teems with references to Classical education in Germany.

The number and nature of the references made to Goethe when Gildersleeve approached the age at which the sage of Weimar departed this earth incline us to believe that Goethe was the guide of Gildersleeve's old age as he had been the guide of his youth. At the age of seventy-six (1908) he writes:[36] "There are four lines of Goethe that come back to me whenever I have been called in my long life to part with a friend forever,

>Nicht in das Grab, nicht über's Grab verschwendet
>Ein edler Mann der Sehnsucht hohen Werth,
>Er kehrt in sich zurück und findet staunend
>In seinem Busen das Verlorne wieder.

On October 26, 1913 we read: "As Goethe says '*Alles ist als wie geschenkt*'."[37] These same words of Goethe occur again in Gildersleeve's eighty-ninth year.[38]

With Schiller's poetry he was also familiar. Still in a martial mood he recalls Schiller's "Siegesfest" saying:[39] "It is an old cry, – 'Ja, der Krieg verschlingt die Besten.' Still, when Schiller says...

> Ohne Wahl vertheilt die Gaben,
> Ohne Billigkeit, das Glück,
> Denn Patroklus liegt begraben,
> Und Thersites kommt züruck,

his illustration is only half right. The Greek Thersites did not return to claim a pension."

Gildersleeve finds another occasion to reprove Schiller for his failure to represent Classical antiquity authentically. This time it is a question of form rather than of fact. It is a matter of metrics. He writes:[40]

> I am even now tempted to call attention to the fact, which I have never seen emphasized, that in the so-called model distich commonly credited to Schiller, though Wilamowitz claims it for Schlegel,
>> Im Hexameter steigt des Springquells flüssige Säule,
>> Im Pentameter drauf fällt sie melodisch herab.
> the poet has constructed an hexameter on lines that are so unpopular in Greek that in 695 hexameters of the Theognidea there is only one spondee in the bucolic diaeresis.

In the Hopkins Collection there is a document marked "Fifth Lecture." It deals with "the inadequacy of translation." It is an enlargement on the preceding. Gildersleeve quotes Coleridge's "not less famous distich"

> In the Hexameter rises the fountain's silvery column,
> In the Pentameter aye falling in melody back.

and concludes:

> So I shall lead Schiller and Coleridge by the ear – the ear by which they have sinned – to the schoolboy bench where they can study the structure of the hexameter and qualify for the metrical heaven. A bucolic cesura, as it is called, ending in a spondee, is sedulously avoided by careful Greek versewrights. And this misplaced spondee figures both in Schiller and his imitator Coleridge.

On another occasion our grammarian makes the following penetrating, and apparently non-complimentary, observation:[41] "The neuter

'It' has of late years become something demoniacal like the ES in Schiller's 'Taucher,' an unsexed, absolute, absorbent Being."

Additional references and quotations indicate the nature of Gildersleeve's acquaintance with the works of Jean Paul Richter, Rückert, Heine and of Nietzsche. The last named he esteems as a fellow philologian. He says:[42]

> Much of Nietzsche's power lies in his style... Nietzsche was a child of seven when I was poring over Thukydides in Berlin and reading Theognis in Göttingen – those two Greeks who either influenced Nietzsche profoundly or responded intimately to his native genius – and now no one can write of Thukydides or Theognis without bringing in Nietzsche... Nietzsche's interpretation of Greek literature is accepted as a canon by persons who write about the Greek Genius.

Gildersleeve's knowledge of German letters was not confined to the Classical period and the nineteenth century. Quotations from and references to Luther are not infrequent. When he tells us in 1909:[43]

> Reading Luther's Table Talk many years ago, I was struck with the fact that whenever the great translator of the Bible was stirred, he quoted Scripture in Latin. – *Führ' uns nicht in Versuchung* of his own *Vater unser* could never have meant the same to him as *Ne nos inducas in tentationem*,

he speaks as a Classical translator who was conscious of the inadequacy of translation.

Of the German author of Latin comedies, Nicodemus Frischlin, he says in 1908:[44]

> In my early pot-boiling days I wrote for the Southern Methodist Quarterly Review for July, 1856, an account of that disreputable person, based on David Strauss's interesting and instructive Life.[45]

Later he expatiates:[46]

> In Hermann's *Lateinische Litteraturdenkmäler des 15. und 16. Jahrhunderts* Walther Janell has edited Nicodemus Frischlin's *Julius Redivivus*, with introductions by Walther Hauff, on Frischlin as a man; Gustav Roeth, on Frischlin as a dramatist; Walther Janell, on Frischlin as a philologian.

Evidence of Gildersleeve's sympathy for Frischlin is contained in his statement of 1912:[47] "I have had occasion from time to time to air my Frischliniana in the Journal." As late as 1916 he quotes from his article[48] "the cry of the ill-fated Swabian scholar and poet" which came back to him "after sixty years." "O wa seind meine Bücher!"

Going even further back to the Middle High German period he informs us: "Kudrun is to me a more interesting personage than Kriemhilde or Brunhilde."[49] In the notes to his edition of *Pindar The Olympian and Pythian Odes* (1885) he writes:[50] "Pindar is a manner of 'Frauenlob', at any rate, but here 'das Ewig-Weibliche' is paramount." Twelve years later Gildersleeve reverts to this theme, noting that Wilamowitz had written in a recent edition of the Choëphoroi:[51] "Eine edle Frau giebt es nicht bei [Pindar]." Gildersleeve retorts:

> That is a hard saying, especially for an editor who has ventured to call Pindar 'a manner of Frauenlob.' Surely Alkemene is not unworthy of her son... The Ninth Olympian [ode] is given up to the Eternal Feminine and the lofty realm of personifications is full of goddesses. If the worship of the Virgin Mary is a tribute to womanhood and motherhood, something is to be said for Pindar's shining forms arrayed in woman's garb.

In a lengthy learned article, "The Legend of Venus,"[52] after declaring that "The story is best set forth in an old German ballad, reprinted by Achim von Arnim in his well known collection, 'Des Knaben Wunderhorn' which he calls the "delight of my youth,"[53] he continues:[54]

> The language does not indicate a great antiquity; it is to our ear very much the racy tongue of Luther's Table Talk, so that the version which we give below... is faulty ... we only hope that even in this imperfect rendering the reader may still trace the rude directness of the original, its lively portraiture, its boldness of transition, its honesty and its earnestness.

Then follows, in the verse forms of the original as found in von Arnim's collection, an English translation, "The Ballad of Tanhuser" in Gildersleeve's own rendition.

THE BALLAD OF TANHUSER

And now I will begin my song,
   And of Tanhuser tell,
And all the wonders done the while
   He did with Venus dwell.

Tanhuser was a right good knight,
    Great wonders he fain would see,
So went he to Dame Venus' mount,
    Where other fair dames be.

'Sir Tanhusèr, I love you much, –
    This you should take to heart:
You sware to me a solemn oath
    No more from me to part.'

'Dame Venus, that I did not do,
    And that I will gainsay:
There's none that saith so, saving you,
    So help me God this day.'

'Sir Tanhusèr, how say you so!
    Here you must spend your life:
I'll give you one of my play-feres
    To be your wedded wife.'

'If I should take another wife
    Than her which I desire,
Then I must burn forevermore
    In brimstone and hell-fire.'

'You talk so much about hell-fire
    And have not been therein –
Bethink ye of my rosy mouth
    And of my dimpled chin.'

'What good doth me your rosy mouth?
    It doth not please me moe;
By all dames' honor, Venus sweet,
    Give me good leave to go.'

'Sir Tanhusèr, if you wish leave,
    I will not give you none:
Now stay, my noble Tanhusèr,
    And fresh your life anon.'

'My way of life hath fallen sick,
    I cannot longer stay;
From your proud body give me leave,
    Sweet dame, to go away.'

'Sir Tanhusèr, nay speak not so,
   You are not in your mind:
Let us go back into my bower,
   Our fill of love to find.'

'I am a-weary of your love,
   In which I wont to revel –
O Venus, noble damosel,
   Methinks you be a she-devil.'

'Tanhuser, how can you speak so?
   Too bitter is your gird.
If you should longer stay with us,
   You'll pay me well that word.

'Tanhuser, if that you will go,
   Take leave of my knights around;
And when you journey through the land,
   My praises shall you sound.'

Tanhuser from the mountain went
   In sorrow and in ruth –
'Unto Rome city I will go
   And tell the Pope the truth.

'Now joyously, with God to friend,
   To Rome I trust to win.
The Holy Father, Pope Urbán,
   Will shrive me clean from sin.

'Lord Pope! O Holy Father mine,
   I am in sore distress
For all the sin which I have done,
   The which I now confess.

'A twelvemonth fully I have been
   With Venus, that ladye;
Now I wish shrift and penitence,
   God's face that I may see.'

The Pope he had a white, white staff,
   'Twas made of a dry, dry tree:
'When this staff beareth leaves, then shall
   Thy sins forgiven be.'

'If I should live not more than a year –
    But one year here below –
I would do penance and repent,
    God's grace again to owe.'

Then gat he him away from Rome,
    And sorely he did grieve:
'O Mary Mother, Virgin pure
    If thee I thus must leave,

'I'll get me back to yon mountain,
    To dwell forever and aye
With Venus, mine own ladye dear,
    Where God will have me stay.'

'O welcome home, Tanhuser dear,
    I've missed you long and sore:
O welcome home, my dearest lord,
    My chosen evermore.'

Mayhap the third day after that,
    The staff again waxed green,
    And criers were sent to every land
    Where Tanhusèr had been.

But he was back in Venus' Mount,
    And there he shall aby
Forever, till the judgment day,
    When God his soul shall try.

Now this is what no priest should do –
    Miscomfort any that live:
If a man do penance and repent,
    His sins he should forgive.

The translator admits that his version is "somewhat doctored"[55] but justly claims that he has "stuck closer to his text than Mr. Bithell."[56] He excuses the latter for omitting "the last feeble verse [stanza]," notes "the prosaic effect of the tag" and concludes: "and yet in view of my sins and the sins of my fellow-translators I am fain to say,

    Dass [*sic*!] soll nimmer kein [Richter] thun,
    Dem Menschen Misstrost geben,
    Will er denn Buss' und Reu' empfahn
    Die Sünde sei ihm vergeben.

And surely my penitence is sincere and poignant enough."⁵⁷

The *Southern Messenger* for February, 1854, contains a short article called⁵⁸ "A Modest Critique of 'A Sketch after Landseer'," introduced by a couplet:

> Ich sehe nichts als einen schwarzen Pudel.
> Es mag bei euch wohl Augentäuschung sein.
> *Faust.*

The author refers to himself as "an old student of *Friderica Guilelma Rhenana*. He speaks of "the Lubber – the common gathering place of students." He goes into details about "Othello," the dog that was once a "frequent visitor at the house where I lodged, which was inhabited by sundry Palatines." He refers to "Sons of Belial flown with lust and wine," and signs the article "Chrysobrachion," which, we have already learned,⁵⁹ was the name given to Gildersleeve in the *Schola Graeca* during his first semester in Berlin.

This is the young doctor's first published article resulting from his sojourn in Germany, but one must wonder whether the article of which this was a "critique," "A Sketch after Landseer, Extract from a Journal of the Rhine," which appeared in the same periodical in the preceding month (January, 1854)⁶⁰ and which introduces the same dog and a group of students returning to Bonn, might not be a product of the same pen, for we know of no other contributor to this Charleston(s.c.) periodical who had recently been at Bonn.⁶¹

In the Gildersleeve Collection in the Johns Hopkins University Library we find these words: "When I was a young fellow in Germany, one of my friends was enamoured of Platen and that led me to write an article, on that German poet." The article, "Platen's Poems", first appeared in the *Southern Review* (Baltimore) for October, 1868.⁶² It was then, and probably remains today, the most authentic evaluation of that poet ever to appear in an English periodical. As the author observes:

> It is not often that a German makes a reputation on this side of the water without undergoing the baptism of the Channel. And the English have never taken to Platen.

The essay is based not only on the most authoritative critical works of the middle of the last century, but on Gildersleeve's long and intimate acquaintance with Platen's writings as well as on an unsurpassed mastery of Classical literature, scholarship and metrics, without which his extensive translations from Platen's dramas, ghazels and ballads would have been impossible. He likewise brought to his criticism a very extensive knowledge of German literature in general, as immediately becomes evident from a perusal of the essay.

Gildersleeve early assayed metrical translations of Platen's "lofty and melodious verses" which "bring back ... the golden music of the past, blending with the roll of the Rhine and lingering among the echoes of the Seven Mountains." He explains that he became acquainted with Platen's poems in Bonn in 1852 and continues: "Several of our set knew long stretches of Platen's poems by heart, and never were his 'lofty and melodious verses' more lustily declaimed than on our trips to Heisterbach and the Siebengebirge."[64]

We are therefore not surprised to discover that the following "Occidental Ghazels" which appeared in the *Southern Literary Messenger* for March, 1854, introduced by a single mutilated German verse[65]

> Verknende nicht indess, Gasele, dem Vaterland
>
> Platen[66]

are creations of the youthful Gildersleeve.

INTRODUCTORY

The sun that is setting will rise again
And brighten to-morrow the skies again,
The heaven, all covered with darkness thick,
Will open its manifold eyes again.
The song of the Persian may perish *there*,
Here let it awake and arise again.

I

Whatever fortune gives in haste collect,
And seize the moment whilst thou mayst collect,
Misguided pilgrims, fainting sore for food,
A meal of berries from the waste collect,
Disporting children on the shore whate'er
The scornful sea hath thither chased collect,
Bold divers headlong plunging precious pearls,
Deep in the ocean's bosom placed, collect,
Unwearied scholars search their volumes well,
And words, that Time had now effaced, collect;
So too dost thou, to whom my songs are due,
The lines my feeble hand hath traced collect.

II

The prisoned spirit is set free at last,
The seed upspringeth to a tree at last;
The truant brooklet wanders through the mead,

But runs to meet his lord the sea at last.
The honey-bee collects all day his store
Yet homeward turns the weary bee at last.
The clouds that hide the beauty of the sun,
Stretch out their misty limbs and flee at last.
The stubborn lock defends the treasure-house,
But cunning lock-smiths find the key at last.
My soul hath sought for bliss in every clime
And finds its only bliss in thee at last.

III

The nightingale displays her craft at night,
Soft breezes softer perfumes waft at night.
The simple merchant setteth sail by day,
The wary soldier floats his raft at night,
The chariot-steering sun drives up the morn,
The hunter's moon lets fly her shaft at night.
The Persian mixes wine with morning dew,
The Occidental drinks the draught at night!

B. L. G.

The second and first of these stanzas Gildersleeve reprints in "Platen's Poems," but not without some modifications.

He holds in high esteem Platen's lyrics in antique meters and calls their author "a master of the form ... still unequalled in this direction."[67] Asserting that:[68] "His lyric poems commend themselves by their exquisite beauty of form," and that "some of his minor pieces quiver with suppressed sensibility," he exemplifies this by presenting the following translation:

O happy time in which a man can love his fellow-man:
Upon my heart there lies a curse, upon my soul a ban.

Once bitter anguish was my lot, I've love and fortune now;
But how can I return the love? I know not how.

All calmness and all joylessness, from East to West I go,
Unutterable frost succeeds unutterable glow;

And if a light and loving hand but chance my hand to press,
I feel at once a sudden pain and deep rebelliousness.

Why, then, in all your beauty's light upon my senses burst,
As if my life were warm and full as was my youth at first?[69]

He recommends that "those who are desirous of enriching our English poetry by classic versification ... study Platen in order to see what has been done in a kindred tongue."[70]

Of Platen's ballads he opines:[71] "In our judgment, some of his pieces, though a little cold, rank among the best of German literature." He considers Platen's "Harmosan" "better and more dramatic than Rückert's poem on the same subject," and presents his own translations of two ballads, "Harmosan" and "Zobir," preserving both the metrical form and the poetic spirit of the originals.

HARMOSAN

The throne of the Sassanidae now lay in dust, the ancient throne,
And Moslem hands were plundering the treasur'd wealth of Ctesiphon;
Now Omar came to Oxus' strand – 'twas after a many a hard fought day,
Where Chosru's grandson, Jezdegerd, a corpse on piles of corpses lay.
As through the wide champaign he went, and countless booty well explored,
A satrap, Harmosan by name, was brought before Medina's lord;
The last that the fearless foe among the mountains dared to strive,
But ah! the hand so bold before, was manacled by heavy gyve.

And Omar sternly vieweth him and saith, 'Perceivest now how slight,
How vain against the God we serve the idol-servers' counter-might?'
And Harmosan thus answers him, 'Thy hands the victory have wrought,
Whose gainsays a conqueror, gainsays from foolish lack of thought.
I venture but a single prayer, well-weighing both thy lot and mine:
Three days I've fought without a draught – O! serve me with a draught of wine.'
The caliph beckons – at his beck a beaker on the captive waits,
But Harmosan suspects a drug and still a while he hesitates.

'Fear not,' outspeaks the Saracen, 'for treachery stains no Moslem soul:
Thou shalt not die, my friend, until thy lips have drained this glowing bowl.'

And then the Persian takes the cup, and quickly, with his
                                              ironed hand,
Instead of drinking, hurls it down with instantaneous self-
                                                  command.

And Omar's followers fall on him and haste to venge the
                                              cunning plan,
Bright gleam their swords above the head of the all too
                                          crafty Harmosan –
'His life be spared,' cries Omar then, while warding off the
                                          threatening sword,
'If aught be sacred on the earth, it is a warrior's given word.'

ZOBIR

All eager for plunder, terrific and poor,
Abdallah has brought to the African shore
The Arabian host,
And suddenly stands upon Tripoli's coast.

Yet ere they lay siege to the wall and the gate,
The noble Gregorius cometh in state –
The victor renowned
Byzantium sent out to make war on Mahound.

While bravely he stems the fanatical tide,
His daughter so winsome rides close by his side,
Her lance in its rest,
The golden-hair'd maiden with steel-covered breast.

She had taken upon her a warrior's part,
And wielded her spear and shot far with her dart
In the roar of the fight,
Like Pallas and yet like Cytheré so bright.

Then up rose her father and looking about,
He fired with valor his warriors stout –
'Come cease with this game,
My men – at Abdallah! – for that is your aim.

Whoever shall bring me the enemy's head,
To-day mine own lovely Maria shall wed,
With riches untold:
Beside her dear self, countless treasures of gold.'

Then thicker the shafts of the Christians they flew,
And the Moslem grew fainter in muscle and thew,
And Abdallah in gloom
Withdrew to his tent from the coming of doom.

Yet one in that host fought with spirit aflame,
A thunderbolt he, and Zobir was his name:
Off rides he in wrath,
And his spur, as it rings, sprinkles blood in his path.

He speaks to his master and says: 'Will you miss
The fight like a boy? What, Abdallah, is this?
By the caliph you're sent
To conquer the world, and you dream in your tent!

Let that which the Christian devised to unnerve
The Moslem, be made his own ruin to serve:
Your promises make
The equal of his, and the same be the stake.

Announce to your soldiers this guerdon of fight:
Whoever the enemy's leader shall smite
On his infidel head,
I'll grant him the lovely Maria to wed.'

Abdallah proclaims it – new light in his eyes –
His soldiers take heart at the glorious prize –
Zobir in the van
With the whirl of his scimitar slaughters his man.

See! the Christians they hide in the town their disgrace!
See! how the gaunt Moslems crowd into the place!
See! floats from the tow'rs
The flag of the prophet – 'the city is ours!'

Long, long did Maria the foeman withstand:
Surrounded at last by a Saracen band,
On the tide she was swept
To the feet of Zobir, and she saw him and wept.

Then outspeaketh one from the midst of the horde:
'We bring you your winsome, your lovely reward,
The beautiful fere
That you fought with us for, and you've gained her, Zobir!'

> Then answers the hero with sneer and with jest:
> 'Who tempteth the manhood that reigns in my breast?
> Catch me like a bird?
> I fight for my God and I fight for his word!
>
> For love of a Christian I vie with you? I?
> Go, girl! for thy freedom is granted thee, fly –
> What seekest thou here?
> Go, weep for thy father and curse thou Zobir.'

The following remarks illustrate the Classicist's critical acumen:[72]

> Rückert was a wonderful poet ... far more masculine than Platen, and gifted with an easier mastery of the language. His playfulness is more spontaneous; his serious verses are deeper; his satiric knout takes out the flesh at every stroke. Platen felt the influence of the stronger genius, and, inspired by Rückert, he attempted to transfer to the German language the form as well as the spirit of that Persian poetry which Goethe's 'Divan' had made so popular.

He then sagaciously reminds us that "if Goethe had commenced with his 'Divan' [as did Platen, with his Gaselen] he would hardly have become the favorite of the Germans."[73]

Gildersleeve's broad tolerance and innate sense of humor made him an ideal interpreter of the comedies of Platen. When he says:[74] "not one Englishman in fifty can see any fun in German wit" just after having written:[75]

> We can admire a 'classicist' without despising a 'romanticist'; we can taste the perfume of Heine's flowers without defiling Platen's memory with the subsoil of Heine's hot-bed; and can enjoy Platen's artistic creations without joining in Platen's injustice to Immermann.

he exhibits some of his qualifications as a critic.

Admitting that: "We may well despair of giving to an English translation the finished perfection of language which is to many the highest, to some the sole charm of Platen,"[76] he presents what was at that time probably the most extensive body of English translation in verse forms of the original from Platen's comedies, "The Fateful Fork" (143 verses) and "The Romantic Oedipus" (150 verses), which dramas he asserts "have made themselves a permanent place in the history of German literature."[77]

As a result of his studies of Platen's comedies, especially of "The Romantic Oedipus," the Classicist concludes:[78]

The imitation of Aristophanes in this piece is also very close, and many of the verses are a direct echo of the great original. But while this close study gives these compositions of Platen a peculiar charm in the eyes of the classical scholar, the general public, even in Germany, has little real relish for such artificial reproductions; and Platen's plays are destined to become at no distant day mere literary curiosities.

After having translated the opening soliloquy of act five of "The Fateful Fork," Gildersleeve restricts himself to mere references to the following lines, "which," he says, "we cannot translate without disgusting the English reader. Scenes like that at the opening of the 'Peace' of Aristophanes are even more to the German taste than they were to the Greek."[79] He thus, unintentionally, adduces one reason why the literature of Germany is almost devoid of great comedies.

In making his translations from these two comedies Gildersleeve took pleasure in collecting German words of exceeding length, as did his friend and contemporary in Göttingen, David Ramsay, and his follower, Mark Twain,[80] with whom he has been compared by one German critic in another connection.[81] But Mark Twain would hardly have passed unnoticed Platen's "der ohnmachtfloskelragoutsteifleindürrnüchterne Houwald" in a line whose translation Gildersleeve did not even cite.[81] Gildersleeve translates Platen's "Froschmolluskenbreinatur" as frog-molluscitude (418),[83] "Demagogenriechernashornangesicht" as demagogue's rhinocerotic smeller-face (p. 427), "Freischützcascadenfeuerwerkmaschinerie" as hydraulicpyrotechnicalities (p. 431). "Obertollhausüberschnappungsnarrenschiff" (p. 444) he does not attempt to render.

When Gildersleeve, the Pindarist, spent sixty days in Greece in 1896 he protested that the revival of the Olympian games was not the reason for his sojourn, insisting that the religious fervor which had been the *raison d'être* of the ancient Grecian games must of necessity be lacking in the new, preponderantly athletic, contests. By way of contrast he cites the enduring religious spirit of the Oberammergau Passion Play as impressed upon him during both visits there, in 1860 and again in 1890. Insisting that his interests in Greece were those of a classical scholar and a devotee of Pindar, he recalls "the old German song

Ich hatt' einen Kameraden, einen besseren find'st du nit,"
and concludes: "There is, after all, no better comrade for a trip to Greece than Pindar."[84]

In 1919 Gildersleeve confessed:[85]

To Pindar I shall probably never say farewell, until I bid the world goodnight... In my student's years in Germany I was

taught to be an admirer of Platen... Among my favourites was a sonnet on the Death of Pindar. Not long ago, trying to work in the dark, I found that I could recall only half of the poem, but while awaiting a transcript by a friendly hand, the familiar story framed itself into a sonnet of my own, only part of which is due to Platen.
The part of Platen's sonnet that escaped my memory betrays his well-known egotism. No one but Platen would have dreamed that a wish for a death like Pindar's would have involved any comparison between the two poets in life or genius.

He then presents his own sonnet based on Platen's:[86]

> When I depart on God's appointed day,
> Quick and unconscious passage be my lot,
> Like stars' that quit the sky and tarry not,
> Unlike the comet's train that fades away.
>
> Such was the end of Pindaros, they say:
> The theatre in Argos holds the spot
> Where, heedless of the play's soul-stirring plot,
> The weary bard in peaceful slumber lay,
>
> A perfect image of serene repose,
> His gray head resting on his favorite's knee;
> His sleep grew deeper as the play went on;
>
> The play was o'er, the audience rustling rose,
> The boy essayed to wake him tenderly, –
> In vain, for Pindar to the gods was gone.

This reminiscence of Platen whom he had admired since his youth as a master of classical form, whose "ghaselen" he had imitated in 1856, whose lyrics he had praised in 1868 for their "exquisite beauty of form" and their "suppressed sensibility" and a quatrain of one of whose sonnets he translated at that time:[87]

> My soul by inner contest rudely jarred,
> Hath felt so oft in this short life of mine,
> How easily I could my home resign;
> But ah! to find a second home, how hard!

indicates that, when Gildersleeve realized that "God's appointed day" was drawing near and he was threatened with Milton's affliction of spending his remaining days "in this dark world," his resort to sonnetry was accompanied by a return to Pindar and to those German poets who loved classical poetry and who were experts in the mechanics of classical metres. In 1920 he wrote:[88]

> My theory of the sonnet, or, to be precise, of that form of sonnet to which I am addicted, is of the same order as my view of the structure of Pindar's triadic odes ... so I look upon the sonnet, and its parts ... the octave representing the hexameter [of the elegiac distich], the sextet, the so-called pentameter, of the elegiac distich.

He continues:[89]

> The other day my attention was called by a true lover and knower of Pindar to a cry of despair uttered by one who is accounted among the leading German poets. It is couched in the measure regularly employed by the Greek epigramatists, and, in further illustration of the theory that the modern sonnet corresponds to the Greek epigram, I have not translated it but transposed it into that form:

> Can Pindar's lays be made to live again,
> Which in Olympia once the Hellenes stirred?
> His words of wisdom deep may still be heard,
> And traces of his upward flight remain.
>
> We have an inkling of the rhythmic strain,
> Which bore aloft his many-storied word.
> To hope for more, however, were absurd;
> Renunciation is our plan, 'tis plain.
>
> And then the myth. What can we do with that?
> What was a living treasure-house to him,
> A tree of life, emotion's fountain-head,
> To us are names, all colorless and flat.
>
> Ho, tireless searchers, resolute and grim,
> The thing is dead. Seek not to wake the dead.

Gildersleeve then subjoins the ten verses of Emanuel Geibel from "Distichen aus dem Wintertagebuche" beginning:

> Nimmer gelingt's dir, Freund, uns Pindar's Lied zu beleben,
> Wie's in Olympias Hain einst die Helenen ergriff, etc.

and comments:

> It will be observed that Geibel has put in the front line the things that remain of Pindar, the 'Tiefsinn seiner Gedanken.' Against the low estimate in which certain Pindarists have held the thought of the great Theban, I have protested more than once and venture to add another protest in the fashion I have affected so much of late:

> Pindar is charged with poverty of thought;
> A slender wit, in royal mantle clad,
> He only gave what he from others had,
> He only taught what he himself was taught.
>
> But we, who deemed his odes with wisdom fraught,
> Heed not his critics' small, fault-finding fad –
> We, who in every time, or good or bad,
> Counsel and comfort from the singer sought,
>
> And not in vain. But when the counsel came,
> Such was its music that we half forgot
> Its sterling value for its silvery ring –
>
> The cherub wisdom for the seraph flame.
> Comfort descended, but they noted not
> The healing for the plumage of its wing.

In March, 1921,[90] Gildersleeve published an article "The Solace of Sonnetry" in which he declares: "I was a rhymster long before I had any claim to be a classical scholar, and in my old age... I have gone back to the 'versus et cetera ludicra' of my youth – my favorite form being the sonnet." (p. 179) Here is presented his best known composition in the genre: "The Cup and the Ball."

> A child I used to play with cup and ball,
> The little globe is tethered with a string;
> You hold the cup and give the ball a swing
> And catch it ere it reach its farthrest fall.
>
> Now at an age men second childhood call,
> When I would play, the sonnet is the thing –
> You give the octave ball an upward fling,
> And catch it in your sextette. That is all.
>
> I know this sonnet-writing is inanity.
> It is not an art. 'Tis nothing but a knack
> With which I while away the darksome hours.

> I'll keep it up, though critics doubt my sanity,
> Till the pale postman comes whose knocks attack
> Alike the poor men's cots and princes' towers.

Here "the cup" and "the ball," the octette ("octave ball") and the "sextette" (cup) seem to echo, in the mechanics of verse, the rise of the "Springquells flüssige Säule" in the "Hexameter" and its melodic fall in the "Pentameter" in the distich for which Gildersleeve had reproved Schiller and Coleridge in 1912.[91]

Yet another sonnet in this essay seems to owe a debt to German inspiration. To quote the sonneteer: "The warning is a versified reproduction of one of Lessing's fables ["Der Besitzer des Bogens," *Fabeln*, 3tes Buch] and of the German proverb 'Allzuscharf macht schartig'."

> An archer once, the fable says, intent
> On rich adornment for his favorite bow,
> Carved on it figures far too deep, and 'lo!
> He tried to bend it, and it snapped ere bent.
>
> A cutler, says another tale, who meant
> To make a blade no fellow-craft could shew,
> Put on the steel too fine an edge, and so
> The falchion into gaps unsightly went.
>
> Crowd not thine octave, heedless sonneteer,
> With far-fetched facts and fancies, lest it break,
> And strew the earth with unrelated spilth.
>
> And make the meaning of thy sextette clear,
> Lest thy keen falchion prove a mimic rake
> Of no real service for the spirit's tilth.

The above should suffice to show whence Gildersleeve obtained much of his solace in sonnetry. The following sonnet will show his pioneer American nature and will explain some of the attitudes assumed in later life:

> I lie on life's lone beach a useless log,
> Erstwhile a dugout – that's the Greek for boat.
> On many a stream of thought I was afloat.
> My freight? Lost Causes. Name? The Under Dog.
>
> In poet sunshine or grammarian fog,
> On open sea or else a stagnant moat,
> The will that drave me on asunder smote
> Pedantic weeds that would my pathway clog.

> Nay, I am rather like a locust tree,
> The Pseudacacia of my native land,
> The farmer's favorite timber for a post:
>
> Leave but a strip of bark and you will see
> How the tough fibre doth the adze withstand,
> And put forth pinnate leaves – arboreal ghost.[92]

These are the thoughts of a nonagenerian, whose active career has about ended, who has forged forward despite "Lost Causes" and still has fibre enough to withstand attack. But what most concerns us here are his "Lost Causes." As we have indicated in our introduction, the Civil War took a heavy toll of the Southern youth who had been educated in Goethe's Germany, and its aftermath cut short potential growth in prominence and fame of numerous others. So one of Gildersleeve's lost causes in the sixties of the nineteenth century was the Civil War which also left him a physical cripple. As he says: "In our Civil War many scholars of military age – the Southerners almost without exception – shewed that the martial notes of Tyrtaios had not lost their edge."[93]

In his first presidential address to the American Philological Association in 1878 Gildersleeve set forth the situation that had confronted Southern scholars, "cut off not only from contact with those who were pursuing the same line of study and pressing forward toward the same ideals, but from every sign of life from without, from new books, new journals, now by the pillar of fire which is called war, now by the pillar of cloud which is called poverty."[94] In the same year the former Göttinger student, lamenting his second "lost cause," published in *Essays and Studies*:[95]

> Since the late war with France it is no secret that the land of scholars has lost much of its attraction in the eyes of scholars, because it has become so despotic.

Again, in the second decade of the twentieth century, the outbreak of World War I and the subsequent entry of his native country into that conflict caused further estrangement. After the beginning of hostilities he wrote:[96]

> The Franco-Prussian War made a deep cleft in my life ... the world has never been the same to me since then. I shall never cease to mourn for the Germany of my young manhood.

He now refers back to his statement of 1878 when he had said that the post-bellum situation *vis à vis* Germany was[97] "inexpressibly sad to anyone who, like the writer, owes all the best impulses of his intellectual life to the contact with German ideals." Returning to his World War I statement (1915) we find further:

> If English scholars were better acquainted with the German language, ... if more of them had been trained in German schools, as have so many of our leading American scholars, there would be less subserviency... He who has profited by his German training, who has learned the secret of German method, of German exhaustiveness, is armed by German "Wissenschaft" against German "Allesbesserwissenschaft."

But in the same commentary, still mindful of the other Germany, he queries: "What has become of that wonderful lay sermon preached by Goethe, the guide of my youth. It begins:

> Willst du dir ein hübsch Leben zimmern,
> Muszt um's Vergangene dich nicht kümmern.

The penultimate verse runs,

> Besonders keinen Menschen hassen.

Interestingly enough it is in this period that Gildersleeve most frequently refers to Heine. In 1916 he repeats Heine's quatrain,[98]

> Ein Posten ist vakant! Die Wunden klaffen.
> Der eine fällt, die andern rücken nach.
> Doch fall' ich unbesiegt und meine Waffen
> Sind nicht gebrochen. Nur das Herze brach.

and remarks: "a favorite [quatrain] not of mine only but of many who pray for a life of endeavor and a quick exit." The following year he observes: "Among German writers Heine was Bywater's[99] favorite – and no wonder. Heine was what the Hebrews call the mouth of the sword, and Bywater was a master of incisive speech." Later he adds:

> When the wielders of Thor's hammer, foretold of Heinrich Heine descendant of the prophets of old, had made some progress in destroying the temples of Christ, the son of an un-German god, there was some discussion among the followers of an un-German creed as to what course was to be pursued after the war, whether to restore what used to be called in pseudo-classic style the sacred fanes that had been demolished or to let them remain to be a perpetual reminder of the ruin that had been wrought." [Berlin's Gedächtniskirche?]

True, Gildersleeve had previously referred to Heine in his earlier articles "Limits of Culture" (1867), "The Legend of Venus,"[100] and in "Platen's Poems" (1868)[101] where he quotes Platen as calling Heine "the shamelessest of human kind."

Gildersleeve's last "Lost Cause" was the desire to maintain the primacy of Classical studies, especially of Greek, in the academic world of America. With the adoption by Harvard in 1883, under the presidency of Charles W. Eliot (1869-1908), of the elective system, a system apparently born of the democratic philosophy of Thomas Jefferson, the founder of the university where Gildersleeve spent the first two decades of his professorial career (1856-1876), and of the reformatory zeal of George Ticknor when freshly imbued with the *Lehr- und Lernfreiheit* of Göttingen,[102] and with the founding in the same year of the *Modern Language Association of America*, the founder and long-time editor of the *American Journal of Philology* surely saw in these innovations the decisive blows which were to result in the collapse of his domain of Classical learning.

But he remained ever loyal to his lore, to which he had dedicated his long life, and to the sources, Classical and Germanic, whence he had acquired inspiration and erudition. He himself expresses this allegiance best in *Hellas and Hesperia* (1909):[103] "That mistress of mine bore a lumbering name – Altertumswissenschaft – imperfectly rendered by 'Science of Antiquity.' But then you cannot translate 'Gretchen,' you can only love her."

Such were the Germanic qualities of the classicist whom Professor Paul Shorey has designated as "The Dean of American Scholars and Arch-Apostle of the Classics,"[104] and of whom his colleague, C. W. E. Miller, in an obituary written shortly after the decease of the Nestorian Gildersleeve in his ninety-third year, writes: "In the American Classical pantheon he sat enthroned as Zeus."[105]

JAMES WOODROW
PRESBYTERIAN DIVINE AND EVOLUTIONIST

SOUTH CAROLINA

James Woodrow, son of a Presbyterian minister, was born on May 30, 1828, in Carlisle, England, whence his family migrated via Canada (1836) to Chillicothe, Ohio, in 1837. The manuscript records in the Archives at the Heidelberg University reveal that Woodrow had between the years of 1834 and 1846 attended schools in Glasgow, Scotland; Brockville, Ontario, Canada; Chillicothe and Athens ("Athenarum"), Ohio; and that in 1846 he was admitted to Jefferson College (Pennsylvania), where he was awarded the degree of Bachelor of Arts in 1849 and the Master of Arts degree in 1853.[1] The first degree at Jefferson was conferred with highest honors. At this same college, later Washington and Jefferson at Cannonsburg, Pennsylvania, Basil Lanneau Gildersleeve, likewise the son of a Presbyterian minister, had been a student in 1846.[2]

Having moved to the South Woodrow served as principal of several small academies in Alabama from 1850 to 1853 and then became professor of Natural Science at Oglethorpe University, then located at Midway, near Milledgeville, Georgia. He was immediately granted a leave of absence to study at the Lawrence Scientific School of Harvard University under the famous Swiss naturalist, Jean Rodolphe Aggasiz, who in his youth had studied at the German universities of Zurich, Heidelberg and Munich. It was not long before Woodrow followed the example of his Swiss mentor and continued his studies at the University of Heidelberg in Germany.

From a biographical sketch written by the Reverend Dr. William J. Flinn in 1907 we learn:[3] "In 1856 he took the degree of A. M. and Ph. D. in Heidelberg University 'summa cum laude' ... completing in four months what students usually require several semesters to accomplish." Dr. Thornwell of the Columbia Theological Seminary visited Heidelberg shortly after Woodrow had obtained his degree there and on his return to America spoke "most warmly of the splendid reputation the young Oglethorpe professor had left behind him there, and how his praises were still on the lips of many."[4]

When James D. Woodrow, on February 21, 1856, applied to the Philosophical Faculty of the University of Heidelberg for permission to take the doctoral examination he stated he had attended at Heidelberg the lectures of the following professors: Leonard in Mineralogy and Geognosy, Bähr in Cicero, Bunsen in Chemistry, Blum in Mineralogy and Petrography, and Leonard (privatissime) in Geology. Among the documents in the Archives of the Faculty is a letter from Dean Röth to his Faculty, dated February 25, 1856, which discloses:

> Er [Woodrow] ist jetzt auf einer wissenschaftlichen Reise in Europa in kurzem begriffen und hat zum Behulfe seiner weiteren Ausbildung auch hier chemische, physikalische und mineralogische Vorlesungen besucht... Er legt unter anderen ein Schreiben an den nordamerikanischen Gesandten in Bern bei, welches allerdings nur ehrenvoll für Herrn Woodrow lautet ...

Among the testimonials presented by the candidate are listed:
1. An excerpt from an American newspaper.
2. A letter of recommendation from the American Minister, H. Fay, in Bern.
3. A letter of recommendation from a Professor at Oglethorpe University.
4. A letter of recommendation from H. Jos. Henry of the Smithsonian Institute in Washington.

The Dean further states that the applicant has brought no academic testimonials with him to Europe, and that shortness of time renders it impossible for the candidate to cause such documents to be forwarded from America, therefore it will be necessary for the Faculty to make its decision on Woodrow's application on the basis of the data herewith presented.

As a part of the oral examination a preliminary in Latin, conducted by Professor Bähr, took place on March 5th. The major examinations, which began a 6 P.M. on the following day, were in the fields of chemistry and mineralogy, the last named being under the direction of Professor Karl Caesar Leonhard; that in chemistry was presided over by the famous Heidelberg chemist, Robert Wilhelm Eberhard Bunsen, who voted to give the candidate "die erste Note." Leonhard was "vollkommen befriedigt." The other members of the committee were also "vollkommen befriedigt." Hence the candidate was voted the degrees of Doctor of Philosophy and Master of Liberal Arts "Summa Cum Laude" as of March 6, 1856.

There was no dissertation; no set of formal theses to defend. Not even formal matriculation as a member of the university was required. A very satisfactory performance in the *Examen Rigorosum* and the payment of a not inconsiderable sum, an examination fee of two hundred and sixteen florins, in addition to four months in residence and attendance at lectures were the only requirements exacted of James D. Woodrow.[5]

Dr. Flinn further states:[6] "Immediately upon Dr. Woodrow's graduation he was offered a full professorship in Heidelberg University," but since "he went to Germany not for the honor she might give him, but to gain and take back to the land of his love Germany's treasures for her enrichment," he rejected the Heidelberg offer and returned at once to his professional duties at Oglethorpe University in his adopted Southland to which region he continued loyal throughout the remainder of his life. At Oglethorpe he continued his duties until 1861.

During this Oglethorpe period a close association developed between the Heidelberg scientist and his pupil, Sidney Lanier (1842-1881), later to become one of the South's truest poets. Woodrow himself reports:[7]

> When he [Lanier] graduated [July, 1860] I caused him to be appointed tutor in the University, so that I became better acquainted with him, and liked him better and better. I ... often took him to ramble with me, observing and studying whatever we saw, but also talking about everything either of us cared for. About the same time I was licensed to preach, and spent Saturdays and Sundays in preaching in feeble churches and in schoolhouses, court houses, and private homes within forty or more miles of home, so that I could drive to the college for my Monday morning sunrise lecture. Every now and then I would invite Lanier to go with me. During such drives we were constantly engaged without interruption in our conversations. In these ways, and in listening frequently to his marvelous flute-playing, we were much together. We were both young and fond of study.

When Lanier began his tutorship he wrote to his father, on October 8th, 1860:[8]

> [I] find the madness growing on me – Mr. Woodrow is to learn [sic!] me French and German. I commence them tomorrow – He also superintends my private classical studies.

He is here referring to his plan, recently conceived, to study at a German university. Lanier himself later (1881) admitted:[9]

> I am more indebted to Dr. Woodrow than to any living man for shaping my mental attitude toward nature and life. His

spirit and method not only guided and enlarged my scientific knowledge, but they had a formative influence on my thought and fancy in all my literary work.

Shortly before the outbreak of the Civil War (January, 1861) a fellow-teacher from the North, who had been associated with Lanier asserted:[10]

> The tutor – Lanier – is studying for a professorship; he is going to remain here about two years, then go to Heidelberg, Germany, remain about two years, come back, and take a professorship somewhere.

This is a clear indication that the tutor was intending to walk in the footsteps of his professor. Philip Graham in an article "Lanier and Science"[11] has pointed out further manifestations of Woodrow's influence on the youthful Lanier, calling his first book, *Tiger Lilies* (1867), which holds a position in Lanier's literary career similar to that held by the German-inspired *Hyperion* in Longfellow's and to that held by *Morton's Hope* in John Lothrop Motley's novelistic activities, "a boyish record of one just initiated into the world of German thought." Graham notes at the same time that Lanier, in his work *The English Novel*,[12] observes the prevalence in Germany of the belief that science would destroy poetry and attributes Lanier's belief "that science and poetry are mutual helps" to the fact that Woodrow's direct influence on Lanier was exerted in the late 'fifties', when "Woodrow was still strongly opposed to evolution." Like Woodrow the young Lanier "saw no danger to religion or poetry in science."[13] The passage in *Tiger Lilies*:[14]

> But how long a time intervened between Humboldt and Goethe; how long between Agassiz and Tennyson? Moreover and what is more, one can scarcely tell whether Humboldt and Agassiz were not as good poets as Goethe and Tennyson were certainly good philosophers!

written in commenting on "all the humbug of Macaulay, that the advance of imagination is inverse to the advance of reason, and that poetry must decline as science flourishes," suggests Lanier's mentor, Woodrow.

Writing of "Sidney Lanier: Man of Science in the Field of Letters,"[15] Aubry Starke rightly remarks: "Never did Lanier lose interest in scientific research, in 'Mineralogy, Botany and Comparative Anatomy,' or in the study of French and German."[16] In the Spring of 1868 Lanier wrote to Milton H. Northrup:[17] "I know few things I should like better than to go [to study in Germany] ... but ... it is like that I, who have loved Germany all my life, must after all, die with only a dream of the child-land." This causes Starke to opine:[18]

> We know from his romantic novel that the conception of Germany which Lanier had formed as a result of much reading of Carlyle, Richter and Novalis, and of long conversations with his friend, Dr. James Woodrow, ... was a land where scientists are musicians and philosophers and poets are professors, musicians, philosophers, and scientists.

In reality Lanier was, in a way, following in the footsteps of his mentor in being a man of science in the field of letters, for after being ordained as a Presbyterian clergyman in 1859[19] and elected to the faculty of the Columbia Theological Seminary in 1860, Woodrow was named "Professor of Natural Science in Connexion with Revelation" and thus became a man of science in the field of revealed religion.[20]

In 1859, the same year which witnessed the publication of Darwin's *Origin of the Species*, Judge John Perkins, Sr. of "The Oaks", near Columbus, Mississippi, munificently endowed at the Columbia Theological Seminary at Columbia, South Carolina, "The Perkins Professorship of Natural Science in Connexion with Revelation", "the design of which shall be to evince the harmony of science with the records of our faith, and to refute the objections of infidel naturalists."[21] Dr. Woodrow, finally approved by the controlling synods of South Carolina, Georgia, and Alabama, assumed the duties of this unique office in 1861. As Woodrow himself subsequently (1884) asserted:[22] "The chair was new; it was without parallel in the world; no theological seminary in America or Europe had anything that could even remotely serve as my guide." The position in which the young Professor of Natural Science now found himself was an unenviable one. But for the fact that the Civil War was already upon the Fundamentalist South the inevitable clash between Science and Religion would have come sooner. Already in his inaugural address, delivered at Marietta, Georgia, on November 22, 1861, before the Board of Directors of the Theological Seminary, Woodrow realizing the gravity of his position declared:[23]

> The offensive feeling of responsibility is greatly increased by the fact that I have been called, not to discharge the duties of an office already well known, in which the experience of many predecessors affords guidance, but to organize an entirely new department of instruction, without a single similar chair in any theological school, in either America or Europe, to serve as a model.

When Dr. Woodrow joined the staff of the Seminary he also assumed additional duties of his church. From 1861 to 1865 he served as treasurer of the General Assembly's Foreign Missions and Sustentation and became editor and proprietor of *The Southern Presbyterian Review*, a prominent theological quarterly which he continued to conduct from 1861 to 1885, and to which he contributed numerous articles during the great controversial period of his ministry.[24]

When the outbreak of the Civil War disclosed a dearth of scientifically trained personnel in the Confederate States, Woodrow was called upon to make practical use of his Heidelberg training. As chief of the medical laboratory in Columbia from 1863 to 1865 he served his beloved Southland in the preparation of drugs and other medical supplies to take care of its war needs. The Reverend William W. Boggs quotes Woodrow as having said after the conflict had ended:[25] "The Confederate government was the only human government that I ever loved."

When the Seminary reopened in September, 1865, Dr. Woodrow resumed his position as a professor on its faculty and continued in that office until 1866, when he was deposed because of the views he expressed on the subject of "Evolution." After the reopening of the Seminary Woodrow was almost immediately (1869) elected to be Professor of Geology, Pharmacy and Mineralogy at South Carolina College also located in Columbia. From this latter position he withdrew in 1872, "when the Reconstruction regime – carpetbaggers, scalawags and Negroes – seized the college and filled its chairs and dormitories with their kind."[26] Even as Basil Lanneau Gildersleeve had studied Spanish in anticipation of taking refuge in South America on the fall of the Confederacy and his fellow Charlestonian, Governor Thomas Caute Reynolds, already a student of Spanish, actually did find refuge in Mexico and Cuba after that War, so this third Charlestonian and doctor of philosophy of a German university, retired to Germany and resumed his scientific studies there in 1872, where he remained with his family until 1874.[27]

This European sojourn and its concomitant studies, contacts and observations served to confirm Woodrow in his views on the subject of evolution and resulted in increased pressure being exerted against him by certain factions in his own church. This led to a series of charges, hearings, trials and expulsions which culminated in 1888 in his condemnation by the General Assembly at Baltimore. The part which his German connections played in the course of this contest is evident in his writings. His publication in the April number (1863) of the *Southern Presbyterian Review*[28] of an article "Geology and Its Assailants" might be regarded as the opening gun in the acrimonious conflict waged between him and Dr. Robert L. Dabney, D.D., Professor of Theology at the Union Theological Seminary of Virginia.

But it was not until Woodrow had spent a year of his sojourn in Germany that the contest was on in earnest. "An Examination of Certain Recent Assaults on Physical Science," he published in the *Review* for July, 1873.[29] It is a rejoinder to four documents which had denounced the physical scientists in the years of 1866, 1869, 1870 and 1871, three of them bearing the name of Dr. Dabney. Here Woodrow calls upon German scientists to uphold his point of view. He writes:[30]

> The leading representatives of natural science maintain that the connexion between mind and matter lies wholly beyond the limits of that science; that it does not know, and it can never hereafter know, anything concerning this subject. The doctrine of scientific men was well stated last August [1872] by Professor DuBois-Reymond, a leading professor in the University of Berlin, in a discourse before the German Association of Men of Science assembled at Leipzig. No one who knows this eminent man of science will suspect him of an inclination to claim too little for Natural Science, or anything at all for revelation. He says: "That it is utterly impossible, and must ever remain so, to understand the higher intellectual processes from the movements of the brain-atoms, supposing these to have become known, need not be further shown. Yet, as already observed, it is not at all necessary to refer to the higher forms of mental activity in order to give greater weight to our arguments ... In this we have the measure of our real capacity, or rather of our weakness. Thus our knowledge of nature is inclosed between these two boundaries, which are eternally imposed upon it: on the one side by the inability to comprehend matter and force, and on the other to refer mental processes to material conditions. Within these limits the student of nature is lord and master; he analyses and he reconstructs, and no one knows the boundaries of his knowledge and his power; beyond these limits he goes not now, nor can he ever go." Ueber die Grenzen des Naturerkennens. Zweite Auflage, pp. 27-29. Thus modestly and truthfully is the real position of science set forth.

Woodrow further along points the finger of scorn at his reverend opponent by recalling his own Heidelberg experience.[31]

> Although the Lectures and Sermons are dated 1871, their author does not give any indication of his having heard of the amazing discoveries of Bunsen and Kirchhoff about

fifteen years ago, or of the applications of the spectroscope with which they enriched the world – an instrument by which not only the chemistry of the heavenly bodies can to some extent be ascertained, but by which incandescent gases – nebulous matter – can be distinguished from solids and liquids.

In an article "Dr. Woodrow and the 'Silence of Scripture'" the Reverend Dr. E. M. Green, at that time Business Manager of the Woodrow-owned *Review* and the *Southern Presbyterian*,[32] informs us that Woodrow's reply to Dabney "was printed in pamphlet form and widely distributed among his friends in Europe and America," a statement easily credited since the author of the reply owned a printing house in Columbia and was at that time commuting between Germany and America. Green relates further: "Taking me into his confidence, he read me numerous letters from various parts of the world, written in German, French, and other languages, from eminent scientists, expressing their indebtedness to him for his luminous exposition of the relations between Revelation and Natural Science."

Naturally Woodrow's reply evoked a rejoinder from Dr. Dabney,[33] which was answered in turn by another reply, "A Further Examination of Certain Recent Assaults on Physical Science," published in the *Review* for April, 1874.[34] As a practical geologist Woodrow invites his opponent to accompany him on some walks to examine "the mighty series of fossil-bearing beds around Saarbruck in the western part of Germany,"[35] which the geologist had visited in the summer of 1873. It is evident that Dr. Woodrow's sojourn in Germany made him more of an evolutionist than ever and that his forthright statements in defense of science and his unequivocal attacks on the detractors of science were stirring up a hornet's nest in the camps of the opposition. We know that Dr. Dabney was no admirer of the Germans, as is manifested in a letter written to his wife from Leipzig on July 22, 1880, and published in *The Life and Letters of Robert Lewis Dabney* by Dr. Thomas C. Johnson.[36] Here he condemns the Germans' "contempt for the scholarship of other nations" as "Absurd and most blamable" and continues:

> If they would consider other people's writings some, perhaps they would not be so everlastingly running after new-fangled crotchets and heresies. They are like Job's fools: "Surely we are the people; and wisdom will die with us."

Describing a visit to Professor Luthardt, he says: "I thought I would amuse and please him by telling him how familiar we were with German lexicons, etc., in Virginia. He swallowed it all gravely, and said, 'Ya; Shermany ist de school-mistress of de vorldt!'"

So it must have been distasteful to Dr. Dabney that many of Dr. Woodrow's speeches and defenses were so fraught with German scientific lore and displayed that he had been influenced in reaching his scientific conclusions by the experiences and observations he had made, not only during his student days at Carlo Ruperto, but also, or even more, during his recent residence in Germanic lands. Although that address on "Evolution" which he delivered before the Alumni Association of the Columbia Theological Seminary on May 7, 1884, and which the editor of *Dr. James Woodrow as seen by His Friends*, his daughter, Miss Marion W. Woodrow, correctly informs[37] "was made the occasion, though it was hardly the cause of a war on Dr. Woodrow which lasted for twenty-five years," is completely devoid of any such geographical reference, most subsequent controversial utterances up to and including the "Argument before the General Assembly at Baltimore, 1888" show plainly the source of Woodrow's erudition.

In his "Speech before the Synod of South Carolina"[38] on October 27 and 28, 1884, he relates his experience in Europe between 1872 and 1874.

> Now as to the belief of naturalists in foreign lands. When I was in feeble health some twelve years ago [1872] ... I spent a portion of my time in the enlightened capital of Saxony, where I was warmly received and invited to become a member of the scientific association of that city [Isis]. I visited the Scientific Association of Switzerland in 1872, and I spent days in conversing with my fellow-members upon this very subject. In 1873 I had the pleasure of attending the meeting of the German Naturalists' Association in Wiesbaden, and there too I pursued my inquiries. Amongst others I had the pleasure of making the acquaintance of one who has been continually named during this discussion, Prof. Virchow, with whom I conversed freely touching this very subject. ... I didn't then believe evolution to be true; I believed it was not true, ... So far as the capital of Saxony was concerned, the Professor of Comparative Anatomy, in whose laboratory I was dissecting day after day, did not believe in evolution. The Professor of Geology, distinguished highly in that kingdom, was in doubt. But every other naturalist in that association [Isis], so far as I could learn, except those two and myself, were decided evolutionists. At the meeting which I referred to at Freiburg, in Switzerland, I found no antievolutionist except one Presbyterian minister, who had paid a little attention to science and so had become a member of that association; but he paid only a little attention to science.

> ... At the meeting of the German naturalists at Wiesbaden, the subject having been brought prominently before the association by Prof. Oscar Schmidt, who delivered ... a lecture that contained much that was offensive and untenable, the greatest interest was felt. Every one was ablaze with regard to the matter; and yet, though I prosecuted my inquiry with great diligence, I could not find a single member who agreed with me. From my conversations with Prof. Virchow, I feel sure he would be greatly amused and amazed if he knew how he has been quoted during this controversy as an anti-evolutionist.

Being a clergyman as well as a scientist Woodrow felt it incumbent upon him to ascertain the attitudes of the churchmen in the countries he visited. He reports:[39]

> But it has been our lot to hear them [denunciations of all modern science as infidel] most frequently from German pulpits; next in frequency come pulpits of the United States, North and South; occasionally we have heard them from the lips of Swiss pastors among their own mountains; and never in the churches of England.

To indicate the change that had come over the minds of men in the last quarter of a century the defendant says:[40]

> When I was scarcely more than a lad, I became Professor of Geology in Oglethorpe University, I found that the honored President, Dr. Talmage, held the view that the world was only six thousand years old, and that the Scriptures so taught... When I came to Columbia I found that the loved Thornwell held the same views, and so did his successor... If I were to go to Union Theological Seminary, I know that a few years ago the three senior professors there believed just as Dr. Talmage did.

Dr. Woodrow gives his definition of evolution[41] "in the three words 'Descent with Modification.'" Nearer the end of his defense, beginning what might be termed his peroration, the accused affirms:[42]

> And I know that isolation is desolation. But if I must stand alone in defense of what I believe to be his [God's] truth, I submit to the decree and to the will of my God. I will not be the first who seemed to stand alone. As I look through the vistas opened before me by the word of God, I see the forms

of three who were cast alone into the furnace... As I look in another direction, I see a form standing alone, in the presence of a mighty emperor and the princes of the empire, and saying, all alone as he seemed to be, "With regard to the charges against me, if any man can prove that they are true by the word of God, I will repent and recant, but until then, here I stand, I cannot otherwise; God help me. Amen." And so stand I.

There can be no doubt that the accused is here consciously endeavoring to call attention to the similarity between his trial for heresy and the trial of Martin Luther at the Diet of Worms held in April, 1521, which is popularly reported to have terminated with Luther's utterance:[43]

And unless my conscience is taken captive by the words of God, I am neither able nor willing to revoke anything, since to act against conscience is neither safe nor honest. Here I stand. I cannot otherwise. God help me, Amen.

Nor, in the light of these two utterances, can one fail to realize that another world-shaking April pronouncement, made by the nephew of Dr. James Woodrow, President Woodrow Wilson, when he concluded his speech before a Joint Session of Congress beseeching a declaration of war against Germany in 1917, was also an echo, not only of the German reformer's pronouncement, made almost four centuries earlier, but also of that of his German-educated uncle of South Carolina, uttered scarcely more than three decades earlier. The President concluded: "God helping her [America] she can do no other."

After having heard the defense of Dr. Woodrow the Synod resolved:[44]

That in the judgment of this Synod the teaching of evolution in the Theological Seminary at Columbia, except in a purely expository manner, with no intention of inculcating its truth, is hereby disapproved.

The controversy did not cause a flight to the Wartburg, but it did "result in the ousting of Dr. Woodrow from his chair in the Seminary. The Perkins Professor was temporarily re-instated, and ceased to act as Professor in May, 1886."[45]

From now on Woodrow was almost continually tried in the religious press. The General Assembly at Augusta, Georgia, on May 29, 1886, did "earnestly recommend" that he be dismissed "as a professor in the said Seminary."[46] On August 17, 1886, the Presbytery of Augusta found him "NOT GUILTY".[47] Finally at the trial of The Presbyterian Church of the United States versus James Woodrow at Baltimore in 1888, the defendant made a lengthy, eloquent and learned argument.[48] As the argument waxed rhetorical, the sentences waxed to the length to such German proportions as Mark Twain admired. The decisions and annulments, etc., of the Presbyteries, Synods and General Assemblies were so varied as to become almost mystifying, and at times evoked demonstrations of amusements from elements who were not in the serious center of the litigation. To quote the Reverend J. W. Flinn:[49]

> The general results of the controversy were: Dr. Woodrow was removed from the Seminary by the controlling Synods; a majority of South Carolina Synod stood by him. He was tried by his Presbytery and acquitted of heresy in his belief by a nearly three-fourths vote. Georgia Synod, on a complaint, annulled this judgment. The General Assembly of 1888 confirmed Synod's annulment, but in doing so declared through its Moderator and Georgia Synod's counsel that whether the Assembly sustained or overruled the complaint, Dr. Woodrow's ecclesiastical status, as fixed by his Presbytery's judgment of acquittal, would not be affected, *i.e.*, that he would still remain as a regular orthodox minister in good standing.

In short it was decided that the geologist-minister might still preach but no longer teach, thus admitting that the *cathedra* is mightier than the pulpit.

Despite the seriousness of the situation and the importance of the conflict some persons preserved their sense of humor. The following examples from among many will suffice to demonstrate how some publications, especially the press, dealt with the controversy in a lighter vein.

> The *Southwestern Presbyterian* says that the 'late Assembly repudiated the Ape as a factor of Presbyterian theology, and recommended the removal of Professor Woodrow, his spokesman, from the Columbia Seminary.'
>
> That's very smart, we suppose. But it is not true. Professor Woodrow is not a "spokesman" for the Ape. He has not intimated that the Ape is the ancestor of the editor of the *Southwestern Presbyterian* or of any other man.[50]

Or, to cite the Springfield [Massachusetts] *Republican* of September 16, 1886:[51]

Whenever things get dull with the Presbyterians of the South, they turn to and try Prof. Woodrow for heresy. The trial usually comes earlier in the season, but this has been an exceptional year for early crops and things are a little – mixed. The Augusta (Ga.) Presbytery has just finished the heresy drama for this year.

The rehearsal of this must recall another evolution trial which occurred in one of the Fundamentalist communities adjacent to the states involved in the Woodrow proceedings, and which attracted the attention of the world and reaped the ridicule of the more liberal (?) elements of Christendom.

This time it was not a clergyman but a public school teacher, J. T. Scopes, who was the victim. He too was brought to trial for teaching Darwinism. He too was removed from his academic position. The following lampooning of this "Trial of the Century" is a foreigner's concept of how America can mingle comedy with tragedy. This indicates the reason why Phineas T. Barnum and Samuel L. Clemens are typical American philosophers. The following persiflage of the civil trial of J. T. Scopes in Dayton, Tennessee, in 1925, might fit *mutatis mutandis* the ecclesiastical trials of Dr. James Woodrow in Georgia, Carolina and Maryland three decades earlier.

COMÖDIA DARWINA[52]

von

ERICH WEINART

In Tennessee, in Tennessee
Da trinkt man keinen Rum,
Da trinkt man keinen Hennessy;
Da geh'n Propheten um.
Herr Bryan reist in Tropendreß,
Mit Pauken und Trompeten,
Zum grossen biblischen Proceß
Nach Tennessee, nach Dayton.

Vom lieben Gott, vom lieben Gott
Sind wir der Gypsabguß!
Der Darwinismus ist bankrott,
Singt man mit Impetus.
Der Gott, der Affen machen ließ,
Hat nichts mit uns zu schaffen.
Wir stammen aus dem Paradies
Und sehen nur aus wie Affen.

United States, United States,
Ihr fühlt euch wieder wohl.
Ihr sucht im Wunder des Gebets
Ersatz für Alkohol!
Kann man, wie dieser Fall beweist,
Sich keinen Whiskey kaufen,
Dann muß man sich am Heiligen Geist
Et cetera besaufen.

In Tennessee, in Tennessee,
Ist man total beschwipst
Und fühlt sich dort, in Frenesie,
Vom Herrgott abgegipst. –
Der alte Gott in seinem Groll
Auf euren Firmenschildern
Hat sich schon die Nase voll
Von solchen Ebenbildern.

After being deposed at the Seminary Dr. Woodrow continued his distinguished career at the University of South Carolina, also in Columbia. From 1888 to 1897 he was Professor of Geology and Mineralogy, serving at the same time as Dean of the College of Arts and Sciences from 1888 to 1891 and as President of the University from 1891 until 1897. In June of the last year he resigned from the Presidency and from his professorship and attended the sessions of the International Geological Congress in St. Petersburg during the Summer. On his return from Europe he was elected President of the Central National Bank in Columbia, which position he retained until 1901.

In addition to being the bearer of many academic degrees, both earned and honorary, Woodrow was a Member of the German Scientific Association, The Swiss Scientific Association, Isis (of Dresden), and the Victoria Institute of London. He was a Fellow of the American Association for the Advancement of Science and a member of the International Congress of Geologists.[53]

He died in Columbia, South Carolina, on January 17, 1907.

Dr. C. R. Hemphill tells us[64] that Woodrow "was at home with the classics, and it was no uncommon thing to find him with some Latin or Greek author in his hand. He had a familiar knowledge of French and German and a good acquaintance with the literatures of these languages." Dr. E. S. Joynes, a well known Southern scholar in the field of modern foreign languages, who has held professorships at several Southern universities, says:[55] "He was a thorough scholar in the classical languages and Hebrew, in English literature, and in modern languages." Yet in spite of these facts and the facts that he had studied in Heidelberg and done research in Dresden and had travelled widely and visited extensively in German lands, references to German literary authors do not manifest themselves in his words or works, nor in references to him and his activities.

Even though Goethe, because of his study of osteology and his active interest in other fields of natural science, has always been considered a precursor of Darwin, and was moreover, in a limited way, a geologist, I have found no mention of Goethe nor of any of his works in the writings of our Southern geologist who was too much condemned for being a disciple of Darwin. This enigma is probably attributable to the fact that Woodrow was a Calvinist, a devoted churchman, and a minister of the gospel; and that a true knowledge of and admiration for Goethe and his works had not penetrated into his conservative regions of the South, and especially not into his circles of devout clergymen. We need only to become aware of the hostile attitude early displayed by Woodrow's protege, Sidney Lanier, toward the sage of Weimar and his philosophy to have a basis for understanding James Woodrow's silence concerning Goethe.[56]

MATH AND AFTERMATH

SOUTH CAROLINA

OSCAR MONTGOMERY LIEBER

The previous chapters have indicated how the careers of Reynolds, Gildersleeve and Woodrow were handicapped by the actual hostilities and their social, political and academic activities encumbered by the restrictions and disadvantages imposed on the representatives of "The Lost Cause" by the aftermath of the martial conflict. It now seems fitting to indicate very briefly by a few examples the wages of war exacted by the grim reaper from too many of the South's distinguished sons who returned from laudable accomplishments at the universities of Germany only to be cut down in the bud or amid their first flowering, or, who, having survived the "math", were unable to flower or even survive during the "aftermath," euphemistically entitled "The Reconstruction."

The case of Oscar Montgomery Lieber (September 8, 1830-July 22, 1862), the Boston-born son of the German refugee, Francis Lieber, who, in America, became a famous scholar and served with distinction both at Columbia, South Carolina and Columbia University in New York, will perhaps most poignantly exemplify the tragedy of our Southern scholars, who returned from academic Germany to shed their life's blood in American Civil War. Oscar lived in Columbia from 1835 through 1839. While in Germany in June, 1844, Francis Lieber reported that he then saw his son Oscar for the first time in five years.[1] Evidently Oscar, who could write German as a child of eight years, had resided with relatives in Germany since 1839 or 1840[2] because his father was of the opinion that Oscar "the apple of his eye" should remain in Europe for an indefinite period since he could not rear his children in the slave-South.[3] Oscar apparently returned to America with his father in February, 1845. There is a letter of his dated "South Boston, June 16, 1845."[4] Evidence indicates that he attended South Carolina College until 1847, for the records at the Berlin University contain what is manifestly a copy of a transcript from Berlin, marked "d.22 Mai 1848," stating: "Oscar Montgomery Lieber, Boston;

Columbia [South Carolina] Univ., Abitur; 20 Oct. 1847. Chemie – Mitscherlich; Physik – Magus; Mineralogie – G. Rose.

Göttingen d. 22 Mai 1848."

The above document is probably a reply to the following communication from Lieber dated April 6, 1848.

Hoch verehrte Herren:
Ich wurde gezwungen Berlin bald nach der großen Revolution zu verlassen und konnte nicht in der Unruhe, welche da herrschte, mein Abgangszeugniß fordern. Ich habe hier erfahren daß es in Ihren Universitäten nicht gebräuchlich ist einzutreten, wenn man nicht von der vorigen Universität eine Zeugnisschrift hat. Ich werde Sie daher bitten mir dasselbe nebst Pass zu senden... Die Herren Professoren, die ich hörte, waren Mitscherlich, Magus und G. Rose.

Ergebenst
J. O. M. Lieber
aus Columbia.

The facts all agree with the "ex-Matrikel" in the Humboldt University; except that in the latter document that student's father is designated as "Professor, Columbia, South Carolina" and the date of the "rite" appears to be 29 (?)/5/48. The matriculation list shows further that Oscar was a student of "Naturwissenschaft" and lived at "3 Breitestrasse."[5]

Concerning the insurrectional activities that made it necessary for Oscar to flee from Berlin to Göttingen we learn that "Oscar had hastened to Berlin and, by coincidence, on his father's forty-fifth birthday [March 18th] had participated in fighting along Breite Strasse, the very street in which [Franz] Lieber had been born."[6]

Lieber remained at the University of Göttingen from Easter, 1848 to Easter 1849 as a student of "philosophy." Hence it was not until the Spring of 1849 that he became a student of the Academy of Mines at Freiberg in Saxony.[7] Freidel reports of the year of 1849:[8] "Eighteen-year-old Oscar fought three or four days on the barricades of Dresden" and quotes from a letter of F. Lieber to Charles Sumner:

> He always stepped forward when volunteers were called out; he defended a richety barricade against pouring attacks; he served ... the cannons. His coat was riddled, his powder flask perforated; the hat shot into, but God protected the ardent lad.

Oscar Lieber spent probably only one semester at Freiberg, for in 1850 he was again in America awaiting in vain the fulfillment of the promise of John C. Fremont to create for him a career as geologist in the West.[9] In the Spring of 1851 he was at home in Columbia still looking for employment. But Lieber was too aggressive a person to wait long. In 1851, he was elected Assistant Professor of Geology at the University of Mississippi from which position he resigned after seven months of service.[10] However on July 15th he was appointed assistant geologist of that state under an act of the legislature of the State of Mississippi of March 5, 1850. From this position he resigned on January 4, 1852.[11] After his return to Columbia, S. C. he published[12] *The Analytical Chemist's Assistant. Translated from the German with Introduction, Illustrations and Copious Additions*, dedicated to its author Friedrich Woehler, Dr. Phil., Professor of Chemistry in the University of Göttingen and to Michael Tuomey, Esq., Professor of Geology and Agricultural Chemistry in the University of Alabama. The preface, dated Columbia, S. C., April 10, 1851, contains the democratic statement "Liebig does not disdain to teach the ploughman" and is signed "Late Geologist of the State of Mississippi." Also in 1852 appeared his *The Assayer's Guide; or Practical Directions to Assayers, Miners, and Smelters, for Tests and Assays, by Heat and Wet Processes, of the Ores of all the Principal Metals and Gold and Silver Coins and Alloys*.[13] The usefulness of this work is attested to by its reprinting in 1877 and its new and revised issue in 1893.

In 1854 and 1855 he was employed as Assistant Geologist of the State of Alabama to conduct a geological survey under Michael Tuomey. On December 22, 1855, he became State Geologist of South Carolina and published a series of *Reports of the Geognostic Survey of South Carolina* at Columbia.[14] This series terminated and he resigned on April 2, 1860. In July he accepted an invitation to be one of the American scientists to participate in the "Astronomical Expedition to Cape Chidley, Labrador" for the purpose of observing the total solar eclipse on July 17th. In his capacity as meteorologist and geologist he was assistant to Professor Charles Scott Venable, a Virginian, who, after studying in Berlin and Bonn, was then a professor at the South Carolina University.[15] Lieber's *Notes on the Geology of the Coast of Labrador*, August, 1860,[16] is based on his manuscript "Journal of a Trip to Labrador in the U. S. Coast Survey Steamship Bibb, Lieut. Murray, commanding, 15 June – 7 August" found in the library of the University of South Carolina.

In addition to the above mentioned publications Lieber contributed almost innumerable scientific articles to periodicals in both America and Germany, ranging from the *New York Mining and Statistic Magazine* and Von Cotta's *Gangstudien*, where he published in 1860 "Der Itacolumit Seine Begleiter und Metallführung desselben,"[17] through the Charleston, S. C. *Mercury* to the "Yorkville Enquirer" and the "Cheraw Gazette."

Nor did he confine his publications to the field of natural science. His monograph *Vocabulary of the Catawba Language, with some Remarks on its Grammar, Constructions and Pronunciation*, Charleston, 1858[18], manifests another interest probably aroused by his friend and mentor[19] Alexander von Humboldt and recalls the fact that two earlier Southern scholars in Goethe's Germany, Joel Roberts Poinsett and Jesse Burton Harrison, had been impressed by the interest of the Humboldt brothers in the languages of American Indians.[20] In the *Southern Magazine* for January, 1873, C.W. Hutson observes:[21]

> In the *Courant*, a weekly which flourished for a short time in Columbia, he published several articles, one of which, Morphology of a Plum-pudding, was intended as a burlesque on the tendency of science at the present day to adapt its processes of reasoning to social problems, and convert analogy, which should be employed simply as illustrative, into serious argument. Had his writings been commensurate in quantity with the fullness and extent of his thought and the largeness of his learning and experience, he would have left a literary name behind him of which the South might well have been proud.

That Lieber, who had published two volumes before he was twenty-two years of age, was dead before he had reached thirty-two, was indeed a calamity. But the rift between father and son was a tragedy. At the outbreak of the Civil War, Oscar, as his father had foreseen, joined the Confederate Army, whereas his father and his two brothers sought and found service in the North. As early as December 27, 1860, the father wrote from New York to G.S. Hilliard:[22] "I am very unhappy. My son Oscar is so imbued with all that I hold worst in South Carolina that hardly anything is left between us but the thread of paternal and filial affection."

Oscar was mortally wounded in the battle of Williamsburg (May, 1862), and died at Richmond on June 27, 1862. Freidel tells us:[23] "Then the crushing story came that his eldest son had died deliriously raving against his father and the North." In Oscar's will, dated Camp Barton, Hampton Legion, 7. Apr. 1862, we read:[24] "To all my dear friends at home I send my best remembrances and the same to my dear relatives in the West Indies and in Germany." Thus perished the Yankee-born, German-educated son of German immigrants whose father had fought against Napoleon at Waterloo, who himself had fought with the rebels in the streets of the capital of

Prussia and also in the capital of Saxony, in the capital of the Confederacy to which he displayed both devotion and loyalty even until his untimely death.

Appropriate are these words of tribute paid to "Oscar M. Lieber ... whose short life was marked by the exhibition of rare talent and uncommon knowledge, and whose early death Science and the South have so much reason to deplore."[25] But, more appropriate and sadder words would be: "It might have been."

DAVID RAMSAY

Likewise a casualty of the "War between the States" was David Ramsay (1830-1863), a graduate of the College of Charleston (1849), who was matriculated at the Göttingen University from Easter 1850 until Easter 1852, with an interruption for the Spring semester of 1851 which he spent at the University of Berlin.[1] He subsequently studied one semester at the University of Heidelberg where he received the degree J.U.D. (Doctor of Laws) with highest honors on August 14th, 1852.[2] He was the grandson of the historian, David Ramsay (1749-1815) a German translation of whose *History of the American Revolution* Goethe borrowed from the Ducal Library in Weimar and studied, October 25-30, 1826, a year after he had received a visit from George Henry Calvert, a quasi-Washingtonian, who was then a student at Göttingen and who, apropos the election of John Quincy Adams as president, instructed the Sage of Weimar on the methods of procedure in our Electoral College.[3]

A letter from Germany dated Monday, April 22, 1850,[4] to "dear Joe" Legaré shows that Ramsay at that early date had already acquired a good German vocabulary and was able to spell correctly every German word attempted. His statement: "They [the postal arrangements] are the type of national character – slow but sure," displays the tyro's knowledge of the German people as well as his Twainian sense of humor. He now signs himself "Stud. jur. David Ramsay."

Just five days later he writes to the same friend:

> You may fancy me comfortably situated in a German Town, studying and then, every now and then, relieving myself & obliging my American-Swiss-English-German and Greek friends either by a visit or a walk – or more ambitious when there is a holiday here, for they have more holidays here than I like, making a journey, going to Berlin. I am going to Warsaw & Copenhagen but before I do so, I shall give you information in case you have any commands. – Then fancy

> me walking out with a yellowish coat, striped pantaloons, blue waistcoat, purple neckcloth and flaming handschuhe *handshoes*. If you would like to know why I thus harlequinized, I tell you briefly, that I am one of the most *modestly* and gravely attired persons in Göttingen. I do *not* conform to the customs of the country, in every respect, but where you can get a suit of clothes for 20 rs = $18 and, if your American suits are torn, you, Joe, would get one – I have – Lord has – Dingle has.[5] Anybody would.

He then closes his letter with five lines of correct German written in excellently executed German script. The letter represents astonishing alertness for an American youth who has not yet attained his twentieth birthday.

The South Carolina State Library possesses the originals of two additional letters, one dated "Hanover City," April 3rd, 1851, and the other Berlin, April 14. The former reports:

> Leaving Göttingen the 2nd I arrived in the Hanoverian majestic capital the 3rd of April. ... I am now en route to Berlin, in which city I shall probably stay for the next Semester.

The second letter informs that he had visited the Sachtleben family in Brunswick[6] and continues:

> From Brunswick I came to Berlin where I received a most hearty welcome from my friends. I have met 8 Charlestonians:[7] Walter, 2 Carrs, Wilson, La-e, [name not legible (Lane?)], 2 Geddings and somebody else I do not remember. I am waiting for a pair of beinkleider (legclothes) to be[8] presented to our Minister & hope he will invite me to dinner, thereby saving me 7½ Silbergroschen. ... our admirable and amiable Minister, decidedly one of the most gentlemanly, polished men I ever met, and at the same time a man of great discrimination invited me to one of his soirees.
> .....
> The old lady [the Minister's wife] had been in Berlin only two months & applied to me for some hints. I gave her a variety of information and anecdotes, which would all guide & assist her should she ever be at a university & determine to frolic. I believe she will find my advise with respect to German life eminently practical & useful.
> I have hired a room here for a month after which time I will determine whether to study here or go to Heidelberg.

From an undated letter in the same collection, evidently from Göttingen and likewise to Joseph Legaré and belonging to the year of 1850, we excerpt the following:

> My dear Beppo:
> Ah je me rappelle gestern war hier eine Volksversammlung. Man sagte daß der berühmte Gauss (hast du von ihm gehört) praesidieren wuerde; this however was not true. This meeting was called to express the feeling – the indignant feeling that pervaded all Germany upon the infamous attack upon Schleswig-Holstein by the Danish king and still more at his shameful conduct in obtaining a victory...[9] ...(talking of long words what do you think of this Constantinoplitanischen-dudelsackspfeifersgesellschäftsgesetzbuch, Journeymensbag-pipersregulationbook.

This letter also contains a description of the German meeting of protest referred to above.

These manuscript letters are all written in a very excellent chirography, be the script Latin or German. The numerous German words, expressions and sentences interspersed are invariably correct in both orthography and meaning. The contents indicate that young Ramsay was a wit. The humor, with which the letters are replete, is suggestive of that later employed by Mark Twain, e.g., the "beinkleider to be presented to our Minister" and the long word (64 letters) which would probably have been accepted as a gem by Mark Twain despite the fact that it is shorter than his word of ninety-five letters coined almost half a century later.[10]

In "An Oration Delivered before the Cincinnati and the '76 Association on the 4th of July 1854"[11] Ramsay imparts to us a poetic bit of his fond reminisences of his Harzreise and commingles with it his patriotic sentiments for his native land.

> Years ago I stood on an outlayer of the Harz. Widespread fields lay beneath, through whose verdant and undulating surface a river sparkled like a silver thread. Some thirty or forty villages lay scattered in the peaceful valley, while the venerable towers of a university town gave dignity to the repose of the scene. But evening drew on, and the landscape lost its brighter hues in the gray tints of twilight, as the sun began slowly to sink behind the opposite mountains. I stood with my countrymen and gazing on the setting sun, we knew that it went to give light to our own land and hailed the omen, that as time to Europe already past, to America was yet to come, so that, although all in the aged hemisphere

grew dark and yet more dark, on our young republic would pour an ever waxing glory.

On June 16, 1854, William Gilmore Simms wrote to the literary historian, Evert Augustus Duykinck: "for notices of Dr. Dvd Ramsay, the Historian, write to his grandson, David Ramsay, Esq., Lawyer of Charleston, a highly educated young man recently from Germany."[12] Simms further informs Duykinck: "Mr. David Ramsay has just left for the North,"[13] and implies that young Ramsay will visit Duykinck. It is therefore assumed that the article on his grandfather in Duykinck's *Cyclopedia of American Literature*[14] was written by the young Ramsay.

The Göttingen Ramsay died on August 4, 1863, as the result of wounds received in the second assault of Battery Wagner. The inscription on the monument raised in honor of David Ramsay in the graveyard of the Circular Church in Charleston was given its final form in June, 1868, by William Gilmore Simms and Samuel Lord who had been Ramsay's close companion in Göttingen from Easter 1850 till Michaelmas 1851.[15] It so eloquently epitomizes his short but brilliant career that it deserves inclusion here.

> David Ramsay A native of the City of Charleston, South Carolina. The grandson of David Ramsay, Historian of that State, he inherited the endowments of his grandsire. Born the 14th day of September, 1830.
>
> Educated in the Schools of Charleston, he completed his collegian studies at the University of Heidelberg, Germany. Here his native gifts of intellect, aided by industry and stimulated by honorable ambition, secured for him the highest honors of his Alma Mater. Returning to his native country he embarked into the practice of law and soon reached an honorable rank among the distinguished of the profession.
>
> Fame and fortune seemed equally within his reach, when, at the call of his country, he repaired to the field of battle. There as Major of Battalion he fell, mortally wounded gallantly fighting in the defense of Battery Wagner on Morris Island on the 18th day of July, 1863. He died on the 4th day of August ensuing. Aged 32 years, 11 months and 10 days.
>
> Quis desiderio sit pudor aut modus
> Tam cari capitis.

THOMAS EDWARDS HART
SCHOLAR AND EXPELLEE

Thomas Edwards Hart was born in Hartsville, Darlington County, South Carolina on June 26, 1833. He entered the Military Academy (The Citadel) at Charleston on January 1st, 1851 and was graduated with the second honor of his class in November, 1854. Immediately after graduation he was appointed Tutor in Mathematics in Furman University where he became later Adjunct Professor of Mathematics. After spending two winters in laboratory work at Harvard University, he went in 1858 to Germany where he was matriculated as a student of philosophy at Göttingen from Easter, 1859, through Michaelmas, 1860.[1] On December 17, 1860, he was matriculated at Heidelberg University as a student of "Staatswissenschaften" (Political Science) and registered in the winter semester of 1860-1861 and the summer semester of 1861 for lectures and "Übungen."On March 7th, 1866, he applied to the Philosophical Faculty to be permitted to take a doctoral examination. The oral examination, embracing a Latin preliminary examination, and the principal examination in mathematics (Hesse), and chemistry by Bunsen and in physics by Kirchhoff, took place on March 13th, 1866. He was awarded the degree of Doctor of Philosophy on March 14, 1866.[2] The title of his "Inaugural Dissertation, genehmigt von der philosophischen Facultät," was *Elemente der Geometrie auf der Geraden Linie.*[3]

Major J. J. Lucas supplements the remarks made by Colonel Asbury Coward[4] by informing us that while at Heidelberg Mr. Hart was selected by one of the professors of the university to correct the proof sheets of his new work in mathematics, "passing over all the native and other students. He had such confidence in the ability and great accuracy of Mr. Hart that he said he would rather trust Mr. Hart than do the work himself." Lucas also states here that Hart submitted "an original problem in mathematics which was so highly thought of by the professors of the university that a sufficient sum of money was appropriated from university funds for its publication."[5] The first claim of Major Lucas seems to be justified by the conditions then obtaining at the university. Professor [Ludwig] Otto Hesse (1811-1874) was, as indicated above, the chief Professor and director of Hart's dissertation. In fact the very subject of the dissertation seems to have grown out of a study which Hesse had published a few months before Hart's examination, *Vorlesungen aus der Analytischen Geometrie der Geraden Linie, des Punktes und des Kreises in der Ebene* von Otto Hesse ordentl. Professor an der Universität zu Heidelberg; Leipzig. Druck u. Verlag von B. G. Teubner, 1865. Vorrede, November, 1865. Under the circumstances the doctoral candidate Hart would be, and probably was, the best qualified man in the department to see the Hesse volume through the press.

Since Hart's dissertation was published, not locally in Heidelberg, as were most doctoral dissertations, but in the same world-famous press in Leipzig which brought out his mentor's popular volume, it seems quite credible that his Heidelberg department might have financed the printing, as Lucas asserts.

Shortly after Hart's return to his native state from Germany on August 1st, 1866, he lost his wife née Susie G. Lanneau to whom he had been married on September 27th, 1860.[6] Of course he found his native state "a scene of wreck and ruin" as a result of the Civil War. When Furman University reopened after the War in 1866 Thomas Edwards Hart and John F. Lanneau were members of the faculty. Under their leadership a new (fifth) school of Civil, Military and Mining Engineering was to be completely organized by the beginning of the scholastic year in August.[7] But, after serving as Professor of Chemistry for only one year at Furman (1866-67), Hart was forced to seek employment in a college in Kentucky in order to earn his bread. It must be remembered that "the constitution adopted in 1868" placed "that State" under "Negro domination."[8]

After a brief stay in Kentucky (1867-68) Hart returned to Furman as Professor of Chemistry. From 1869 until June, 1872, he was Professor of Mathematics, and Civil and Military Engineering and Construction at the University of South Carolina. For several months in 1870-71 he also taught subjects in the department of Natural and Mechanical Philosophy and Astronomy.[9] "From this honorable position he was removed with other members of the faculty by the alien Negro government forced upon the state."[10] Thus, in June, 1872, at the same time that James Woodrow, who had earned his doctor's degree at Heidelberg almost exactly ten years before Hart, was removed from the direction of the School of Chemistry and Geology to make room for the Reverend T. N. Roberts, Hart had to yield his position to the Reverend A. W. Cummings, D. D.[11] Thus ended Dr. Hart's public employment in the field of educational enlightenment.

A slight limp which he had brought back with him from Europe developed into lameness and ultimately into paralysis of the lower limbs. His mind, however, remained good and he was able to enjoy his scholarly interests until he passed away on December 3, 1891.

EPILOGUE

The facts have been presented, but what are the implications?
One fact is that Philip Tidyman of South Carolina received in 1800 the earliest doctoral degree ever earned by an American at Göttingen, or, as far as known records reveal, at any other German university, when he presented a dissertation on an agricultural product of his agrarian state and dedicated it to his brother-in-law, John Drayton, Governor of South Carolina.

The first of the twenty Americans who visited Goethe in Weimar and who was feted at the Ducal Court there (1810) was likewise related by marriage to a Governor of South Carolina. He was Aaron Burr, the third vice-president of the United States. Of course Burr, having been born in the North of Puritan ancestry was not a Southerner. But at the time of his European exile he was a quasi-Southerner, having fled to the South to be feted and defended there after his deadly duel with Alexander Hamilton, and because his only offspring, Theodosia (1783-1813) had married Joseph Alston, later to become Governor of South Carolina. When Burr returned to America "the only two persons dear to Aaron's heart" (Edwin G. Gudde, *op. cit.*, p. 367) were this daughter and his young grandson, Aaron Burr Alston, both South Carolinians.

Burr was a duellist, an avocation in which some of the Southern scholars who later visited Goethe's Germany, unlike their New England counterparts, are known to have indulged. Michel Musson of New Orleans, perhaps the most widely regarded of the American students who ever attended a German university, thanks to his portrait included in the immortal painting "The Cotton Market, New Orleans" (1873) by Edgar-Hilaire-Germain Degas, the brother of his son-in-law, René Degas, according to an entry in the *Göttinger Journal* (May 28, 1829) of his fellow Göttinger student, Henry Wadsworth Longfellow, "fought a duel of 12 Gängens with a Hildesheimer – neither was wounded." We know that on July 4th, 1833, four students, Amory Coffin, Mitchell King (both of Charleston, South Carolina) John Lothrop Motley and Otto von Bismarck, celebrated American Independence Day in Göttingen "indem sie versuchten sich gegenseitig unter den Tisch zu trinken" (*Hochschule und Ausland*, März 1930; XIII, 3, 11-20). This indicates a Burresque tendency among some of our Göttingener Southerners. That King on August 31, 1832, became a member of the *Corps Hannovera* in which Bismarck was the outstanding duellist suggests another Southern dueller. Thomas Caute Reynolds of Virginia who spent a month in Weimar in 1839 later wounded Gratz-Brown in a pistol duell in Missouri.

The observation of Gudde (*op. cit.*, p. 363): "The larger part of Burr's entries [in his Weimar *Diary*] is concerned not with men but with lovely and clever women of whom there was certainly no lack at the Thuringer residence" recalls that our young Southern cavaliers, although none of them was a roué, as Grandpa Burr seems to have been, definitely did devote considerably more time and attention to the social life in Weimar than did any, or all, of Long's New England Pioneers. Calvert, who spent about three weeks in Weimar, even though he impressed the Grand Duke as being a "Quaker," remarked on the "unusual number of handsome unmarried ladies" in Weimar and on the "particular favor" with which foreign beaus were received.

Burr records [*Diary*, I, 351 f] "Princesse Marie (de Russie), a very interesting face *et les plus belles mains*. Marie is very handsome and does credit to her rank and birth." Later (January 7, p. 357) he says: "La Princesse speaks English extremely well, ... Fine hands and arms. Elbow perfect." Jesse Burton Harrison who spent over a month at this court two decades later seems to be echoing Burr, whom he had visited shortly before leaving New York and from whom he had received a return visit even after he had embarked on his departure from that city, when he writes of "the decided charm of countenance" of the same Marie Pavlowa, and of her display of the "finest pair of shoulders that I have ever seen" (p. 31).

Both Burr and Goethe are very laconic about the two visits the American paid to the latter while in Weimar:

> Goethe's *Tagebuch*. January 4: "Herr von Humboldt, Obrist Burr aus Nord Amerika"
> Burr's *Diary:* "Went first to Wieland's 77. To Goethe's 58. There Humboldt."

Why the silence? Although Goethe's interest in the silver mines of Mexico was probably not as great then as it had become later when Herzog Bernhard tarried two months in New Orleans (1826) definitely desiring to visit the Weimar mining interests in Mexico, he had already been displaying at least an academic interest in that country even before Burr's arrival (*see Tagebücher*, Bd. 4; 1809, June 9, 10, 11; August 3, 6, 7; December 30, 31; 1810, January 3, 4, 6) and, in general, ever since Alexander von Humboldt had set out on his expedition to Latin America. He must have known of the supposed interest of Aaron Burr in divorcing Mexico from Spain. But Goethe almost positively did know that Burr was, at the very moment of his presence in Weimar, under the surveillance of the secret agents of Thomas Jefferson, President of the United States, his opponent and enemy. The very presence of "Herr Humboldt," whose great brother became a friend and correspondent of President Jefferson, might also have contributed to the taciturnity.

The fact that Burr was a colonel might have embarrassed Goethe, if we can judge by his alarm evoked by the presence of the American Colonel Pearce in Weimar in 1793. And finally, in our opinion, Goethe was less loquacious in the presence of mature foreigners than he was with our youthful American scholars.

Although Burr spent scarcely one week in Weimar and departed in sudden terror "in Nacht und Nebel," this was not his last contact with the Weimar court. In June, 1826, he received a visit from Herzog Bernhard, the younger brother of the Reigning Duke of Weimar, shortly before the former's termination of his lengthy American sojourn. On this occasion Burr "spoke of a remarkable good reception [in Weimar] on the part of my father" (Bernhard, *Travels*, II, 196). Almost three years later Jesse Burton Harrison on his way to Göttingen called on Burr who showed him "extreme courtesy" and informed him of some aspects of his visit in Weimar. It is also significant that Harrison *en route* from Paris to Germany visited Duke Bernhard.

As far as research has until now disclosed, no other American scholar who visited Weimar in the first half of the nineteenth century tarried there as long as the Charlestonians, George Henry Guerard and Thomas Caute Reynolds. Practically all the information we have of that visit stems from the records of Ottilie von Goethe who seems to have served as their adviser and friend. Shortly after this Weimar visit Reynolds and Ottilie's son Wolfgang were fellow students of law at both Heidelberg and Berlin. The fact that a Eugen von Egloffstein (a name well-known in the Goethe circle at Weimar) also matriculated in the Law Faculty on the same day as did Reynolds (May 9, 1840) and that both, at one time, had the same Heidelberg address, "Panzer, Wittib," seems to indicate more than a coincidental presence of these Weimar-connected persons at Germany's oldest university.

After Reynolds had transferred to the University of Berlin and spent two semesters there Wolfgang von Goethe matriculated in the Faculty of Law on October 30th, 1841, thus becoming a "Kommilitone" of Reynolds for another semester. The American's testimonial of departure from this university is dated June 6, 1842, that of Wolfgang Maximilian von Goethe, March 3, 1842.

As is the case of H. W. Longfellow records fail to disclose any visit of B. L. Gildersleeve to Weimar despite the fact that this learned classical philologian was, like the Harvard professor, an enthusiastic admirer of Goethe's works.

Walter Wadephul's monograph *Goethe's Interest in the New World* (1934) indicates that his researches in Weimar were hastily forced to a premature conclusion and suggests that much additional information on the subject of Americans in Weimar is awaiting disclosure, **but will** have to await the reopening of the Road to Weimar.

NOTES

INTRODUCTION

[1] *The Journal of English and Germanic Philology*, XLI (January, 1942), 1-45.
[2] Cram, de Gruyter, Hamburg, pp. 235.
[3] *The Miscellaneous Writings of Joseph Story*, edited by his son, William W. Story, Boston, 1852, "Sketch of the Character of Hugh S. Legarê, pp. 820-824.
[4] 1844 (May 1843-April 1844, Inclusive), pp. 43ff.
[5] Heidelberg, Band 4, 232f.
[6] *Southern Literary Messenger*. Vol 1 (1835), p. 222.
[7] Long, O. W., *Op. cit.*, p. 64.
[8] *Ibid.*, p. 108.
[9] *Ibid.*, p. 160.

SOUTH CAROLINA - HUGH SWINTON LEGARÉ

[1] *German American Annals*, N.S. VIII (1910), pp. 199-254. My search reveals 18 South Carolinians for this period.
[2] Sonderdruck aus dem *Göttinger Jahrbuch*, 1955-1956, p. 23.
[3] *South Carolina Historical and Genealogical Magazine*, Berlin: Michaelmas 1860 - Michaelmas, 1861: Pringle, J. R., Phil.; Pringle, E. A., Law. Heidelberg: Dec. 17, 1860 through the Easter semester, 1861.
Pringle, John Julius, formerly at Berlin.
Member: Saxo-Borussia, 1860.
Then all three Pringles withdrew. War!
[4] *Travels through North America, during the Years 1825-1826*, Philadelphia, 1828, II, 11. See also pages 5, 7 and 10, and p. 23 *Infra*. Note that Mr. Lowndes is mentioned each time Dr. Tidyman is and that a J. Lowndes of Charleston, S. C., was a student of philosophy in Göttingen, Michaelmas, 1855 to Easter, 1856, the latter undoubtedly a younger member of the same prominent family. James Lowndes registered at Bonn Summer Semester (April 19) 1855.
[5] *Reise Sr. Hoheit des Herzog Bernhard zu Sachsen-Weimar-Eisenach durch Nord-Amerika in d. Jahren 1825 und 1826*, Weimar, 1828, II, 10f.: Derselbe Dr. *Tidymann* gab mir zu Ehren ein *Diner d'apparat*. Bei demselben traf ich mehere der angesehensten hiesigen Einwohner wie Herrn *Lowndes;* einen Major *Garden*, Sohn jenes schottischen Arztes, welchem zu Ehren Linne der bekannten Planze den Namen *Gardenia* beigelegt hat; einen Herrn J. *Allen Smith*, der 17 Jahre seines Lebens in Europa, und besonders in Rußland zugebracht, und sich des besondern Wohlwollens des Kaisers Alexander erfreut hatte: er war bei meines Bruders Heirath zugegen gewesen, und erkundigte sich nach demselben angelegentlichst.

Dieser äusserest liebenswürdige und interessante Mann hat den grössten Theil seines Vermögens verloren.
[6] *South Carolina Hist. and Geneal. Mag.*, XLIII (1942), 33.
[7] Charles J. Stille, "The Life and Services of Joel R. Poinsett," *The Pennsylvania Magazine for History and Biography*, XII (1888), 137 ff.
[8] Matthew L. Davis, editor, *Private Journal of Aaron Burr*, 2 vols., New York, 1858, p. 389. See also Erwin G. Gudde, "Aaron Burr in Weimar," *South Atlantic Quarterly*, 40 (October, 1941), 360-367 and my "Young Southern Scholars in Goethe's Germany," *Jahrbuch für Amerikastudien*, Bd. 4 (1959), 220. Research has yet to confirm the statement of William MacClure (1765-1840) "the father of American Geology", reported by Herzog Bernhard (*Reise*, II, 138): "McClure ist ein berühmter Gelehrter, der eine geologische Charte der Vereinigten Staaten herausgegeben hat. Er sagte mir, im Jahre 1802 sei er in Deutschland gewesen, und sei auch nach Weimar gekommen, wo er die Bekanntschaft aller dortigen Gelehrten gemacht habe." It is strange that no further record has been discovered to indicate any personal contact between him and Goethe who was interested in geology. Mary Effie Cameron James informed me on Jan'y 31, 1960, that she and her husband in preparing their biography of MacClure "have found no material relevant to his presence in Weimar other than the above statement of Duke Bernhard.
[9] *American Literature*, IX (Nov., 1937), 356-357.
[10] *Ibid.*, p. 356.
[11] See note 8, *supra*. Since Burr's only offspring, his daughter Theodosia, was, at the time of his sojourn in Weimar, a resident of South Carolina, and, since 1801, the wife of Joseph Alston, shortly to become governor of that state (1812-1814), her father, being otherwise without domicile, was a quasi-resident of her state. Hence it was quite natural for the Duchess Maria Paulowna and her entourage to speak with Burr about these two distinguished South Carolinians who had recently been so intimately associated with her Imperial Russian family in St. Petersburg, and whom the Weimaraner knew either personally or through family association. Burr would naturally gladly record the celebrity of these citizens of the home state of his daughter and of his only grandchild Aaron Burr Alston († June 13, 1812).
[12] This identification renders untenable Eduard Castle's speculation (*Der grosze Unbekannte*, Wien und München, 1952, p. 367), for Sealsfield would not have addressed the dedication of his *Der Legitime und die Republikaner* to an "A. J. Smith" who had died five years before the novel was published. See *South Carolina Hist. and Geneal. Mag.*, II, No. 3 (July, 1901), 217.
[13] *South Carolina Hist. and Geneal. Mag.*, XL III (1942), 33, "Poinsett – Campbell Correspondence."
Göttingen
[13a] King, W. *sic!*, for McMillan C., #2 Michaelmas 1831, Charleston, Amer.; Jur.; W. Keil, Jüden 462.
King. M. C., [# 3], Michaelmas, 1831, Charleston, Amer.; Med.; O.R. Meyer, Jüden 459. Remained at Göttingen 4 semesters, i.e. through August, 1833.
McMillan King after one semester went to Berlin, matriculated on May 21, 1832 and remained until Oct. 8, 1832.
[14] *Writings of Hugh Swinton Legaré*, 2 vols. Charleston, S. C., 1846, p. xi.
[15] University of South Carolina, manuscript copy of "memoirs of Hugh Swinton Legaré."
[16] The seriousness of the disturbances in the Summer of 1818 can be judged by the fact that the student enrollment which had been 1150 during the previous semester (Easter, 1818) fell to 658 in the Winter Semester, 1818,

when Legaré would have, and Bancroft did, matriculate. Not until Easter, 1820, did it really recover from the shock. Then 1118 students matriculated. Three years earlier (Spring, 1815) almost the opposite had happened to George Ticknor. Under the direct influence of Thomas Jefferson, Ticknor had intended to sojourn in France, but: "The political turmoil in Europe made travel directly to France precarious ... Ticknor ... changed his plans and concluded to proceed at once to Göttingen." O.W. Long, *Thomas Jefferson and George Ticknor, A Chapter in American Scholarship*, Williamstown, Mass., 1933, p. 11 f.

[17] Rhea, Lina, *Hugh Swinton Legaré, Charleston Intellectual*, Chapel Hill, N. C., 1934, p. 55.

[18] *Ibid.*, To appreciate that our *Southern* scholars in Europe were less confined to *studies* alone witness the following reminiscence from a letter of July 13, 1852, from Washington Irving at Sunnyside to Wm. C. Preston, Esq.:
Do you recollect our pleasant scenes at Mer Craig's in Fourth Street where you had poor Legaré for your house mate, who use to play snake at his window, ogling and "charming" a bevy of serving girls in an opposite house?" (University of South Carolina Collection).

[19] *Writings of Hugh Swinton Legaré*, p. xlviif. Although engaged in the study of law Legaré was still very actively interested in Classical Languages and Literatures.

[20] Lina Rhea, *op. cit.*, p. 61 f.

[21] See *Writings*, pp. li-lx.

[22] Vol I (Feb., 1828), 1-49; also *Writings*, II, 19.

[23] Vol. III (Feb., 1829), 192-207. Se also *Writings*, II, 168. Also in New England and the Middle Atlantic States this work enjoyed reviews by two other distinguished American scholars: Peter S. Du Ponceau in Walsh's *American Quarterly Review*, Philadelphia, September, 1828, and George Bancroft in the *North American Review*, Boston, January, 1829.

[24] *Writings*, II, 299 ff.

[25] *Ibid.*

[26] *Ibid.*, II, 356-410, p. 382.

[27] *Ibid.*, II, 400.

[28] *Ibid.*, II, 425 ff.

[29] *Ibid.*, II, 426-430.

[30] *Ibid.*, II, 435-437, 439.

[31] *Ibid.*, II, 502.

[32] The originals are found in the manuscript division of the Library of Congress, "The J. Burton Harrison Papers." Since the handwriting is very difficult to decipher, several emendations have been ventured. Cf. *Writings*, I, p. 151: "Note by the Publishers": "The difficulty of deciphering the manuscripts may have led to many verbal errors, especially in the names of persons and places."

[33] *Cf. Writings*, II, 36. Tiedemann, Dietrich T. (1748-1803), "Dialogorum Platonis argumenta, exposita et illustrata", (1786).

[34] Vol. IV, No. VII (Aug., 1829), 136-176.

[35] He was a Professor of German, instruction in which language ceased at South Carolina when he went to Europe in 1831. See LaBorde, M.; *History of the South Carolina College*, Charleston, S. C., 1874, p. 145.

[36] *Writings*, I, 12, 24, 34.

[37] *Ibid.*, p. 1-100.

[38] Falkenstein's *Tempelherren-Orden*, Dresden, 1833. See catalog of his library in Columbia University Library.

[39] *Writings*, I, 237.

[40] *Ibid.*, p. 243.

[41] *Ibid.*, p. 114 ff.
[42] See *Writings*, I, 135, Later in Berlin (April 27) Legaré writes: "[I] Say the merit of Tocqueville's book consists in his being the only foreigner, except Herren, who has seen that *republicanism* is the primordial law and condition of American society, and that our revolution was merely *external* and confined to the question of sovereignty."
[43] For further enlightenment on American visitors to A. W. Schlegel in Bonn see Long, *Literary Pioneers*, p. 55 and 60; 172; Ticknor, G., *Life, Letters and Journals*, Boston, 1877, I, 453 f., II, 101; Hatfield, J. T., *New Light on Longfellow*, New York, 1933, p. 37; Calvert, this volume p.32; Dwight, Henry E., *Travels in the North of Germany in the Years of 1825 and 1826*, New York, 1829, p. 19; Jesse Burton Harrison, this work chapter, page 53f. (*supra*).
[44] *Writings*, I, p. 119. *Cf.* "Catalog of Rare and Valuable Private Library of Hugh S. Legaré", Washington, 1848, Item 121, Karl Simrock's translation, Berlin, 1827 and item 421, Schlegel's *Dramatische Kunst und Litteratur*, Heidelberg, 1817. Rhea's statement (*op. cit.*, p. 204) that his German books were mostly connected with jurisprudence, philosophy, and history, "though he had a few additional ones in that language" is misleading. It were better stated that most of his books connected with jurisprudence were German and he had a considerable number of German volumes dealing directly with literature. In addition to the titles mentioned in Rhea's note 16 add: "*Sämmtliche Werke*, Klopstock, 12 vols.; Herder, 34 vols.; Lessing, 25 vols.", etc. I have counted in the list of 1843 (Library of Congress) 61 German titles, some of which embrace many volumes.

The following lines from a letter written by Legaré on October 10, 1841, should be noted in this connection: "I am quite sure if I had gone to Göttingen, as I intended, in my youth, instead of going to England, I might have dispensed with half the books I have since found to be unworthy of notice from a critical student. The Germans are now, and have for some time past, been treating this very study of the philosophy of society and legislation in a style peculiar to themselves, for they distance all other inquirers, both in vast and accurate research and in acute criticism." Charleston *Self Instructor*, I, 77-80 (Jan., 1854); Also given in full in Guy A. Caldwell's "Charleston Periodicals, 1795-1860" (University of North Carolina dissertation). *Cf.* Hubbel, Jay B. *The South in American Literature*, Duke University Press, 1954, p. 266 and p. 946.
[45] Rhea, *op. cit.*, p. 132. It is strange that he should have written to Harrison within two days two letters containing identical phrases. *Cf.* p. 13 *supra*.
[46] *Life, Letters, and Journals*, I, 453.
[47] Underlining mine. *Cf.* The wording of Legaré's account *supra*. Ticknor regretted the absence of Legaré from Brussels when he passed through there on Nov. 6, 1835 (*Life, Letters, etc.*, p. 450). For Ticknor's remarks on his visit to Schlegel in 1817 see Long, *Literary Pioneers*, p. 30 ff.
[48] *Ibid.*, p. 454.
[49] *Literary Pioneers*, p. 172. Underlining mine to indicate identity with Legaré's account *supra*. *Cf.* Hatfield, J. Taft, *New Light on Longfellow*, Boston and New York, 1933, p. 37.
[50] *Memoirs of John Quincy Adams, Comprising portions of his Diary from 1785 to 1848*, edited by Charles Francis Adams, 12 vols., Philadelphia, 1874-1877, IX, 399. See also *University of South Carolina, Vol. I, South Carolina College*, by David Walker Hollis, Columbia, S. C., 1951, p. 26. The other congressmen referred to are George McDuffie and Francis W. Perkins. Note too a comparison of Legaré with Edward Everett, New England literary pioneer at Göttingen, made by a Maryland student of Everett at Harvard, who was also a Southern pioneer at Göttingen, who

later became a New Englander and co-worker of the Everett brothers, George Henry Calvert, written in his *Autobiographic Study*, Boston and New York, 1885, p. 180f.: "He [Legaré] was more of a scholar than Everett, having a stronger and less superficial mind." "Legaré had a larger calibre, and, unlike Everett, to whom literature was chiefly a help to rhetoric or display, loved literature, especially poetry, for its own sake."

51 *Writings*, I, pp. 119ff., 124, 125f.
52 *Ibid.*, pp. 137ff. See also *Southern Literary Messenger*, IX, 642ff.
53 *Writings*, I, p. 141f.
54 *Ibid.*, p. 146. *Cf. George Eliot, Life as related in her Letters and Journals*, ed. J. W. Cross, Boston and New York, 1908, II, 94, (July 7, 1858). "I was glad to say a last good-bye to the quaint pepper boxes of the Frauenkirche."
55 *Ibid.*, p. 148. His library contained: *Herder, Sämmtliche Werke*, 34 vols. in 22, Carlsruhe, 1820.
56 *Ibid.*, p. 150.
57 *Ibid.*, p. 229. The date of the letter should be March 25, 1836, instead of 1835 as printed in *Writings*. *Cf.* the following letter, p. 230f.
58 *Ibid.*, p. 231f.
59 *Ibid.*, p. 232.
60 *Ibid.*, Legaré's library contained Schiller's *Sämmtliche Werke*, 12 vols., Stuttgart, 1835.
61 *Ibid.*, p. 233. See catalog of library cited *supra*.
62 *Ibid.*, p. 234f., republished in *Writings*, I, 367-442; 502-558, "The Origin, History and Influence of Roman Legislation."
63 *Writings*, I, 443-501.
64 *Ibid.*, lxvii; *New York Review*, IX, No. 1 (Mar., 1841).
65 "Legaré Papers", University of South Carolina.
66 Rhea, *op. cit.*, p. 184f. Cogswell had been a student in Göttingen and Edinburgh with Ticknor, was dear to Goethe and was responsible for the founding of the Astor Library in New York City. See also O. W. Long, *Litarary Pioneers*, p. 104f.
67 *Writing*, I, lxiiif.
68 *Ibid., Writings*, p. lxix, and (Rhea, *op. cit.*, p. 212). His library contained Eichhorn, *Grundsätze des Kirchenrechts*, 2 vols., Göttingen, and the same author's *Staats- und Rechtsgeschichte*, 4 vols., Göttingen, 1821. See "Roman Legislation", *Writings*, I, 1 p. 504, p. 523, p. 524.
69 "Diplomatic Correspondence", *Writings*, I, p. 201.
70 Library of Congress, E340, LSH8, copy 2 Name of author not given but was Thomas Caute Reynolds. See *Southern Literary Messenger*, September, 1843.

MARYLAND - GEORGE HENRY CALVERT

1 *Travels through North America during the Years 1825 and 1826*, Philadelphia, 1828, I, 180.
2 *George Henry Calvert, American Literary Pioneer*, by Ida Gertrude Everson, Columbia University Press, 1944, p. 75.
3 "Die ersten amerikanischen Studenten an der Universität Göttingen," von Hertha Marquardt, Sonderdruck aus *Göttinger Jahrbuch*, 1955-56, p. 30ff. Was Noel Clark a Georgian? His two registrations in Göttingen read: Clark, Noel, [#31364] Amerika, philos.; V[ater] Consul-General aus Boston, 1824, Oct. 25.
32650, 1826, Noel Clark, Amerika, philos.; 25 Oct. 1824, No. 185 war

seither auf Reisen. V[ater] Ambassador in Cuba wohnhaft in Georgia, Apr. 25 [1826].

Clark was a friend of the Emersons and known in the New England circle. He might have dwelt in Georgia while his father was functioning in Cuba. I have not yet been able to discover any evidence that he was a Georgian.

[4] See note 2 *supra*.
[5] *Autobiographic Study*, by George Henry Calvert, Boston; Lee and Shepard. New York: Charles T. Dillingham, dedicated 1885, Columbia University, Folio, B812; c, 13, p. 65. Quitman became Governor of Mississippi in 1850. His father, Friedrich Henry Quitman, a native of Germany, who had studied theology at Halle, migrated *via* Curaçao to Philadelphia, where he had an interview with George Washington and subsequently served a Lutheran pastor at Rhinebeck, New York. Harvard University honored him in 1814 with the degree of Doctor of Sacred Theology. "When M. Edward Everett and Mr. [George] Ticknor were going to Germany, he provided them with letters to the most eminent professors. At Göttingen, these American students made so favorable an impression that Professor Eichhorn wrote a special letter of thanks to the doctor for the introduction of 'such agreeable young barbarians'." (*Life and Correspondence of John A. Quitman*, by J. F. H. Claiborne, New York, 1860, I, 22). John A. Quitman was tutored (1809-12) by the Rev. A. Wackerhagen, a German divine in Schoharie, N.Y. and then by his father in Rhinebeck before enrolling in Hartwick Academy (Lutheran) at Otsego, N.Y. (1816-1818). *Cf. op. cit.*, p. 27 f.
[6] *Ibid.*, p. 179 and Everson, *op. cit.*, p. 50, 58. Everett's degree at Göttingen was awarded, "without examination," Orie W. Long, *Literary Pioneers*, Harvard University Press, 1935, p. 239, note 36.
[7] *Ibid.*, p. 144 and p. 66, respectively.
[8] *Autobiographic Study*, p. 150. On his visit to Germany in 1841 Calvert lamented: "Thence [Köln] to Göttingen was ... hardly more than a two day's journey. It would have been but a melancholy pleasure to revisit the noble old university, now made ignoble by the basemindedness of her rulers ... Göttingen had ceased to be what Napoleon called her 'l'Université de l'Europe'. *Travels in Europe. Its People and Scenery*, 2 vols. in One, Boston, 1860, II, 36.
[9] Everson, *op. cit.*, p. 71.
[10] *Ibid.*, p. 72 and *First Years in Europe*, Boston, 1866, p. 83, previously printed in part in *Putnam's Monthly Magazine*, vol. VIII No. XLVIII (Dec., 1856), 595-607 "Göttingen in 1824."
[11] "Göttingen in 1824," *Putnam's Monthly Magazine*, VIII, p. 595.
[12] *Ibid.*, 595 f. Letter IV.
[13] *Ibid.*, p. 595. Johann Friedrich Blumenbach.
[14] *First Years in Europe*, p. 88.
[15] Everson, *op. cit.*, p. 74. C. soon moved to the house of Municipal Senator Berg "on a quiet side street" [Nicolaistrasse] (*First Years*, p. 105-109). The American colony record book gives two additional addresses, "bei Breda, Johanis St.," and "bei Keil, Jüden St." (MS in Columbiana, C.U.) Everson, p. 261, note 16.
[16] O. W. Long, *Literary Pioneers*, p. 109.
[17] *Putnam's Monthly Magazine*, VIII (Dec. 1856), p. 596. Everson notes, *op. cit.*, p. 260 f., that "Wm. Emerson [on April 1, 1824] mentions beginning German with 'Dr. Bodenburg'," and suggests "this may have been Calvert's 'Dr. B.'" She is probably correct.
[18] *Ibid.*, p. 598.
[19] Everson, *op. cit.*, p. 75.

[20] *Putnam's Magazine*, VIII, 600.
[21] *Ibid.*, p. 599.
[22] Pp., 97-99.
[23] *Putnam's Magazine*, VIII, p. 597. Henry Edwin Dwight of Yale, another cultural pioneer, in his *Travels in the North of Germany in the Years of 1825 and 1826*, New York, 1829, gives the same figures (p. 205). Dwight's book was reviewed by George Bancroft in *The American Quarterly Review*, VI (Sept., 1829), pp. 189-216.
[24] *Putnam's Mag.*, VIII (Dec., 1856), p. 600f.
[25] *Op. cit.*, p. 43.
[26] *First Years*, p. 109.
[27] *Travels*, p. 105. See also Everson, *op. cit.*, p. 92. I surmise this admired companion was Pusey, Edward B. See Note 31, *infra*. Dwight matriculated at the University of Berlin in the Winter Semester, 1825-26, and lived at Dorotheenstrasse 13.
[28] P. 109.
[29] *The Letters of Ralph Waldo Emerson*, ed. Ralph L. Rusk, New York, 1939, I, 154, note 64.
[30] Everson, *op. cit.*, p. 78. Dr. William Hume, born July 26, 1801, graduated from Yale, took medical degree in New York. Met Humboldt in Paris. Elected third professor at the Citadel, May 20, 1844, assigned to Department of Chemistry, Geology and Mineralogy. Was the only member of the ante-bellum faculty present at the Citadel at the fall of Charleston, February 18, 1865. See *The Story of the Citadel*, by Col. O. J. Bond, Richmond, Copyright 1936, p. 78f. No matriculation of Hume found at Berlin University.
[31] One of Calvert's fellow-students at Göttingen was Edward Boverie Pusey, later famous as the Oxford High Church leader. See Everson, *op. cit.*, p. 78 and p. 262.
[32] See Everson, *op. cit.*, p. 85 and p. 93.
[33] *First Years*, p. 207.
[34] *Putnam's Magazine*, Dec., 1856, p. 603 and "Some Unpublished Letters of George Henry Calvert (1825)" by Ida G. Everson, *Maryland Historical Magazine*, vol. 42, No. 3 (Sept., 1947) 197-205, p. 202f.
[35] *Travels*, p. 84 note. In the same letter is noted that "a fete for Blumenbach's fiftieth anniversary as a professor and one hundredth semester of lecturing" has been celebrated "a few evenings since."
[36] *First Years*, p. 120.
[37] *Putnam's Magazine*, VIII, Dec. 1856, p. 605f.
[38] *Ibid.*, p. 606f.
[39] *First Years*, p. 200.
[40] Everson, *op. cit.*, p. 81.
[41] *Putnam's Magazine*, VIII (Dec., 1856), p. 600. See also Calvert's essay *Coleridge, Shelly, Goethe, Biographic Aesthetics Studies*, Boston and New York, 1880. There Calvert adds: "Wordsworth thought that by his visit to Germany he [Coleridge] was drawn astray from poetry. By learning German he was enabled to read Kant and Schelling."
[42] *First Years*, p. 134.
[43] *Ibid.*, p. 137.
[44] Rusk, *op. cit.*, I 161f note.
[45] *Ibid.*, p. 162.
[46] *Ibid.* For a full account see Rusk, *op. cit.*, p. 161-162 and VI, 34, note 38. See also *Goethe's Gespräche*, hrsg. Flodard Frhr. von Biedermann, Leipzig, 1909-1911, III, 130f.
[47] Everson, "Unpublished Letters" etc., No. 1, April 11, 1825. See note 34, *supra*.

[48] *Putnam's Monthly Magazine*, VIII, No. XLV (Sept., 1856), 257-267, p. 257. Note 1) Both arrive about dinner time and are sent away because Goethe is engaged. 2. Both return later and are admitted about 4 P.M. 3. Each "doctors" his visiting card by connecting his name to a famous name already known to Goethe. 4. Each remains "half an hour". One is inclined to believe that Calvert has copied the M. O. invented by Emerson the preceding September, who must have revealed it to his Göttingen comrade, since he actually reported it twice across the Atlantic in writing. See *supra* p. 29, note 44.
[49] *Supra* note 11.
[50] *Putnam*, VIII, 258.
[51] For a full account of this visit see *Goethes Gespräche*, Biedermann, III, 175 f.
[52] *Ibid.*, p. 178.
[53] Vol. XIX, pp. 303-325.
[54] Weimar Ausgabe X, 36; see also p. 34 and p. 35.
[55] *Putnam's Magazine*, VIII, (Sept., 1856), p. 260. See "Unpublished Letters," note 48 *supra*. Weimar, April 11, 1825.
[56] Everson, "Unpublished Letters," See note 147, *supra*.
[57] *Ibid.*, p. 200.
[58] *Putnam's Magazine*, (Sept., 1856), p. 260.
[59] "Unpublished Letters," *Maryland Historical Magazine* (Sept., 1947), p. 200 f.
[60] Everson, *op. cit.*, pp. 87-90.
[61] *Putnam's Magazine*, VIII (Sept., 1856), 264.
[62] P. 83, *cf.* note 10, *supra*.

In retrospect (1841) Calvert meditated: "At the time of my visit in 1825, the Grand Duke and his congenial Duchess, and the greatest of his poetic band, Goethe, were still alive; over the hospitalities of the Palace, the remarkable beauty of the ladies of the Court threw a fascination that made it like a fairy castle." (*Travels in Europe: Its People and Scenery*. Two volumes in One, Boston, 1860, II, 37.) In the Summer of 1850 he revisited Weimar and wrote: "I walked again in my old paths through the tranquil town of Weimar ... after twenty-five years, the scenes of my careless, laughing youth," (*Ibid.*, I, 55 f.). "I passed before Goethe's house. At that door I had knocked ... and within I had met, shining with kindliness, that great glittering eye...

Besides the holy remains we lingered with feelings of cheerful elevation. It was not a place of sadness ... I stood between them, [Goethe's and Schiller's sarcophagi] with my hands resting one on either coffin" (*Ibid.*, I, 56) "In the study of Schiller I sat down one morning at his desk, and with ink dipped in an inkstand of Goethe, I took phrenological notes on a cast of Schiller's head." (p. 57). Calvert concludes his chapter fittingly with the verses:

Was ich besitze seh' ich wie im Weitem,
Und was verschwand wird mir zu Wirklichkeiten

which he translates:

What I possess I see as in a distance,
And what is gone comes back in firm consistence.

[63] *Bayard Taylor and German Letters*, by John T. Krumpelmann, Hamburg, 1958, p. 17 or "Bayard Taylor and Schiller" by the same author, *Contributions to the Humanities*, Louisiana State University Press, 1954, pp. 11-24.
[64] "Unpublished Letters," *loc. cit.*, Göttingen, May 27, 1827.
[65] *Ibid.*
[66] *Ibid.*, Letter No. 7.
[67] P. 38. Later incorporated into *Travels*, etc. as volume II. Niebuhr, Barthold Georg, professor of history.

[68] *First Years* (1866), p. 204.
[69] *Ibid.*, p. 82.
[70] *Op. cit.*, p. 110. See also p. 110 and p. 269 f. for text of hymn.
[71] P. 67. It is interesting to compare this rendition with that of Bayard Taylor and to recall that Taylor's first serious attempt to make his Faust translation was a rendition of this same hymn. "The Archangelic Chorus was the first thing translated." See Krumpelmann, *Bayard Taylor and German Letters*, p. 39 and note 127.
[72] See Everson, *op. cit.*, p. 300. Note also Bayard Taylor's interest in this poem. (Adelaide)
[73] P. 179.
[74] Vol. 39, No. LXXIV, p. 1-30.
[75] "Bayard Taylor's Adaptation of Schiller's *Don Carlos*," *Journal of English and Germanic Philology*, Vol. 16 (Jan., 1917), 27. Bayard Taylor made a new verse translation of this same drama in 1876-77. It would be interesting to inquire into the relationship between Taylor's translation (adaptation) and the translation of his contemporary and neighbor, Calvert.
[76] "George Henry Calvert, Admirer of Goethe" in *Studies in Honor of John Albrecht Walz*, Lancaster, Pa., 1944, 117-161. See also pp. 134-137.
[77] See note 53 *supra*.
[78] Vol. 43, pp. 528-529.
[79] P. 161.
[80] Philadelphia, 1849, p. 308.
[81] Everson, *op. cit.*, p. 120.
[82] Vol. 43 (October, 1836), 528-529.
[83] 8 Bde. Breslau, 1826-1833, Richter, Christian Otto; Ernst Foerster.
[84] Vol. 1, pp. 251-279.
[85] *Ibid.*, p. 276, 279, respectively.
[86] II (June, 1839), 495-500.
[87] V, (June 19, 1847), 5. See also Calvert's *Goethe* (1872), p. 149.
[88] Note the acceptance of Calvert's second line in Longfellow's revised translation in the *Atlantic Monthly*, 26 (September, 1870), p. 362.
[89] Everson, *op. cit.*, p. 153. *Cf.* Longfellow's informative, interesting and amusing remark in a letter to Freiligrath, Marienburg, July 22, 1842 (*Life*, I, 430, *Works*, XII, ed. Samuel Longfellow, Boston and New York, 1891): "A countryman of mine, Mr. Calvert, of Baltimore, arrived here yesterday, with his wife. I want them to know you and Mrs. Freiligrath, and you to know them. He is a young man of fortune, and an author, having published a translation of Schiller's *Don Carlos*." Calvert was born in 1803, Longfellow, in 1807. Calvert matriculated at Göttingen on February 3, 1824, Longfellow, on May 26, 1829. What made Calvert "young" in 1842?
[90] *Op. cit.*, XI, 387.
[91] V. (April 15, 1848), 184, reprinted in his biography of Goethe in 1872, p. 271 ff. See also Everson, *op. cit.*, p. 149 and p. 236.
[92] VIII, September, pp. 257-267 and December, pp. 595-607, respectively.
[93] See Everson, *op. cit.*, p. 306 f.
[94] *Ibid.*, p. 202, and note 19, "Calvert's long and interesting signed inscription to Mr. Freiligrath regarding the work, and Schiller's Maid of Orleans" contained in a presentation copy.
[95] Everson, *op. cit.*, p. 194.
[96] *Life of Goethe*, p. 260.
[97] *Ibid.*, p. 274.
[98] John T. Krumpelmann, Hamburg, 1959, p. 136. Taylor's biography was never written. With the very titles of Taylor articles *Atlantic Monthly*,

XXXV, 26-39, XXXVI, 229-237 and XXXIX, 61-69, 1875, 1877 compare Calvert's "Weimar in 1825" and "Göttingen in 1824" published in *Putnam's Monthly Magazine* (Sept. and Dec., 1856 respectively). My words "Above, before and after all things, Goethe was a lover" (*Goethe After Two Centuries* ed. Carl Hammer, Baton Rouge, 1952) were probably inspired by my study of Bayard Taylor long before I was acquainted with Calvert who says in the work under discussion (p. 193) "As Goethe was born a poet, so was he born a lover."

[99] P. 207.
[100] *Life and Letters of Bayard Taylor*, ed. by Marie Hansen-Taylor and Horace E. Scudder, 2 vols., New York, 1884, vol. II, 554 (Apr. 8, 1871). In *Brief Essays and Brevities* (Boston, 1874, p. 126) Calvert comments: "Of all his [Goethe's] poems, Faust is the most difficult [to translate]. And yet Faust must be translated... And we can say without being charged with American brag, that the two best translations of Faust into English have been made by two of our countrymen, Mr. C. T. Brooks and Mr. Bayard Taylor."
[101] *Life of Goethe*, p. 262.
[102] *Introduction to Social Science. A Discourse in Three Parts*, Henry Calvert, New York, 1856.
[103] *Life of Goethe*, p. 263.
[104] *Ibid.*, p. 231.
[105] *Ibid.*, p. 241.
[106] *Life of Goethe*, p. 233 and p. 235.
[107] *New York Times*, January 11, 1877, p. 5. col. 6.
[108] Everson, *op. cit.*, p. 293 and Orie Long, *Frederic Henry Hedge, A Cosmopolitan Scholar*, Portland, Maine, 1940, p. 48.
[109] *Coleridge, Shelly, Goethe, Biographic Aesthetic Studies*, p. 261. Note the Goethe-Luther evaluation in *Scenes and Thoughts in Europe* (1846), p. 57, dated 1841. "No man of the age has so widened the intellectual horizon of his country, so deepened and freshened the common sea of thought, so enriched the minds of his contemporaries with images of beauty and power. Among the heartless, senseless complaints against Goethe ... that of his want of patriotism is the most vapid. Let the man be pointed out who has done so much to enlighten, to elevate Germany. He has thus contributed more towards the liberty of his country than any score of 'Liberals' ... There is a fitness in his being born at Frankfort, at once the capital of Germany and a free town. Saving Luther, there is none other who better deserves the title of Father of his country."
[110] *Ibid.*, pp. 276 and 290 respectively.
[111] *Ibid.*, p. 294.
[112] *Coleridge, Shelly, Goethe*, see note 105, *supra*.
[113] Published in *Anyta and other Poems*, 1886, p. 161. Also *Coleridge, Shelley, Goethe*, 1880.
[114] *Op. cit.*, p. 213.
[115] *E.g.*, p. 161.
[116] *Passim*.
[117] P. 192f. (ed. 1886).
[118] P. 134.
[119] P. 132.
[120] P. 26, *supra*.
[121] P. 260.
[122] *Op. cit.*, (note 70, *supra*), p. 158.
[123] See Everson, *op. cit.*, p. 229f. and p. 241, note 39.
[124] MS., Archives, Weidner Library, Harvard University, especially p. 7 and p. 20.

VIRGINIA - JESSE BURTON HARRISON

1. *Aris, Sonis Focisque, being a Memoir of an American Family The Harrisons of Skimino, edited by* Fairfax Harrison from material collected by Francis Burton Harrison, 1910, p. 84.
2. *Literary Pioneers*, Orie W. Long, Harvard University Press, 1935, p. 6.
3. *Aris Sonis Focisque*, p. 86.
4. *Jefferson Papers*, Series 2, Vol. XLV, No. 98.
5. *Aris Sonis Focisque*, p. 88.
6. *Ibid.*, p. 103.
7. *History of the University of Virginia, 1819-1919*, by Philip A. Bruce, New York, 1920, II, 151 f.
8. The Jesse Burton Harrison Papers (manuscript) Library of Congress. *Cf. The Works of Charles Follen with a Memoir of his Life in Five Volumes*, Boston, 1842. p. 233. "21 st. [Jan. 1828]. In the morning I rode out with Professor Ticknor, who told me that he had written to Mr. _____, who was going to Germany, that, whenever they should ask about me, or Beck, or Lieber, he might tell them that we are esteemed and loved by all."
9. *History of the University of Virginia, 1819-1919* (Bruce), II, 154.
10. *Aris Sonis Focisque*, p. 104.
11. See Ticknor to William H. Prescott, Monticello, Dec. 16, 1824 (*Life, Letters and Journals of George Ticknor*, Vol. I, p. 348): "The family consists of Mr. Jefferson, Mrs. Randolph, his sister, about 52 years old, Mr. Trist, a young Louisianian, who is married to her fourth daughter ... Mr. Harrison, a young lawyer of Lynchburg... Mr. Long, just from Cambridge, England, apparently an excellent scholar, and now a professor in the University of Charlotteville." Two weeks after Harrison's departure from Weimar Goethe on May 14, 1830, borrowed from the Ducal Library, Thomas Jefferson's *Memoirs, Correspondence and Private Papers*.
12. Jesse Burton Harrison Papers (manuscript), Library of Congress. Nicholas Philip Trist (1800-1874) was a native Virginian but he had many connections with Louisiana where his father had once lived and some members of his family still dwelt.
13. *Aris Sonis Focisque*, p. 99 and Legaré, *supra*, p. 10. The latter part of the citation refers to Harrison's remarks in his Hampden-Sidney "Discourse." One of the exceptions must have been their mutual friend, George Ticknor.
14. Jesse Burton Harrison Papers, Library of Congress.
15. *Cf.* Henry E. Dwight (1797-1832) *Travels in Germany in the Years 1825 and 1826*, New York, 1829, p. 43 and *infra*, p. 174, note 38.
16. Jesse Burton Harrison Papers, Library of Congress.
17. *Ibid.*
18. See *supra*, Legaré, p. 10 ff.
19. *Aris Sonis Focisque*, p. 105.
20. Jesse Burton Harrison Papers, Library of Congress.
21. *Aris Sonis Focisque*, p. 107.
22. *Ibid.*, p. 110.
23. *Travels through North America during the Years 1826 and 1826*, by his Highness Bernhard, Duke of Saxe-Weimar-Eisenach. In two Volumes, Philadelphia, 1828, II, 203.
24. *Ibid.*, II, 196.
25. *Aris Sonis Focisque*, p. 112.
26. September, 1828, Philadelphia, edited by R. Walsh.
27. *Aris Sonis Focisque*, p. 112. The letters were evidently to Goethe, Froriep and Luden, in Jena. See *infra*, p. 60ff.

²⁸ Letter date September 27th, 1829. J. Burton Harrison Papers, Library of Congress.
²⁹ Letter, October 20, 1829, Library of Congress.
³⁰ *Ibid.*
³¹ This book should be collated with his letters found in the Library of Congress and be published *in toto* in a separate volume.
³² *Diary*, pp. 1-6, entry, September 12.
³³ The manuscript (University of Virginia) of 14 pages, 8" × 5", written in black ink on white paper which has now become yellow. In the account of this trip in his letter home to Wm. W. Norwell on February 24, 1830, he adds: "In this excursion one sweeps across sections of Hannover, Brunswic, Anhalt & Prussia – at Alexisbad we were 65 English miles from Göttingen." The verses at the end of this paragraph must have been written by Thomas Green Clemson (1807-1888) for whom Clemson College (South Carolina) is named and who studied in Paris from the fall of 1826 to June 1831. He also attended the *École de Mines Royale* (1828-1832). Since Harrison's "Harzreise" took place in October, 1829, the date heretofore given for Clemson's "Harzreise", 1831, must be incorrect, especially since the latter's article descriptive of his visit to the "Hartz" mining district was published in the January, 1831, number of the *American Journal of Science and Arts*, XIX, No. 1, (January, 1831), p. 105 ff. *Cf.* also *Thomas Green Clemson; His Life and Works* by Alester G. Holmes and George R. Sherril, Richmond, 1937.
³⁴ *Aris Sonis Focisque*, p. 112. His matriculation at Göttingen is dated Nov. 14, 1829.
³⁵ Library of Congress, No. 13.
³⁶ Library of Congress, also published in part in *Aris Sonis Focisque*, p. 113 ff.
³⁷ *Aris Sonis*, etc., p. 115 f.
³⁸ *Cf.* H. E. Dwight's figures, *op. cit.*, p. 205, Professors, 89; students, 1545.
³⁹ See Legaré's remarks *supra*, p. 18. Plum? See OED, "plum, 4b. *fig.* 'a good thing', a tid-bit; also the pick or best of a collection of things, animals, etc., 1780. 5. The sum of 100,000, *slang* now rare." Hence something monstrous, outstanding, e.g., Little Jack Horner ... put in his thumb, and pulled out a plum (from a Christmas pie).
⁴⁰ *Cf.* "George Calvert", *supra*, p. 24.
⁴¹ *Diary* (Univ. of Virginia), p. 9 f.
⁴² *Cf. Weimar, von Paul Kühn*, bearbeitet von Hans Wahl, Leipzig, 1921, p. 153. John Diederich Gries (1775-1842) *Gedichte und Poetische Übersetzungen*, Stuttgart, 1829. 8⁰
⁴³ See *supra* "Calvert", notes no. 38 and 39 and *supra* p. 53 f., note 30.
⁴⁴ Printed in *Aris Sonis Focisque*, p. 117 f and in *Goethes Gespräche*, hrsg. von Flodard Frhr. von Biedermann, Leipzig, 1910, 4. Bd., 252 f. in almost identical form. I have endeavored to preserve the idiosyncrasies of the manuscript.
⁴⁵ Note that the two Southerners, and they alone of all Goethe's American visitors, inform us that they undertook to instruct Goethe. See *supra* p. 30 "Calvert." Also note Legaré and A. W. Schlegel, *supra* p. 13 ff.
⁴⁶ See Biedermann, *op. cit.*, 5. Bd., S. 173 f., 2834, where it is said that Goethe coined this phrase.
⁴⁷ See *Aris Sonis Focisque*, p. 107, note.
⁴⁸ David Ramsay (1749-1815) *History of the United States from the First Settlements as English Colonies, in 1607, to the year of 1808, or the Thirty-Third of their Sovreignity and Independence*, Philadelphia, 1816-17.
⁴⁹ See following note and also note 52.
⁵⁰ Account is from "Diary." A letter dated, Berlin, June 15, 1830, presents a few different details but gives basically the same account with a note:

"Tho' Russell has published a hint of this, yet I would by no means have it made public: it is not generally known in Germany." See John Russell *A Tour of Germany and some of the Southern Provinces of the Austrian Empire in the Years of 1820, 1821, 1822*, Boston, 1825, pp. 49, 52, 53. Russell merely says that "Madame J-n" who "drove Goethe from the direction of the theatre ... has long possessed peculiar sources of influence over the Grand Duke."

[51] See *Goethes Gespräche*, hrsg. von F. von Biedermann, Leipzig, 1911, V, 399, 1: "ihr geheimer Vater war der König Jérôme v. Westfalen."
[52] See note 49, *supra*.
[53] In the "Diary" are 8 loose pages (blue-green) closely written and marked "Memorabilia for the Road." They constitute, in great part, information gleaned from Russell's work.
[54] See *Aris Sonis Focisque*, p. 366, note. Here he excepts Russell's volume when condemning other travel books.
[55] *Cf.* note 15, *supra*.
[56] Letter, Berlin, June 15, 1830, Library of Congress.
[57] Library of Congress.
[58] *Ibid.*
[59] A careful search in the archives of the Humboldt University at Berlin (July, 1963) has failed to reveal any mention of Jesse Burton Harrison in the official registration records. Of the 1787 students matriculated that Spring, (1909 in the preceding semester) the only American was "George W. Haven, U.S., N. Amerika, Phil.", who had transferred from Göttingen. He left Berlin on July 1, 1831.
Amory and Cunningham, both of Boston, to whom Ticknor had commended Harrison (*cf.* p. 48, *supra*) had left Berlin before Harrison's arrival The matriculation records show:
Michaelmas, 1827 – Easter, 1828:
"Amory, W., Boston, Phil., 9 Unter den Linden.
Cunningham, Francis, Boston, Phil., 9 Under den Linden."
Amory came from Göttingen and quitted Berlin on April 4, 1828; Cunningham from Halle, left Berlin on Feb. 16, 1829. During his last semester he dwelt at 12 Dorotheenstrasse with Alfred C. Post, New York, Medicine.
[60] *Aris Sonis Focisque*, p. 119f.
[61] *Supra*, p. 66.
[62] "Discourse," III, No. 7 (Sept., 1827), 193-208; "Remarks," III, No. 77 (Jan'y., 1828), 321-337; especially p. 323 and p. 331.
[63] Pp. 379ff reprinted in *Aris Sonis Focisque*, pp. 337-399.
[64] Richmond, pp. 12ff. The author, a son of the Chief Justice Marshall.
[65] *Aris Sonis Focisque*, p. 347 and 392, respc. See also p. 363, p. 366.
[66] Library of Congress.
[67] Vol. 12, No. 75, pp. 5-24. The quotation is from p. 34. It is an indirect report of Harrison's remarks printed in the report of the meeting, especially pp. 334, 336, 337.
[68] See *infra*, p. 150.
[69] *History of the University of Virginia*, p. 155.
[70] Letter, München, August 24, 1830, Library of Congress.
[71] Letter, postmarked August 24, 1830, Library of Congress.
[72] *Aris Sonis Focisque*, p. 120f.
[73] Library of Congress, Letter, No. 17.
[74] To Froriep, Sept. 1, 1831, *Aris Sonis Focisque*, p. 126f.
[75] *Op. cit.*, p. 130.
[76] *Op. cit.*, p. 131.
[77] No. XVI, 462-491. Reprinted in *Aris Sonis Focisque*, pp. 301-336.

⁷⁸ *Aris Sonis Focisque*, p. 132.
⁷⁹ *Ibid., loc. cit.*
⁸⁰ *Ibid.,* p. 323.
⁸¹ *Ibid.,* p. 319.
⁸² *Ibid.,* 326f. and note. See also p. 330f.
⁸³ Vol. XII pp. 379ff. (December, 1832).
⁸⁴ Both letters in the Library of Congress.
⁸⁵ *Aris Sonis Focisque*, p. 128ff. "Ashland, Sept. 11, 1831."
⁸⁶ *Ibid.,* p. 134.
⁸⁷ New Orleans (E. Johns and Co.), 1839-1840.
⁸⁸ Library of Congress. Re the picture of Goethe by Stieler see *Aris Sonis Focisque*, p. 117, note 2 and *supra*, p. 61.
⁸⁹ *Louisiana Historical Quarterly*, XXIII, No. 4 (Oct., 1940), p. 1039, "The Career of Henry Adams Bullard," by Dora J. Bonquois. See also *Ibid.*, XIX (1936), p. 21, by Walter Prichard.
⁹⁰ XLIII (July, 1837), 281. Doubtless the corresponding secretary (Harrison) communicated to this end with his new acquaintance, the Editor of the *N. A. Review.* Such had probably been the method of having the Colony of Liberia noticed in the *Bulletin of the Geographical Society* in Paris by D. B. Warden. See *supra* p. 68 and *Aris Sonis Focisque*, p. 139, note.
⁹¹ Boston, Sept. 28, 1835, Library of Congress.
⁹² *Loc. cit.*
⁹³ Sept. 18, 1837, Library of Congress.
⁹⁴ *Die Vereinigten Staaten von Nordamerika*, Stuttgart und Tübingen (Cotta), 1827, Bd. 2, S. 203.
⁹⁵ *Aris Sonis Focisque*, p. 136.
⁹⁶ See *ibid.*, pp. 136ff.
⁹⁷ *Ibid.*
⁹⁸ *Ibid.,* p. 137.
⁹⁹ Library of Congress.
¹⁰⁰ *Aris Sonis Focisque*, p. 134.
¹⁰¹ Published, New Orleans, 1841. *Address*, etc.
¹⁰² *Aris Sonis Focisque*, p. 141f.

THOMAS CAUTE REYNOLDS, SOUTH CAROLINA, VIRGINIA, MISSOURI

¹ "There are a number of gaps in the story of Reynolds' life." *Missouri Historical Review* XXXVI, No. 4 (July, 1942), 442.
² *Glimpses of the Past*, "Letters of Thomas Caute Reynolds, 1847-1885", *Missouri Historical Society*, X, No. 1 (January, 1943), 26. To G. P. R. James, Esq., of Norfolk, Va., one of Reynolds' Heidelberg acquaintances, dated St. Louis, 20th June, 1850.
³ *Writings of Hugh Swinton Legaré*, I, 231f.
⁴ *Ibid.,* p. 232.
⁵ *Ibid.* It is noteworthy that while Thomas Caute was now a student of law in Berlin his brother, Dr. William Sims Reynolds, M. D. (1812-1888) had a year earlier published in the *Southern Literary Journal* for June, 1838, an article "Reflections on Prussian Law." See *The Letters of William Gilmore Simms*, edited by Mary Simms Oliphant, *et. al.* University of South Carolina Press, 1952-1959, I, CXXXIII.
⁶ *Writings of Hugh Swinton Legaré*, I, 234.
⁷ *Ibid.,* p. 235f. Underlining his. *Cf. Southern Literary Messenger*, IX (September, 1843), 570-574. See also *The South in American Literature, 1607-1900*, by Jay Hubbell, Duke University Press, 1954, p. 266.

⁸ Information supplied by Dr. David W. Smith, Director of the Amerika Haus, Heidelberg, through the good offices of Dr. Hans Krabusch, Director of the University Archives in Heidelberg, in a letter dated January 30, 1959. Additional facts are contained in the same letter: Reynolds matriculated at Heidelberg University on May 9, 1840. He lived from 1839-1840 in Munich; the Summer semester of 1840 he spent in Heidelberg, the winter semester, 1840-41 in Berlin. From then on he made private studies until he took the doctor's degree..."

⁹ C. A. Oswald, 83 p., 1b., VI, p., 22 1/2, Latin and German.

¹⁰ Huntington Library, San Marino, California. Manuscript.

¹¹ Mittermaier, Karl Josef Anton (1787-1867), called to Heidelberg in 1821, he remained until his death. He corresponded with Simon Greenleaf (1783-1853) and Judge Story, both of the Harvard Law School, was a close friend of Reynolds' friend, Franz Lieber. He associated much with Charles Sumner (later Senator Sumner), of Massachusetts, during the five weeks Sumner spent in Heidelberg in 1840.

¹² Edited by Peleg W. Chandler, Boston, VI (May, 1843) 43 f. The reviewer quotes from Reynolds' diploma, "in virum doctissimum et clarissimum Thomam Cauteum Reynolds ... examine rigoroso summa cum laude superato Gradum Doctoris summos in utroque jure honores rite contulimus." Although he observes that the thesis is dedicated to "Mr. Legaré, the Attorney General" and says it related to the trial by jury, "a British institution, which is more instinct with the spirit of freedom than anything which has proceeded from the Campus Martius or the banks of the Tiber," he could not have known that Reynolds' mentor, Mr. Legaré, had discussed this same subject with A. W. Schlegel when he was a visitor at the latter's home in Bonn exactly eight years previously, May, 1845. See "H. S. Legaré", *supra* p. 14 f. It is also interesting to note with Sumner that the "dissertation bears date at Prague ... – *Scribebam Prague (Bohem.) M. Decemb. 1841.*" See note 8, *supra*.

¹³ *Cf. Memoir and Letters of Charles Sumner*, by Edward L. Pierce, Boston, 1877; II, 120 f. A reminiscence of Sumner's visit to Heidelberg is evident in the review of the dissertation, where the reviewer concludes by quoting Longfellow's *Hyperion:* "Next to the Alhambra of Granada, the castle of Heidelberg is the most magnificient ruin of the middle ages."

¹⁴ Note the same quotation *supra* p. 78 and note 12.

¹⁵ IX, No. 7, 448.

¹⁶ IX, No. 9, 570-572, especially p. 572.

¹⁷ IX, No. 10, 579.

¹⁸ The first quatrain has not been located in *The Poetical Works of Howitt, Milman and Keats*, Philadelphia, 1847, but the second poem "Paradise" occurs in that volume, page 104 f; under the title "This World and the Next" in the identical words of the lines quoted here, with only a few changes in punctuation.

¹⁹ IX, No. 11, 641-646.

²⁰ *Ibid.*, p. 642. Reynolds wrote on May 28, 1839, from Berlin to Mr. Stevenson [American Embassy, London]:
It is nearly three months since I heard from America... And when (as I expect to be in a few months) I am in Bavaria or "gay Vienna," (Library of Congress, And. – John White Stevenson Papers).
This seems to indicate that his mail was first sent in care of our London Embassy. We know that he carried letters of introduction in Brussels, Bonn and Berlin and that the ones to Schlegel in Bonn and Wheaton in Berlin were delivered (*Writings of H. S. Legaré*, I, 232). This indicates he probably went to Bonn before going to Berlin, where he must have arrived too late to matriculate for the Winter Semester (November through

February). Evidently he and Guerard remained in Berlin without formally enrolling at the University and were now about to set out en route to Munich via Weimar.

[21] "Journal of the Rhine", *Writings of Hugh S. Legaré*, I, 137 ff.
[22] *Southern Literary Messenger*, IX, No. 12, 746-749.
[23] *Ibid.*, p. 749. *Cf.* Duke Bernhard of Saxe-Weimar, *Travels*, II, 11, Dec., 1825: "I talked with a person from Erfurt, Mr. Siegling, who had established a music store here."
[24] *Ibid.*, p. 747.
[25] *The Letters of William Gilmore Simms*, I, cxxxiii. See also J. Wesley Thomas, "The Sources of William Gilmore Simms", *Anglo-German and American-German Crosscurrents*, Chapel Hill, 1957; I, 150 f.
[26] Bergland Verlag, Wien, I. Band, 1962.
[27] *Op. cit.*, p. 3. The publishers of the volume are evidently uninformed as to the identity of these two Charlestonians as the "Namenregister" identifies them only as "Guerar" [*sic!*] aus Amerika" (p. XI) and "Mr. Reynolds." (p. XXI)
Cf. also *op. cit.*, pp. 4, 5, 6, 7, 8, 9, 10, 11, 46, 48.
[28] Undoubtedly Karl Friedrich Philipp von Martius, Botanist, b. April, 1794, at Erlangen, died December 13, 1868, at Munich. Shortly after the arrival of Guerard and Reynolds in Munich, Martius was made first curator of the Botanical Gardens, Institutes and Collections in Munich. In a letter to Martius on October 6, 1828, Goethe enclosed a letter from Ottilie to the wife of Martius. *Cf.* Goethe's poem "An Frau v. Martius, Weimar, 11. August, 1831, *Goethe Sämtliche Werke Jubiläums Ausgabe*, III, 178 (356 f.).
[29] P. 77, *supra*.
[30] *Op. cit.*, p. 46. See also p. 48.
[31] *Cf.* Note 25, *supra*. Ottilie surely had reason to be interested in this American divine, of whom she had heard much praise as early as December, 1837, from her friend Anna Jameson. *Cf. Letters of Anna Jameson to Ottilie von Goethe*, edited by G. H. Needler, Oxford University Press, 1939, especially pp. 95-99 incl.
[32] Bluhm, *op. cit.*, p. 48.
[33] *Ibid.* (1840), p. 70.
[34] See note 78, *infra*.
[35] Pp. 755-757.
[36] *Letters of William Gilmore Simms*, I, 397.
[37] Letter to Francis Lieber, October 22nd, 1843, (The Huntington Library, San Marino, California) "I do not expect to be admitted to the Bar before Spring."
[38] *Letters of W. G. Simms*, V, 382 ff.
[39] *Loc. cit.*, note 3. "Reynolds was editor of the *Republican* (Petersburg, Va.) a newspaper which ran during 1843-1850. We have not had access to a file of the *Republican* of 1844." On April 18, 1849, Reynolds wrote to Thomas N. Carr: "I have been an editor." To this the author of *Glimpses of the Past*, "Letters of Thomas Caute Reynolds, 1847-1885", *Missouri Historical Society* adds (X, 18) "Reynolds took charge of the Petersburg (Va.) *Republican* in the summer of 1848." An extensive search has failed to yield convincing evidence on this point aside from the report from the Alderman Library of the University of Virginia: "Margaret Martin has located the October 31, 1844, issue of the Petersburg *Republican* which is the only one in this library covering that period. T. C. Reynolds is listed as the editor."
[40] "Thomas C. Reynolds Papers (1840-1906)"; Missouri Historical Society, Jefferson Memorial. (Folder), Item No. 4. The letter to Woodley is No. 5

in the same folder. A note found among these papers discloses that Reynolds told Denton J. Snider that he [Reynolds] "had been a pupil of the celebrated Thiersch." Friedrich Wilhelm Thiersch (1784-1860), the famous "Altphilolog" and "Pädagog" migrated to Munich in 1806 and was known as the "Prinzessinnen-Erzieher." Re: Reynolds' method of learning Danish and Swedish we note: A fellow-student of law at Berlin was Jochem de Billé of Copenhagen. He matriculated on Oct. 9, 1841, one year later than Reynolds, and withdrew on June 6, 1842. Also a T. de Billé from "Amerika" studied law at Berlin for three semesters, Michaelmas, 1841 till Easter, 1843. Hence he was also Reynolds' contemporary in the Prussian capital.

[41] Bruce, P. A., *History of the University of Virginia*, 1819-1919. The following statement of Charles Kraister, "A Hungarian wanderer," who succeeded Prof. Blättermann, the first Professor of Modern Languages at Virginia, will elucidate the situation. "They [the Board of Visitors] kicked Dr. Blaettermann out because he had whipped his wife, and they have kicked me out because I have been whipped by my wife. What did they really want?" (Bruce, *op. cit.*, II. 161.). The answer was Schele de Vere who served with success and distinction fifty one years. A Swede, who became Prussian, he came as a bachelor but married twice, each time with a daughter of Judge Alexander Rives of Albermarle County, Va., first in 1849 and then in 1860, with a sister of his deceased first wife. (III, 81-84).

[42] Item No. 7 in same Folder indicated above.

[43] *Loc. cit.*, Item No. 6.

[44] Photostat copy of "List of U.S. Diplomatic Officers by Countries, 1789-1939, Vol. 3"; Archives of the United States, Washington, D. C. The nature of the last expression could easily have been the source of the inferential connection made by Reynolds' opponents that he was responsible for the "leak" commented on in the *Missouri Democrat*, that "an offer to purchase Cuba ... was made known through the *New York Herald*, even though the correspondence was 'not published' but was intended to be a State secret." *The Brown-Reynolds Duel*, ed. Walter B. Stevens, St. Louis, 1911, p. 18.

On February 27, 1849, Reynolds wrote from Charleston to Thomas N. Carr:
> The idea of forcing me out (if so intended) by stating me to be actually engaged in annexing Cuba (!!) is a master-stroke. . . . .
> I shall be forced, in defining my position, to make some disagreeable disclosures concerning the course of Mr. Saunders [Romulus Mitchell Saunders, appointed U.S. Minister to Spain in 1845 by President Polk] on the Cuba question, and the injury his bungling has done to the Annexationists...
> I never wrote to Botts on Annexation; it was to a *friend* in Richmond of secrecy & discretion that I wrote from Madrid.

Missouri Historical Society, Glimpses of the Past, "Letters of Thomas Caute Thomas, 1847-1885", X, 15f, Letter No. 4. In letter No. 7 he writes from Charleston, April 11, 1849, to Edward W. Johnstone, Esq. "*Private:* I design to expose the Cuba Annexation political plot or humbug..."

[45] *Letters of W.G. Simms*, II, 491.

[46] *Ibid.*, II, 491f., note 49, letters 471 and 472.

[47] *Ibid.*, II, 492.

[48] *Ibid.*, V, 407f.

[49] *Ibid.*, I, 397.

[50] I, N.S., No. 1 (April, 1850), 75-123.

⁵¹ II, N.S., No. 3 (September, 1850), 273-313; No. 4 (November, 1850), 274-313.
⁵² James L. Reynolds (1814-1877), a brother of the critic, had published in the *Southern Quarterly Review*, XVI, No. 10 (October, 1849), 205-223, an article on *El Buscapié*, signed J.L.R. (See Simms' *Letters*, II, 492, note 52. This same brother had also published in the *Southern Literary Messenger*, XIV (February, 1848) 106-111 "Dies Irae" in which he refers to Goethe's use of this hymn in *Faust* and otherwise gives proof of German erudition.
⁵³ *Letters of W.G.Simms*, I, cxxxiii.
⁵⁴ *Ibid.*, III, 46f, No. 541.
⁵⁵ *Glimpses of the Past, op. cit.*, X, 14, Letter No. 3.
⁵⁶ *Letters of W.G.Simms*, V, 518 and II, 492; also *Glimpses of the Past*, X, 9.
⁵⁷ *Ibid.*, X, 22, Letter No. 9.
⁵⁸ *Ibid.*, p. 23, Letter No. 10.
⁵⁹ *Ibid.*, p. 23 f.
⁶⁰ *Memoirs of Gustav Koerner*, edited by Thomas J. McCormack, 2 vols., Cedar Rapids, Iowa, 1909, II, 583. N.B. On Oct. 20, 1863, Gustavus A. Koerner, age 18, of Belleville, Illinois registered at the University of Heidelberg as a student of law, where Reynolds had received his JUD in 1842. In 1863 student Koerner's father was United States Minister in Madrid, having succeeded Carl Schurz, another German refugee, to this post. Reynolds had earlier (1846) served as our Secretary of Legation in Madrid.
⁶¹ *The Brown-Reynolds Duel. A Complete Documentary Chronicle of the Last Bloodshed under the Code between St. Louisians.* From the Manuscript Collection of William K. Bixby, Edited with Explanatory Narrative by Walter B. Stevens. The Franklin Club of St. Louis, 1911, p. 3 ff.
⁶² *Ibid.*, p. 37 ff.
⁶³ Published in the *Missouri Republican*, March 17, 1855. The brewery was incorporated on March 5, 1855. See *Brown-Reynolds Duel*, etc., p. 38.
⁶⁴ Heinrich Börnstein, *Fünfundsiebzig Jahre in der Alten und Neuen Welt. Memoiren eines Unbedeutenden*, 2 Bde., Leipzig, 1881, II, 252.
⁶⁵ Floyd C. Shoemaker, *Missouri and Missourians*, Chicago, 1943.
⁶⁶ *Brown-Reynolds Duel*, etc., p. 128.
⁶⁷ *Missouri Historical Review*, XXXVI, 443. See *The Struggle for Missouri* by John McElroy, Washington, 1909, p. 23 ff.
⁶⁸ *Ibid.*, XLV, (1950-51), 130-136.
⁶⁹ XVI, No. 16. (December 23, 1864).
⁷⁰ *Missouri Historical Review* XLV, 136 f.
⁷¹ W. C. Nunn. *Escape from Reconstruction*, Fort Worth, Texas, 1956, p. 32.
⁷² *Glimpses of the Past*. Missouri Historical Society, X, 36.
⁷³ *Ibid.*, p. 42. Reynolds had doubtless retained his active knowledge of Spanish as his wife "was a native of Spain, though of an American family, her father having been consul at a Spanish post when she was born." "Diary of Judge Wm. B. Napton" (A Scrap Book of Miscellaneous Clippings), Missouri Historical Society, Jefferson Memorial, St. Louis, p. 716). Not only was her native tongue Spanish, but her obituary indicates that she remained Spanish till death: "Heloise Marie Reynolds, Daughter of Horatio and Victorine Sprague, Born at Gibraltar, Spain, March 25, 1828. Died in Saint Louis, Missouri, January 26, 1872. Rev. F. X. Santois, S. J.; Calvary Cemetery: Requiescat in pace." (*Central Magazine*, Vol. 3, No. 2, St. Louis, *loc. cit.*, p. 543).
⁷⁴ W. C. Nunn, *op. cit.*, p. 38.
⁷⁵ A. H. Noll, *General Kirby-Smith*, Sewanee, Tenn., University Press, 1907, p. 273.
⁷⁶ Nunn, *op. cit.*, p. 110. Reynolds in a letter to Prof. Schele de Vere at the

University of Virginia on Jan. 13, 1879, (Folder, *Mo. Hist. Soc.*, Jefferson Memorial, St. Louis) "sojourned in the City of Mexico Sept. 1865, to Nov. 1867; then to April 1869 at the city of Vera Cruz."
[77] Missouri Historical Society, St. Louis. Folder: Thomas C. Reynolds, 1804-1906."
[78] Reynolds' Matriculations
Munich
#436. Am 28, Nov. 1839, Reynolds, Thomas, Charleston − Nordamerika, Cam[eralistics].
Heidelberg
#134. 1840, 9. Mai., Thomas Reynolds, 18; Charleston, Nordamerika; [Vater] Sklavenbesitzer; pr., J.U.; [früher] München; 7.20. [Adressbuch] Reynold, Thom.; Ost[ern] 40.; Charleston, Amerika. Panzer, Wittib.
Berlin
#3.1840, Am 21. Okt., Thomas Reynolds, Süd Carolina, Jura; [Vater] Rentier, Sklavenbesitzer; [früher] Heidelberg; Rechte; 34 Mohren[str.] 1, 10 Jäger[str]; 10 Jäger[str.].
Abgangszeugnis rite 6/6/42.
Goethe's Matriculations
Heidelberg
#168. 1840. 12. Mai; Wolfgang Maximilian Goethe, 19-1/2; Weimar; [Vater] † Geh. Kammerrath, Weimar; Vo[rmund] Regierungsrath Gatterer, ev.; J.U., [früher] Bonn.
Wittib. Büttner.
Also Wintersemester, 1840-41; Sommersemester, 1841. Doctor of Laws, 1845.
Berlin.
#291. 1841, Am 30 Okt., Wolfgang Maximilian v. Goethe, Jura. [Vater] Geh. Kammerrath 2 Hinter d. kath. Kirche [früher] Heidelberg. Abgangszeugnis 20/3/42. Doctor of Laws, 1845.
Matriculation Egloffstein
Heidelberg
#129. 1840, 9. Mai, Eugen v. Egloffstein, 19, Stuttgart. Vo[rmund] Kanzleirath Haug, Stuttgart; J.U. [früher] Tübingen; bei Förster, Bäcker.
[79] *Missouri Historical Review*, XV, 546 and Nunn, *op. cit.*, p. 35.
[80] *Missouri Historical Review*, XV, 719.
[81] Missouri Historical Society, Jefferson Memorial, also two additional communications dated Mexico City, March 6 and May 10, 1866.
[82] Kansas City, p. 123; also *Missouri Historical Review*, XIX, (1925), 440ff.
[83] Missouri Historical Society, St. Louis, "Reynolds Papers."
[84] L. C.; M.S., Ac, 2176, "Private Papers of Thomas C. Reynolds, Relating to the Emperor of Mexico." A third letter to the same addressee at Washington and dated City of Mexico, 19th May '66, is too faded to be legible. Corwin had been U.S. Chargé de Affaires in Mexico City.
[85] Missouri Historical Society, St. Louis, "Reynolds Papers, 1840-1906," Folder: Letter dated New York, April 18, 1869.
[86] To Prof. Schele de Vere, Jan. 13, 1879. In same Folder as in note 85, *supra*.
[87] *Missouri Historical Review*, XXXVI, 443.
[88] *Ibid.*, X, 43; XXIII, 461; XLV, 137.
[89] See *infra*.
[90] Library of Congress, Manuscripts. "Francis Lieber's Correspondence," Vol. 2, 1862-1867, p. 414f.
[91] *Ibid.*
[92] A reference to the verses in the poem:
    Aber Oranien und Du −
    Unvergängliches Zwillingsgestirne −

⁹³ The copy of the poem in the Library of Congress is introduced thus: "Als im Februar 1843 das Arbeitsschwert (service-sword) Washington's von einem Erben des grossen Bürgers durch einen Congressmitglied dem Congresse als Geschenk Für die Vereinigten Staaten übergeben wurde." A note says: "Dr. Francis Lieber's Lines on Washington's Schwert. Given by him to T.C. Reynolds at Charleston, S. C., 1843.
⁹⁴ Frank Freidel, *Francis Lieber Nineteenth Century Liberal*, Baton Rouge, L.S.U. Press, 1947, p. 414f.
⁹⁵ All Reynolds' letters thus far from Library of Congress.
⁹⁶ St. Louis, August 12, 1872. Henry E. Huntington Library, San Marino, California.
⁹⁷ See *supra*. We are told (*William Gilmore Simms Letters*, I, cxxxiii) he was a "good scholar and able Baptist minister." He "held professorial posts in various Southern Colleges," was twenty years at South Carolina College, ending his career at Furman University. See Green, Edwin L. *History of the University of South Carolina*, Columbia, 1916, p. 451f. James L. Reynolds, Belles Lettres and Elocution, 1851-1857; Roman Literature, 1857-1865; Mental and Moral Philosophy, Sacred Literature and Evidence of Christianity, 1865-1873. Furman University. Romance Languages, 1875-
⁹⁸ Library of Congress, Oct. 3, 1872.
⁹⁹ Scrapbook of Miscellaneous Clippings, Missouri Historical Society, Jefferson Memorial, p. 716.
¹⁰⁰ i.e., *Missouri Republican*.
¹⁰¹ Lieber to Reynolds, Sept. 7, 1871, Library of Congress.
¹⁰² Scrapbook of Miscellaneous Clippings, etc.
¹⁰³ Jonas Viles, *The University of Missouri, A Centennial History*, Columbia, Mo. 1939, p. 173.
¹⁰⁴ *Glimpses of the Past*, Missouri Historical Society. St. Louis, 1943, X, 53ff.
¹⁰⁵ William E. Curtis, *The Brown-Reynolds Duel. A Complete Documentary Chronicle of the Last Bloodshed under the Code between Saint Louisians. From a Manuscript Collection of William K. Bixby*, edited with Explanatory Narrative by Walter B. Stevens. The Franklin Club of St. Louis, MDCCCXI, p. 131.
¹⁰⁶ *Glimpses*, etc. X, 54.
¹⁰⁷ "Reynolds Papers," Jefferson Memorial.
¹⁰⁸ See Thomas C. Reynolds to Norman J. Coleman, Washington, D. C., "Reynolds Papers," Jefferson Memorial.
¹⁰⁹ Daniel M. Grissom, *Encyclopedia of the History of Missouri*, New York, Louisville and St. Louis, 1901, V, 340.
¹¹⁰ *Ibid*.

BASIL LANNEAU GILDERSLEEVE, SOUTH CAROLINA, VIRGINIA, MARYLAND

¹ *Cf. infra*, p. 133.
² *Forum*, X (February, 1891), p. 614.
³ *Loc. cit.*, p. 614.
⁴ *American Journal of Philology*, XXIII (1902), p. 110f.
⁵ *Goethe's Poems*, selected and edited by Julius Goebel (New York, 1901), Holt.
⁶ Zahme, Xenien, VII, *Jubiläums Ausgabe*, II, 168, 323, and IV, 112.
⁷ *Forum*, X (1891), p. 614f.
⁸ Data concerning the matriculations of Gildersleeve taken from the official archives of the universities indicate:

Berlin: Michaelmas 1850-Easter 1851, # 901. Reg. Oct. 2, 1850, Basilius Lanneau Gildersleeve, Charleston, S.C., U.S.A., phil.; V[ater] Prediger. Departure: Apr. 14, 1851.
Residence, Dorotheenstr. 22.
Göttingen: Easter 1851-Michaelmas 1851, # 40. Home, Richmond, Am.; Philos.; Residence, Wedenmeyer, Weenderstr. 58.
            Michaelmas 1851-Easter 1852
As above except Residence: Deuerlich, Weenderstr. 59.
Bonn: Summer Semester, 1852.
Lanneau-Gildersleeve, Basil; Richmont [*sic!*], 26 Apr., 1852. Residence: 180 Sterngasse.
          Winter Semester 1852-1853 as above.
Ex-Matrikel (transcript) Am 8. März, 1853.
[9] A typescript in the Gildersleeve Collection (thereafter cited as "Collection") in the Johns Hopkins University Library of an article "Professional Types" published in *The Hopkinsian* (1893). See also "A Novice in 1850" contributed by Gildersleeve to the *Johns Hopkins Alumni Magazine*, I, No. 1 (November, 1912) pp. 3-6, especially p. 5.
[10] The starred titles are in the "Collection."
The following data copied from the Archives of the Bonn University are interesting and informative.
Abgangszeugnisse, daß Herr Basil Lanneau-Gildersleeve geboren zu Charleston, Sohn des Rentiers H. Lanneau-Gildersleeve zu Richmond in den V.S. von America, zu den acad. stud. in Princeton vorbereitet, auf dem Grund des Abgangszeugnisses der Univ. Gött. am 26. April 1852 bei uns immatriculiert.
           Studienbuch am 28. April 1852
Angenommene Vorlesungen [Sommer Sem. 1852]
Bei Welcker, Griechische Kunstgeschichte
 ("mit unausgesetztem Fleiß," Welcker.)
Bei Ritschl, Kritik u. Hermeneutik
 ("mit rühmlichem Fleiß," Ritschl.)
Bei Ritschl, Aristophanes Ranae u. Geschichte d. Griechischen Komödie (*Privat*)
Bei Aschbach, Alte Geschichte.
 ("Mit ausgezeichnetem Fleiß u. regester Teilnahme bis zum Schluß," Aschbach)
Bei F. Ritter, Lateinische Literaturgeschichte
 ("mit ausgezeichnetem Fleiß u. stets reger Teilnahme," Ritter.)
Bei F. Ritter, Horace Satiren.
Bei Schmidt, Theoretische Systeme d. Tragiker.
 ("mit ausgezeichnetem Fleiß u. reger Teilnahme bis zum Schluß" Schmidt).
Bei Overbeck, Erklärung d. antiken Kunst-denkmale im Gypsmuseum.
 ("Ausgezeichnet fleißigen u. teilnehmenden Besuch bis zum Schluß bezeugt. 19. Aug. 52," Oberbeck.)
Bei Bernays, (privat) Über d. Politik von Aristotles.
 ("Mit unausgesetzterm Fleiß u. regester Teilnahme," Bernays.)
[11] "Brief Mention," *American Journal of Philology*, XXII, 229.
[12] *Amer. Jour. of Philol.* XXXVI, 368f.
[13] See *infra*, p. 153ff.
[14] *A History of the University founded by Johns Hopkins*, by John C. French, Baltimore, 1946, p. 35 and p. 430f.
[15] *Ibid.*, p. 79.
[16] *Ibid.*, p. 135f. Remsen had studied and worked at the universities of München, Göttingen and Tübingen between 1867 and 1872.

[17] *Ibid.*
[18] *Baltimore Sun,* January 10, 1924.
[19] An article, "Professorial Types", written for *The Hopkinsian,* Johns Hopkins University, 1893. See note 8, *supra.*
[20] Phillip August Boeckh, 1785-1867.
[21] New York, 1909, p. 40 ff. See also "A Novice" in 1850, note 8, *supra.*
[22] P. 33f, See "Novice in 1850," p. 7.
[23] This account of Welcker and the following of Jakob Bernays are from *Amer. Jour. of Philol.*, XXXIV (1913), 232 and XXXII (1911), 360f. respectively.
[24] "Brief Mention," *Amer. Jour. of Philol.*, XXXVII, 501.
[25] *Ibid.*, V, 340.
[26] *Op. cit.*, XX (1899), 460f.
[27] *Ibid.*, XXXVIII, 64.
[28] *Ibid.*, XXVIII, 234. See also *op. cit.*, XXIII, 111 and XXXVII (1916), 108 and also *Goethe After Two Centuries,* ed. Carl Hammer, Louisiana State University Press, 1952, p. 45, "for above, before and after all things, Goethe was a lover."
[29] *Hellas and Hesperia,* p. 40f.
[30] *Amer. Jour. of Philol.*, (1909), 232.
[31] *Creed of the Old South,* Baltimore, 1917, p. 14; also *Atlantic Monthly,* vol. 69 (January, 1892), p. 77.
[32] "Brief Mention," *Amer. Jour. of Philol.*, XXXVII (1916), p. 372f.
[33] *Op. cit.*, XXXVI (1915), 241.
[34] First published in the *Southern Review,* October, 1859, later in *Essays and Studies,* Baltimore, 1890, pp. 297-351. See pp. 301, 304, 325, 330, 344, 346.
[35] *Essays and Studies,* p. 361.
[36] "Brief Mention," *Amer. Jour. of Philol.*, XXIX, 125. See also: "The measles of love go hard with an old boy. Think of Goethe's last love affair." *Ibid.* XXXVIII (1917), 65 and "Sei nur nicht halb', says Goethe." *ibid.*, p. 70.
[37] "Basil L. Gildersleeve, An Intimate View," by Charles Forster Smith, *Sewanee Review,* XXXII (April, 1924), 162-175, p. 171. For Oct. 25, 1915. We find on p. 173 the same Goethean phrase again.
[38] *Amer. Jour. of Philol.*, XLI (1920), 402.
[39] *Creed of the Old South,* p. 17. See note 26, *supra.*
[40] "Brief Mention," *Amer. Jour. of Philol.*, XXXIII (1912), 228. Illustrative of his loyalty to his German mentor G. continues: "It is interesting to note that in the 'faultless distich' of 'der romantische Oedipus', Platen has built both hexameter and pentameter on Greek lines, the third trochee caesura in the one, the polysyllabic ending in the other."
Möge die Welt durchschweifen der herrliche Dulder Odysseus
Kehrt er zurück, weh' euch, wehe dem Freiergeschlecht.
"These breaks are all important for the effect of the hexameter."
[41] *Amer. Jour. of Philol.*, XXV (1904), 112f. Note Walter Silz's analysis of the same poem, *The Germanic Review,* XXX, No. 4 (December, 1955), 256ff. "The indefinite pronoun 'es' is used a dozen times to convey the indefinable dread of the whirlpool. Once 'es' occurs with nice visualization for the as yet indistinct whiteness of the human body before it breaks through the surface (74). At the very end 'es' stands for the Princess, giving her a generalized character as the impersonation of the patiently waiting love." But what about the other one score and two "ES"'s?
[42] *Amer. Jour. of Philol.*, XXXVII (1916), 116. Four years earlier (*op. cit.*, XXXIII, 106) G. had written: "Nietzsche became a student of Theognis and drew from him the inspiration of the 'Übermensch'."
[43] *Hellas and Hesperia,* p. 85.

⁴⁴ *Amer. Jour. of Philol.*, XXIX, 500.
⁴⁵ *Quarterly Review of the Methodist Episcopal Church, South*, X, No. 3 (July, 1856), 348-362. This routine article is a review, neither inspired nor inspiring, of Strauss's *Leben und Schriften des Dichters und Philosophen Nicodemus Frischlin. Ein Beitrag zur deutschen Culturgeschichte des sechzehnten Jahrhunderts*, Frankfurt a. M., 1856.
⁴⁶ *Amer. Jour. of Philol.*, XXXIII (1912), 230 ff.
⁴⁷ *Ibid.*, XXXIII, 230. See also *op. cit.*, VIII, 253 and XXIX, 499 ff.
⁴⁸ *Op. cit.*, XXXVII, 234.
⁴⁹ *Atlantic Monthly*, vol. 79 (1897), p. 631.
⁵⁰ American Book Co., Copyright, 1885, p. 201.
⁵¹ *Amer. Jour. of Philol.*, XVIII (1897), 124.
⁵² *Essays and Studies*, 161-205, especially p. 188; Composed between 1867-1869. See p. 165 and p. i.
⁵³ *Amer. Jour. of Philol.*, XXX (1909), 357.
⁵⁴ *Essays and Studies*, p. 188 f.
⁵⁵ *Amer. Jour. of Philol.*, XXX (1909), 357.
⁵⁶ Jethro Bithell, 1878 – *The Minnesingers*, London and New York, 1909.
⁵⁷ In *Amer. Jour. of Philol.*, XXVII (1906), 103. G. calls his Venus essay "a very inadequate performance as judged by the light of recent research."
⁵⁸ XX, 118-120. Landseer, Sir Edwin, 1802-1873, an English painter, held the very highest rank among animal painters.
⁵⁹ See p. 109 *supra*.
⁶⁰ XX, 45 f.
⁶¹ David Ramsay of Charleston, friend and fellow-student of Gildersleeve in Göttingen (1850-1852) completed his studies at Heidelberg. J.U.D., 1852.
⁶² IV, 434-465. Art. VII, *Platen's Poems*.
⁶³ *Essays and Studies*, p. 403.
⁶⁴ *Ibid.*, p. 404 f.
⁶⁵ Verkünde mich indes, Ghasele, dem Vaterland! *Platens Sämtliche Werke in vier Bänden*, hrsg. von Karl Goedeke, Stuttgart, II, 14.
⁶⁶ *Essays and Studies*, p. 407, note. Cf. *Southern Literary Messenger*, XX, 173.
⁶⁷ *Essays and Studies*, p. 445.
⁶⁸ *Ibid.*, p. 411.
⁶⁹ Platen "Lieder und Romanzen," *op. cit.*, I, 131 (1830).
⁷⁰ *Essays and Studies*, p. 445.
⁷¹ *Ibid.*
⁷² *Ibid.*, p. 406.
⁷³ *Ibid.*, p. 408.
⁷⁴ *Ibid.*, p. 404.
⁷⁵ *Ibid.*, p. 402.
⁷⁶ *Ibid.*, p. 403.
⁷⁷ *Ibid.*, p. 404.
⁷⁸ *Ibid.*, p. 444 f.
⁷⁹ *Ibid.*, p. 427. *cf.* also: "Und eine Magd im Putz, das ja ist mein Geschmack" [*Faust*, 831]. That is a German figure and it is precisely in the sphere of metaphor that the natural genius manifests itself; it is precisely in this sphere that the aesthetic judgments of antique critics are hardest to follow with full sympathy." "Brief Mention," *Amer. Jour. Philol.* XXX (1909) 231.
⁸⁰ See p. 155 *infra* and my *Mark Twain and the German Language*, Louisiana State University Press, 1953, p. 15 f.
⁸¹ G. reports in 1911: "One of my German critics has called me recently the Mark Twain of Greek syntax – and as Mark Twain is immensely popular in Germany, I ought to be pleased with the tag." "An Intimate View," *Sewanee Review* XXXII (April, 1924), p. 169. See also *Amer. Jour. of*

     Philol., XXXVIII (1917), 42. "No one who has cheerfully survived being called by a German well-wisher the Mark Twain of Greek systax ... has anything more to dread."
82 *Sämtliche Werke*, "Die verhängnisvolle Gabel," III, 264.
83 Pages referred to are in *Essays and Studies*.
84 *Atlantic Monthly*, vol. 79, p. 634.
85 *Amer. Jour. of Philol.*, XL (1919), 450.
86 *Platens Sämtliche Werke*, II, 104; 800 (XVIII), 8 März, 1826.
87 *Essays and Studies*, p. 412. *Cf.* also Platen, *op. cit.*, II, 110 (No. 92).
              Mein Geist, bewegt von innerlichem Streite,
              Empfand so sehr in diesem kurzen Leben,
              Wie leicht es ist, die Heimat aufzugeben,
              Allein wie schwer, zu finden eine zweite.
88 *Amer. Jour. of Philol.*, XLI, 199.
89 *Ibid.*, p. 201.
90 *The Johns Hopkins Alumni Magazine*, IX, 3, 175-185; republished in the *New York Times*, January 11, 1924, p. 16, cl. 6.
91 See p. 113ff. *supra*.
92 *Cf. Amer. Jour. of Philol.*, XXVI (1905), 358 "'Musst immer thun wie neugeboren' – and this is the nearest approach an old scholar can make to Goethe's 'new birth'."
93 *Ibid.*, XXXVIII (1917), 392.
94 "University Work in America and Classical Philology," *Princeton Review*, May, 1879, p. 519.
95 P. 53 "Classics and Colleges" (1878); Lament for Goethe's Germany *in extenso*.
96 *Amer. Jour. of Philol.*, XXXVI (1915), 240ff.
97 *Essays and Studies*, p. 54f.
98 *Amer. Jour. of Philol.*, XXXVII, 232.
99 *Ibid.*, XXXVIII, 399. Bywater, Ingram (1840-1914). *Cf.* "An Oxford Scholar," *loc. cit.*, pp. 392-400 and p. 459.
100 *Essays and Studies*, pp. 193, 184.
101 *Ibid.*, pp. 402, 449.
102 See *Thomas Jefferson and George Ticknor, A Chapter in American Scholarship*, by O. W. Long, Williamstown, Mass., 1933, pp. 32-39, but especially the final paragraph.
103 P. 41.
104 *New York Times*, January 27, 1924, IV, 3.
105 *Amer. Jour. of Philol.* XLV (1924), 100.

JAMES WOODROW, SOUTH CAROLINA

1 Phil. Facultät. *Acten pro 1856*. Decanat des Herrn Professor Röth, p. 51.
2 In this year rhetoric was to appear "in the catalogue as a regular college subject, taught by an alumnus, Dr. Joseph Wilson, minister of the Hill Church and the father of Woodrow Wilson." *Banners in the Wilderness. Early Years of Washington and Jefferson College* by Helen Waite Turnbull Coleman, Pittsburgh, 1956, p. 88.
3 *Dr. James Woodrow As Seen by His Friends.* Part I, *Character Sketches by His Former Pupils, Colleagues and Associates.* Part II, *His Teachings As Contained in His Sermons, Addresses, Editorials*, etc., Collected and Edited by his daughter, Marion W. Woodrow, Columbia, S.C., 1909, p. 10f.
4 *Ibid.*, p. 57.
5 Archives of the University Ruprecht-Carolus, Heidelbergae. See Note 1, *supra*, but pp. 50-56. N.B. "Bei der Chemischen Doktor-Promotion in

der philosophischen Fakultät zu Heidelberg wurde eine Dissertation nicht offiziell verlangt." *Geschichte des Chemischen Universitätslaboratoriums zu Heidelberg seit seiner Gründung durch Bunsen,* hrsg. von Prof. Dr. Theodor Curtius und Dr. Johannis Risson, Heidelberg, 1908, S. 36.

[6] *Dr. James Woodrow,* etc., p. 10. "Sketch" published in *The State* of Columbia, and *The News and Courier,* of Charleston, January 18, 1907. in *op. cit.,* pp. 4-32. No evidence has been found in the Heidelberg Archives to verify the statement that such an offer was ever made. Bunsen was then, as later, employing "assistants" for his growing laboratory. *Cf. American Colony Book* (M.S.) II, 24 (Goettingen University) August, 1879: "Treadwell from Heidelberg" "T. had made his Dr. but a few weeks previously and had been here but a few weeks when he received and accepted a call as Assistant to Prof. Bunsen in the Chemical Laboratory at Heidelberg." It seems incredible that a young Doctor (Woodrow) so suddenly should have been offered a full professorship at the Mother of Universities in Germany.

[7] *Sidney Lanier* by Edwin Mims, Boston and New York, 1905, p. 29f.

[8] *The Centennial Edition of the Works of Sidney Lanier,* General Editor, Charles R. Anderson, Baltimore, 1945, VII, 29.

[9] *Dr. James Woodrow,* etc., p. 12.

[10] "Recollections and Letters of Sidney Lanier" by Milton H. Northrup, *Lippincott's Magazine,* LXXV (March, 1905), 302-315.

[11] *American Literature,* IV, No. 3 (November, 1932), 288-292.

[12] *The Centennial Edition,* etc., IV, 33-38.

[13] Mims, *op. cit.,* p. 313.

[14] Book I, Chapter XV, Centennial Edition, V, 89. Also *op. cit.,* IV, 34. Lanier states in this connection: "If indeed we go over into Germany, there is Goethe, at once pursuing science and poetry."

[15] *American Scholar,* II, No. 4 (October, 1933) 389-397, p. 390.

[16] See also *Bayard Taylor and German Letters,* by John T. Krumpelmann, Hamburg, 1959, p. 148f.

[17] March 8th. See Aubrey Starke, *loc. cit.,* p. 390 and Lanier's Letters, *Centennial Edition, Works,* VII, 379f.

[18] *Loc. cit.,* p. 390.

[19] *Cf. Dr. James Woodrow,* etc., p. 56f.

[20] *Ibid.,* p. 56f. and note. Also *The Tensas Gazette,* St. Joseph, La. (no date), Louisiana Room, Louisiana State University.

[21] *Dr. James Woodrow,* etc., p. 13f. and p. 730.

[22] *Ibid.,* p. 726.

[23] *Ibid.,* p. 365ff.

[24] *Ibid.,* p. 21ff.

[25] *Ibid.,* p. 82.

[26] *Ibid.,* p. 23.

[27] Re Gildersleeve, see *The Forum,* X (February, 1891), p. 616; Re; Reynolds see *supra,* p. 95ff..

[28] Reprinted in *Dr. James Woodrow,* etc., pp. 388-406.

[29] Reprinted in *Dr. James Woodrow,* etc., pp. 407-459, with a note explaining that it "was in answer to assaults on Natural Sciences made by the Rev. Dr. R. L. Dabney," etc. (p. XVI).

[30] *The Southern Presbyterian Review,* XXIV (July, 1873), 327-377. See p. 335f. Reprinted in *Dr. James Woodrow,* etc., p. 415f. Note that the theme of this entire passage is Du Bois-Reymond's aphorism "Ignoramus, Ignorabimus" which epitomizes his work here cited.

[31] *Review,* p. 344f.; *Dr. James Woodrow,* etc., p. 425. N.B. Woodrow was examined by Bunsen in Heidelberg in 1858 and Gustav Robert Kirchhoff (1824-1887) was called to Heidelberg to fill the Chair of Physics in the

Fall of 1854, hence about the time Woodrow arrived there. Kirchhoff had earlier been a colleague of Bunsen in Breslau.
[32] Reprinted in part and "with additions" in *Dr. James Woodrow*, etc., p. 47 ff. The original article appeared in *The Central Presbyterian*.
[33] *Southern Presbyterian Review*, October, 1873.
[34] Reprinted in *Dr. James Woodrow*, etc., pp. 460-507.
[35] *Op. cit.*, pp. 476, 479. We have evidence that Woodrow did not neglect field work in favor of research in the laboratories in Germany. "While there [in Europe] he spent much time in traveling over regions most interesting to geologists, and in making personal inspection of remarkable formations, and otherwise adding to his store of learning upon this subject ... on one of his excursions near Dresden ... [he] discovered a most important fossil (*calamites gigas*) for which many noted geologists had been long searching." (*Dr. James Woodrow*, etc., p. 53 f.).
[36] Richmond, Virginia, 1903, p. 422. See *Dr. James Woodrow* etc., p. 11. Sixteen days later (August 7th) he wrote to his wife from Göttingen announcing that their son Charles William, Jr., (later to become President of the University of Tennessee, 1887-1904) had successfully passed his *rigorosum* for the Doctor's degree in chemistry and mineralogy. (See *op. cit.*, p. 421 and 413). The records at the Göttingen University disclose that Charles W. Dabney was registered there for four semesters, Michaelmas, 1878 – August 1880, as a student of chemistry. He wrote a dissertation *Ueber eine[r] Isopikra – aminsäure* (Göttingen, 1880, 8°). The "American Colony Book" (MS.) shows that he was the thirty-eighth Patriarch of the Colony and that his father, the Rev. Mr. Dabney, President of the Theological Seminary, Nashville, Tennessee," visited the "Colony" in July, 1880, and they left Göttingen in August (II, 67).

The son's home address was given during his first two semesters as "Edward, America" and for the last two as "Richmond." His Göttingen address was "Hofer, Herzenbergerstr. 9A" until the final semester when it became "Reinhauser Chausee 8A," care of Meyer. The Göttinger student was Charles, Jr. because his grandfather was Charles Dabney. He also had an uncle Charles William Dabney. (*Cf. Sketches of the Dabneys of Virginia*. Chicago, 1888, pp. 127-129).
[37] *Op. cit.*, xvii.
[38] *Ibid.*, p. 721-784; see p. 753.
[39] *Ibid.*, p. 466.
[40] *Ibid.*, p. 759.
[41] *Ibid.*, p. 761.
[42] *Ibid.*, p. 767.
[43] *Cf. The Revolt of Martin Luther* by Robert Herndon Fife, New York, 1957, p. 666 and especially note 103; and *Martin Luther. His Life and Work*, Hartman Grisar, S.J., adapted from the second German edition edited by Frank J. Eble, Westminster, Maryland, p. 185.
[44] *Dr. James Woodrow*, etc., p. 784.
[45] *Ibid.*, p. 54, also p. 103.
[46] *Ibid.*, p. 839 f.
[47] *Ibid.*, p. 840.
[48] *Ibid.*, pp. 913-970.
[49] *Ibid.*, p. 25.
[50] *Ibid.*, p. 853.
[51] *Ibid.*, p. 852.
[52] Copied from *Der Montag Morgen*, Berlin, d. 20. Juli 1925 when the author was a student in Berlin. Note: William Jennings Bryan (verse 5) was a vital force in obtaining at the Democratic National Convention of 1912 the nomination of Woodrow Wilson, the uncle of Dr. James Woodrow,

for the presidency of the United States. When Wilson was elected president of the United States, Bryan became his first Secretary of State. He resigned from Wilson's Cabinet before the declaration of war against Germany in 1917. He was a Fundamentalist and played a leading role in the legal prosecution of Scopes. Five days after he succeeded in convicting Scopes, he died in his sleep.

[53] See *Dr. James Woodrow*, etc., p. 55.
[54] *Ibid.*, p. 113.
[55] *Ibid.*, p. 140.
[56] *Cf. e.g.*, To Mary Day, April 24, 1863: "Friend of mine, never read Goethe to *believe* him –. Goethe is either a God or a Devil: he is not *our* God, but very different: there is only one God ... and so Goethe is a Devil, therefore, a Liar –." (*Works, Centennial Edition*, VII, 89. To Virginia Hankins, May 17th, 1869. "Surely, in the wretched Goethe-doctrines of self-culture, and the like, I, for one, put no reliance, nor ever have. Not only do I disagree with them, but I contemn and utterly despise them. That which hath to do with Self comes of the Devil." (*Works*, VIII, 31).

MATH AND AFTERMATH, SOUTH CAROLINA

a. OSCAR MONTGOMERY LIEBER

[1] Frank Freidel, *Francis Lieber, Nineteenth Century Liberal*, Baton Rouge, 1947, p. 216.
[2] *Cf.* his German letters (Huntington Library Collection).
[3] Thomas Sergeant Perry, London, 1882, pp. 143, 147f.
[4] Huntington Library.
[5] Franz Lieber was born at 17 Breitestrasse.
[6] Freidel, *op. cit.*, p. 245.
[7] Not at "Freiburg," as Lewis R. Hawley and Frank Freidel erroneously state in the biographies of Francis Lieber, p. 59 and p. 243, respectively. *Cf.* Letter: F. Lieber to G. S. Hilliard, June 24, 1849: "Our beloved Oscar, when he had returned from Freiberg to Dresden." Perry, *op. cit.*, p. 222. A careful search of the records of the University of Freiburg, Breisgau, fails to disclose the name of Oscar Lieber.
[8] *Op. cit.*, p. 248f. Letter dated July, 1849. *Cf.* also letter to G. S. Hilliard, June 24, 1849, quoted also by Hawley, *op. cit.*, p. 222 from which Freidel's quote is taken. Note also Hawley's sequence of universities (*op. cit.*, p. 59) is most likely. Freiberg-Dresden is commuting distance.
[9] Freidel, *op. cit.*, p. 251f.
[10] J. A. Holmes, "Mineralogical, Geological and Agricultural Survey of South Carolina," *Journal of the Elisha Mitchell Scientific Society*, VII, 89-117 (Biographical Notes).
[11] Thomas C. Johnson, Jr., *Scientific Interests in the Old South*, New York, 1936, p. 186f.
[12] Philadelphia, 1852.
[13] Philadelphia, H. C. Baird, 1852, 117 p.
[14] I, 1857; II, 1858; III, 1859; IV, 1860. *Cf.* J. A. Holmes, *loc. cit.*
[15] *Cf.* "Report of the Superintendent of the Coast Survey during the year of 1860," Washington, 1861, 36 Congress, 2nd session, Ex. Doc. No. 14, 229-275. Also Laborde, *History of South Carolina College*, p. 476f. for C. S. Venable.
[16] Library of Congress, Sketch No. 38, 7 pp.
[17] Freiberg, III, 309-507. *Cf.* also Über neue Goldgewinnungs-Apparate," *Berg- und hüttenmännische Zeitung*, Leipzig, XIV, No. 47 (21, Nov. 1855).

For further details see "Oscar Montgomery Lieber Scrapbook, 1852-1856" MS.; also "Geology Note Book" University of South Carolina. Judging by the sketches in his note book he must have been a good portrait artist.
[18] James and Williams, Printers.
[19] Humboldt wrote to Oscar: "Ich schäme mich, mein theurer Lieber, der liebenswürdige Sohn meines edlen Freundes, so lange ohne Antwort, ohne Dank für Ihr interessantes Geschenk gelassen zu haben, das ich durch Gustav Rose in der Kn. Sammlung habe einverleiben lassen ... etc." Copy of letter in Huntington Library.
[20] See *supra*, p. 67.
[21] P. 88.
[22] Perry, *op. cit.*, p. 313.
[23] *Op. cit.*, p. 326.
[24] Oscar M. Lieber MS., *University of South Carolina*.
[25] Laborde, *History of South Carolina College*, etc., p. 476f.

b. DAVID RAMSAY

[1] *Berlin:* Registered as No. 541 on April 26, 1851 as student of "Jura" from Charleston; [father] Rentier. Rite [transcript] Nov. 2, 1851.
Heidelberg: Registered as No. 14 on April 21, 1852: David Ramsay, 22, Charleston, America; [father] David Ramsay, Charleston; Catholic, "Jura." From Göttingen; [Fee] 70 Gulden, 20 Kreutzer.
[2] Archives of the University of Heidelberg
Ramsay Jur. Fac. Acta. 1852, Vangerow.
Davidum Ramsay, Americanum Examine rigoroso summa cum laude superati
Gradum Doctoris summos in utroque jure honores P.P. Heidelbergae in Universite literaria
D. XIV Mensis Augusti MXCCCLII.
[3] *Cf.* Walter Wadephul, *Goethe's Interest in the New World*, Jena, 1934, p. 69 and p. 84. Also *supra*, Calvert, p. 30 and note that the only mention of Washington in *Goethes Gespräche* (Biedermann) is in connection with Calvert, *op. cit.*, V, 439 (III, 176). N.B. also the use of the Ramsay historical work at the neighboring University of Jena, *supra*, Harrison, p. 64.
[4] South Carolina State Library, Columbia, S.C.; manuscript. "Ramsay, David (fl. 1850). 5 ALp. S."
[5] S. Lord, W.D.B. Dingle and David Ramsay, all students of law from Charleston, registered at Göttingen together. Their registration numbers were 15, 16, 17, respectively. The addresses of Lord and Ramsay are given as W. Kramer, Weenderstrasse 40 and Zindelstrasse 642, respectively The following semester they both lived at "W. Kramer, Zindelstrasse 642. G.W. Dingle had registered in Göttingen (law) at Easter 1848. He spent seven semesters there and two in Berlin. He matriculated at Heidelberg, October 25, 1852, where he obtained his degree J.U.D. in the course of the semester.
During Ramsay's last semester in Göttingen he, B.L. Gildersleeve and G.W. Dingle all lived at the Deuerlich house, Weenderstrasse 59, where G.W. Dingle had dwelt since the Spring of 1848 and which had come to be a sort of residential headquarters for Southern students in Göttingen.
[6] Probably the family of a Charlestonian. "A. Sachtleben, German born, was Professor of Modern Languages 1867-70. For many years previous he

had taught in the public schools of Charleston." Edwin L. Green, *History of the University of South Carolina*, Columbia, 1916, p. 405; also p. 453.

[7] The following Charlestonians were registered at Berlin, Michaelmas 1850-Easter 1851.
Carr, Henry W., Philos.; Carr, Joseph P., Philos.; Geddings, Dr. V., Med.; Geddings, G. W. Philos.; Gildersleeve, B. L., Philos.; Starr, Robt. C., Philos.; Wilson, J. H., Philos.
Walter, W. D., Med. and Dove, Walter, Med.; lived at 32 Mittelstrasse where Dr. Geddings had lived until Michaelmas.
Lane, G. M., Philos., who lived in the preceding semester with G. W. Dingle, (Law) at 91 Dorotheenstrasse, was possibly in Berlin when Ramsay arrived. He was not a Charlestonian, but a "Charlestownian."
See also Hinsdale, *op. cit.*, p. 612.

[8] I.e., to wear when I am presented to our Minister. A sample of the student's sense of wit and humor.

[9] See *supra*, Gildersleeve, note 12.

[10] Personaleinkommensteuerschätzungskommissionsmitgliedreisekostenrechnungsergänzungsrevisionsfund.
See my *Mark Twain and The German Language*, Louisiana State University Press, Baton Rouge, 1953, p. 16.

[11] Charleston, 1854, p. 13.

[12] *Letters of W.G.Simms*, II, 308.

[13] *Ibid.*, p. 313.

[14] By Evert and George L. Duykinck, 2 vols., New York, 1856 "David Ramsay," pp. 304 f. See *Letters of W.G.Simms*, III, 308, note 117.

[15] See *Letters of W.G.Simms*, IV, 439, note 54 and Shumway's list, p. 117.

C. THOMAS EDWARDS HART

[1] Shumway, "The American Students of the University of Göttingen," *German American Annals*, N.S., vol. 8 (1910), pp. 171-254. The official registration records show: Ostern-Michaelis, 1859.
T. E. Hart, 160, Ost. 59, Süd Carolina, Am., Philos., Wiederhold, Prinzen-[strasse] 528.
The two succeeding semesters give the identical data. It is interesting to note that one of the Gibson brothers of Kentucky and Louisiana first registered at Göttingen shortly after Hart: T. Gibson, Louisiana, Rechte, [Registration No. 185] Schepler, 77 Weender[strasse].

[2] Information supplied by Dr. Hans Krabusch of the Department of Archives, Heidelberg University, March 4, 1959.

[3] Druck von B. G. Teubner in Leipzig, [O. J.], iv, 49. The following data from: "Akten der Phil. Facultät [M.S. Heidelberg Archives] 1865-66, Dekan Zelter, III, 5a, 00. 93"
Thomas Edwards Hart aus Amerika, der seit 1858 in Göttingen ..., hier naturwissenschaftliche Studien gemacht hat ... sich zu Examen in Mathematik als Hauptfach, Chemie u. Physik als Nebenfächer; zugleich überreicht er eine mathemathische Abhandlang (ohne Titel) ... u. vita beilegt.
Herr College Hesse spricht sich in der Anlage für Annahme der Abhandlung u. Zulassung zu Examen aus. In der Voraussetzung, daß die übrigen Herren Sachverständigen beistimmen, schlage ich Dienstag, d. 13. d. Abends 6 Uhr als Prüfungstermin vor.

Zelter

Heidelberg d. 8. März 1866.
The committee of examiners was: Bähr, Latein; Hesse, Mathematik;

Bunsen, Chemie; Kirchhoff, Physik. Report on Examination:
Bähr, Caesar's Gallic Wars: "Ich fand mich befriedigt."
O. Hesse, Mathematics: "befriedigt."
Bunsen, Chemistry: "Ganz befriedigt."
Kirchhoff, Physics: "Ich wurde von den Antworten des Candidaten theilweise befriedigt."
"Die Facultät beschloß den Candidaten mit der Note 'insigni cum laude' zur Promotion zuzulassen
                    Zelter
                    O. Hesse
                    Bunsen
                    Kirchhoff
                    Weil
                    Kapp
                    Reichlin-Waldegg
Original registration in Heidelberg: #233: 1860, Dec. 17, Thomas Edwards Hart, 27, South Carolina, U.S.A. [Vater] Pflanzer †, pr., Cm., (früher) Göttingen, Klingelshorst 20, v. Leonhart, Geh. Rat.
N.B. #235: 1860, Dec. 17 John Julius Pringle, 19, South Carolina, U.S.A. [Vater] Gutsbesitzer, ev. J. U. [früher] Berlin.

[4] "Tribute to Dr. Thomas E. Hart, offered to the Annual Meeting of the Association of Graduates of the South Carolina Military Academy," July 7, 1892. "To the Dead of 1891-92." See note 6, *infra*.
[5] *Ibid.*, p. 30, "Remarks" added by Major J. J. Lucas. Lest we forget: The examiners were well renumerated from the 240 guldens paid by Hart as his examination fee. In those days a 53 page paperback did not cost as much to publish as it would today.
[6] J. L. Coker, *Hartsville, Its Early Settlers*, 1911, p. 8.
[7] Robert Norman Daniel, *Furman University, A History*, Furman University, Greenville, S. C., 1951, p. 81.
[8] Green, *History of the University of South Carolina*, p. 92.
[9] *Ibid.*, p. 93 and pp. 453-54.
[10] Coker, *op. cit.*, p. 9f.
[11] Green, *op. cit.*, p. 93.

INDEX

Adams, Charles F., 166
Adams, John Quincy, 18, 30, 153
Aggasiz, Jean R., 134, 137
Alexander, Czar, 7
Allen, Henry W., 94
Alston, Aaron Burr, 159
American Journal of Philology, 104, 111, 133, 182-186
American Literature, 164, 187
American Quarterly Review, 53, 68, 71, 165, 169
Amory, W., 48, 57, 175
Arconati, 14, 16
Aristophanes, 126
Aristoteles, 110
Arndt, Ernst M., 110-111
Arnim, Achim von, 115
Arrivabene, M., 13, 19, 77
Arthur, Chester A., 102
Aschbach, Joseph, 106, 183
Atlantic Monthly, 171, 184-186

Bähr, Prof. Johann C. F., 135, 191
Baird, H. C., 189
The Baltimore News, 33
Baltimore Sun, 184
Bancroft, George, 2-4, 23, 30, 35, 41, 165, 169
Barnum, Phineas T., 146
Bassano, [Maret], 52
Baumeister, A., 107
Bayard Taylor and German Letters, 1, 40, 170, 187
Bayard, Thomas F., 102
Beach, Mrs., 66
Beal, Daniel, 101
Beauclere, Henry, 66
Beck, Carl, 28, 37, 48, 173
Becker, Immanuel, 20
Bekker, Albert, 20, 109
Benecke, George F., 25, 27, 28
*Bergmann, Prof., 48
Bernays, Jacob, 109, 110, 183, 184

*Prof. in Bonn 1828

Bernhard, Herzog, 7, 10, 23, 31, 52-53, 60, 63-64, 160-161, 163-164, 173, 178
Beulwitz, Friedrich A., von, 62-63
Bielke, Friedrich Wilhelm, 62
Billé, Jochem de, 179
Billé, T., de, 179
Bismarck, Otto von, 3, 159, 160
Bithell, Jethro, 118, 185
Bixby, William K., 180, 182
Blaettermann, George, 179
Blair, Francis P., Jr., 92, 101
Bluhm, Heinz, 81, 82
Blum, Reinhard, 135
Blumenbach, Jo. Fr., 6-7, 27, 32, 55-56, 58, 168-169
Bode, Fr. Wm. A., 59
Boeckh, Phillip Agustus, 10, 108, 110, 184
Boehme, Charles, 2
Boernstein, Heinrich, 92, 93, 180
Boggs, William W., 139
Bond, Col. O. J., 169
Bonquois, Dora, 176
Bouterweck, Friedrich, 25, 28, 90
Brooks, Charles Timothy, 38, 40, 172
Brooks, Sidney, 16
Brown, B. Gratz, 92, 98, 101, 160
Brown, James, 52
Bruce, Philip A., 173, 179
Bruen, Matthius, 50
Brunhilde, 115
Bryan, William Jennings, 188-189
Bryant, W. C., 41
Bullard, Henry A., 73
Bulletin de la Société de Géographie, 68, 176
Bunsen, Robert Wm. E., 135, 140, 157, 187, 192
Burr, Aaron, 7, 8, 52-53, 63, 159-161, 164
Burr, Theodosia (Alston), 164 (see Alston)

193

Byron, Lord (George Gordon), 10, 64
Bywater, Ingram, 132, 186
Cabell, Robert Henry, 52-53, 58, 68
Caldwell, Guy A., 166
Calvert, George Henry, 1, 2, 23-39, 42-44, 50, 60, 81, 86, 88, 90-92, 153, 160, 167-172, 174, 190
Calvin, John, 43
Carl Friedrich, Herzog, 7
Carlyle, Thomas, 34, 72, 104, 138
Carr, Henry W., 154, 191
Carr, Joseph P., 154, 191
Castle, Eduard, 164
Cervantes, 89, 90
Chandler, Peleg. W., 2, 177
* Chandler, Mr. 60
Channing, William, 82
Chase, Salmon P., 71
Chronicle of the Times, 33-34
Claiborne, J. F. H., 168
Clark, Noel, 23, 167-168
Clay, Henry, 51-52, 67, 70, 72, 74
Clemens Samuel L. (Mark Twain), 126, 145-146, 153, 155, 185-186
Clemson, Thomas G., 55, 174
Cleveland, Grover, 102
Coffin, Amory, 59, 159
Cogswell, Henry, 21
Cogswell, Joseph G., 21, 45, 167
Coker, J. L., 192
Coleman, Norman J., 182
Coleridge, S. T., 28, 35-36, 71, 113, 130, 169, 172
Conta, 62
Conti, Comte, 63
Cooper, James F., 50, 69
Corwin, Wm. H., 97, 181
Coward, Col. Asbury, 157
Cumberland, Duke of, 24, 56
Cummings, A. W., 158
Cunningham, Francis, 48, 175
Curtius, Theodor, 187
Cushing, Caleb, 72

Dabney, Charles W., Jr., 188
Dabney, Robert L., 139-142, 187-188
Daniel, Robert Norman, 192
Darwin, Charles R., 138, 148
Davis, Jefferson, 94-95
Day, Mary, 189

* Cf. Goethe, *Tagebücher* (W. A.) 12, 214, 4.

Degas, Edgar -H. -G., 159
Degas, René, 159
Demosthenes, 20
Dichtung und Wahrheit, 35, 44-45
Dingle, G. W., 154, 190-191
Dissen, L. G., 56
Don Carlos, 34, 35, 36
Donelson, A. J., 88
Dorr, Joseph H., 59
Dove, Walter, 191
Drayton, John, 7, 159
Du Bois-Reymond, 140, 187
Dugilson, Robley, 49
Duponceau, Peter S., 53, 165
Dürer, Albrecht, 19
Duyckinck, E. A., 156, 191
Dwight, Henry E., 26-27, 50, 66, 166, 169, 173-174
Dwight, John S., 37-38

Early, J. A., 94
Eble, Frank J., 188
Edwards, John R., 96
Eglofstein, Countess Julie von, 31, 63
Egloffstein, Eugen von, 161, 181
Eichhorn, Johann Gottfried, 25, 27, 167-168
Eliot, Charles W., 108, 133
Eliot, George, 167
Emerson, Ralph Waldo, 27
Emerson, William, 23, 27, 29, 168, 170
Euripides, 15, 16, 110
Everett, Alexander, 34, 56, 61, 71, 75
Everett, Edward, 4, 21, 23, 34-35, 56, 61, 71, 73, 166, 168
Everson, Ida G., 8, 23, 34, 167-172
Ewald, Georg H. A., 105

Faust, 10, 13, 18, 25, 34, 37, 38, 40-43, 70, 111, 112, 119, 185
Fay, Theodore S., 135
Fife, Robert H., 188
Fischer, Peter, 19
Fletcher, 68
Flinn, Wm. J., 134, 136, 145
Foerster, Ernst, 171
Follen, Karl, 48, 173
Forum, 182, 187
Franklin, Benjamin, 6
Franz, Johannes, 109
Frauenlob, 115
Frederick, The Great, 80
Freidel, Frank, 182, 189

Freylinghuysen, Fredrick T., 102
Freiligrath, Ferdinand, 37, 171
Fremont, John C., 151
French, John C., 184
Frischlin, Nicodemus, 114, 185
Fritsch, Gräfin, 63
Froelix, Jean Jacques, 78, 85
Froriep, Fr. Ludwig, 30, 40, 60-62, 64, 66, 69, 173, 175
Frothingham, Ellen, 39

Garden, Major, 7, 163
Gauss, C. Fr., 25
Geddings, G, W., 154, 191
Geddings, Dr. V., 154, 191
Geibel, Emanuel, 128-129
George III., 24, 56
Germanic Review, 184
Gersdorff, Ernst Christian August von, 63, 65
Gibson, Tobias, 191
Gildersleeve, Basil Lanneau, 1-3, 33, 139, 162, 182-184, 190-191
Gilman, Daniel Coit, 107
Gmelin, Dean, Johann F., 6
Goebel, Julius, 105, 182
Goedeke, Karl, 185
Goethe, August, 61
Goethe, Johann Wolfgang, 2, 7-8, 10, 13, 18, 24, 28-31, 33-45, 52-54, 59-61, 64, 70-72, 82, 95, 99, 104f., 111f., 125, 132, 137, 148, 153, 159, 160-162, 167, 169-174, 180, 184, 186-187, 189-190
Goethe, Ottilie, 3, 6, 30, 61, 65, 81-82, 84, 95, 161, 178
Goethe, Wolfgang Maximilian, 161-162, 181
Goetz von Berlichingen, 104
Goode, G. W., 91
Graham, Philip, 137
Grant, U. S., 150
Greely, Horace, 100
Green, Dr. E. M., 141, 181, 191, 192
Greenleaf, Simon, 177
Gries, Johann Dietrich, 59, 174
Grisar, Hartmann, 188
Grissom, Daniel M., 102, 182
Grosvenor, Wm., 100
Guerard, George, 2, 19-20, 77, 81, 161, 177
Gudde, Edwin G., 164

Hammer, Carl, 172, 184
Hankins, Virginia, 189
Harbinger, The, 37-39
Harmosan, 122f.

Harrison, Fairfax, 173
Harrison, Francis Burton, 173
Harrison, Gessner, 49, 69
Harrison, Jesse Burton, 1-2, 4, 8, 11-12, 17, 31, 41-55, 57, 59-76, 81, 90, 152, 160, 161, 165-166, 173-175, 190
Hart, Thomas E., 191-192
Hartmann, Prof. Ferdinand H., 70
Hatfield, J. T., 166
Hauff, Walther, 114
Hausmann, J. Fr. L., 105
Haven, George S., 59, 175
Hawley, Lewis R., 189
Hedge, Fr. H., 41, 172
Heeren, A. H. L., 25, 32, 70
Hegel, Georg W., 33
Heine, Heinrich, 55, 114, 132-133
Hellas and Hesperia, 108, 133
Hemphill, C. R., 147
Herder, Joh. Gottfried, 19, 166-167
Hermann, Karl F., 21, 51, 106, 108-110, 114
Hermann and Dorothea, 39, 63
Hesse, L. Otto, 157, 191-192
Hilliard, G. S., 152, 189
Hoeck, K. H., 105-106
Hollis, David W., 166
Holmes, J. A., 189
Holmes, Oliver W., 41
Homer, 17, 64
Houwald, Christoph E., 125
Howitt, Mary, 79, 177
Howitt, Wm., 82, 89
Hubbel, Jay B., 166, 176
Hübner, Emil, 107
Hudson Views (Milbert), 66
Hugo, Gustav, 16, 23
Humboldt, Alexander, 33, 152, 161, 169
Humboldt, Wilhelm, 67, 131, 152, 190
Hume, William, 27, 169
Hutson, C. W., 152

Iphigenie, 35, 112
Irving, Washington, 50, 165

Jackson, Claiborne, Gov., 93
Jagemann, Mad., 65
Jahrbuch für Amerikastudien, 3, 164
James, G. P. R., 176
James, M. E. Cameron, 164
Jameson, Anna, 178
Janell, Walther, 114

195

Jantz, Harold S., 1
Jefferson, Thomas, 46-47, 52, 61, 70, 74, 90, 133, 161, 165, 173, 186
Jenningros, General, 95
Johnson, Dr. Thomas C., 141, 189
Johnstone, Edw. W., 179
Journal of the Elisha Mitchell Scientific Society, 189
Journal of English and Germanic Philology, 163, 171
Joynes, E. S., 147

Kant, Immanuel, 27, 33, 169
Kapp, Hermann, 192
Karl August, Grand Duke, 7, 31
Keats, John, 177
Kent, Duke of, 24
Kepler, Johannes, 33
King, McM., 78, 164
King, Mitchell, 8, 83, 159-160, 164
Kirby-Smith, General, 94, 95, 180
Kirchhoff, Gustav R., 140, 157, 187-188, 192
Klopstock, Friedrich G., 166
Klueber, J. L., 37
Koerner, Gustav, 92, 180
Koerner, Gustavus A., 180
Kossack, H., xii
Kossuth, Louis, 92
Kotzebue, August von, 69
Krabusch, Hans, 177, 191
Kraister, Charles, 179
Kriemhilde, 115
Krumpelmann, John T., 170-171, 187
Kudrun, 115
Kunst und Alterthum, 10

Laborde, M., 165, 189, 190
Lachmann, Karl, 109
Lafayette, Marquis de, 46
Laffert, Herr von, 24, 32, 56, 58
Landseer, Sir Edwin, 185
Lane, G. M., 154, 191
Langenbeck, Konrad J. M., 25
Lanier, Sidney, 136-138, 148, 187
Lanneau, John F., 158
Lanneau, Susie G., 158
Lavater, John. Kaspar, 42, 43
Lawrence, James, 63
Legaré, Hugh Swinton, 1-3, 6, 8, 9-13, 16-22, 33, 50, 52, 70, 77-80, 83, 87, 90, 164-167, 173-174, 176-177

Legaré, Joseph, 153, 155
Leibnitz, Gottfried Wilhelm, 33
Leonard, Karl Caesar, 135
Lessing, Gotthold Ephraim, 25, 33, 71, 130, 168
Leutsch, Prof. Ernst L. von, 106, 109
Lewes, George Henry, 39
Lieber, Francis, 48, 69, 78, 98, 100-101, 149-150, 173, 177-178, 181, 189
Lieber, Oscar M., 69, 98, 189-190
Liebig, Justus, 151
Lieder, Fr. C. W., 35
Linné, Carl von, 164
Lippincott's Magazine, 187
Livingston, Edward, 9
Long, George, 47, 173
Long, Orie William, 1-3, 17, 25, 164, 166-168, 173, 186
Longfellow, Henry Wadsworth, 3-4, 13, 17, 34, 36-37, 41, 99-100, 159, 162, 166, 171, 177
Longfellow, Samuel, 171
Lord, S., 154, 156, 190
Louisiana Advertiser, 74, 75
Louisiana Historical Quarterly, 176
Louisiana, Historical Society of, 73
Lowndes, 7, 163
Lowndes, J., 163
Lucas, J. J. 157, 192
Luden, Prof., Heinrich, 64-65, 173
Luthardt, Christoph E., 141
Luther, Martin, 18, 33-34, 41, 80-82, 89, 114, 144, 172, 188

McClure, William, 164
McClurg, Joseph W., 89
McCormack, Thomas J., 180
McDuffie, George, 166
McElroy, John, 180
McIntosh, James, 15-16
Macaulay, Thomas B., 137
Madison, James, 48-49
Magnus, Heinrich Gustav, 150
Magruder, John B., 94
Manfred, 10
Marquardt, Hertha, 6, 23, 167
Marshall, John, 68, 175
Martens, G. F., 48
Martin, F. X., 72
Martin, Margaret, 178
Martius, Karl Fr. Ph. von, 81, 178
Maryland Historical Magazine, 169
Mathisson, Friedrich, 34
Maxcy, Virgil, 77
Maximilian (Habsburg), 95-98

* Meade, Mr. 60
Melanchthon, 18, 80, 82
Menzel, Wolfgang, 110
Merck, Heinrich, 42
Michaelwitz, Edward M., 12
Middleton, Harry, 19, 60
Miller, C. W. E., 133
Milman, Henry Hart, 177
Milton, John, 3, 127
Mims, Edwin, 187
Mississippi Blaetter, 99
Missouri Democrat, 92
Missouri Historical Review, 176, 180, 181
Missouri Republican, 180, 182
Mitscherlich, Christoph Wilhelm, 105, 150
Mittermaier, Karl J. A., 78, 177
Monroe, James, 74
Moore, Thomas O., Gov., 94
Motley, John L., 2-3, 137, 159
Mozart, Wolfgang A., 59
Mueller, Otfried, 25, 32
Müller, C. O., Prof., 54
Müllner, Adolf, 69
Musson, Michel, 159

Napton, Wm. B., 101, 180
Nassé, Dr., 16
Needler, G. A., 178
New Orleans Bee, 73
Newport Mercury, 39
New York Review, 20-21, 30, 167
New York Times, 41, 111, 172, 186
Nibelungenlied, 16, 28
Niebuhr, Barthold G., 10, 16, 32, 48, 70, 170
Nietzsche, Friedrich, 114, 184
Nimmo, R. M., 92
Noll, A. H., 180
North American Review, 21, 30, 35-36, 73, 165, 176
Northrup, Milton H., 136, 187
Norwell, Wm. W., 174
Novalis (Hardenberg, Fr. von), 138
Nunn, W. C., 180

Oberammergau, 126
Oldenburg, Grand Duke, 63
Oliphant, Mary Simms, 176
Overbeck, Prof, (Bonn), 183

Paine, Thomas, 25
Palfrey, John G., 73

* Cf. Goethe, *Tagebücher* (W.A.) 12, 100, 4.

Pappenheim, 63, 65
Passy (i.e. Parry), James Patrick, 60
Patton, Robert Bridges, 23
Paul, Czar, 7
Paulowna, Maria, 7, 67
Peabody, Dr. Oliver W. B., 71
Pearce, Colonel, 161
Percival, James Gates, 50
Perkins, Francis, 166
Perkins, Judge John, 138, 144
Perry, Bliss, 45
Perry, Thomas S., 189, 190
Pfund, Harry W., 35, 44
Phaedra, 15
Picayune, Daily, 76
Pindar, 56, 111, 115, 126-128
Platen, August, Graf von (Hallermünde), 119-122, 125, 127, 133, 184-186
Plunkett, Randal Edward, 60, 64, 66
Poe, Edgar Allan, 36
Poinsett, Joel R., 7, 8, 83, 152, 164
Polk, James Knox, 179
Porter, Alexander, 72, 73, 75
Pozzo di Borgo, 14
Prescott, W. C., 173
Preston, William C., 9, 165
Preston, Wm., Gov., 94
Preston, John Smith, 75
Princeton Review, 186
Pringle, Sir John, 6
Pringle, E. A., 163
Pringle, John Julius, 163, 192
Pringle, J. R., 163
Pritchard, Walter, 176
Pulitzer, J., 100
Pusey, Edward B., 27, 169
Putman's Monthly Magazine, 39, 168-170, 172

Quarterly Review, Methodist Episcopal Church, 114, 185
Quitman, Friedrich H., 168
Quitman, John A., 23, 168

Racine, 15
Ramsay, David, 64, 107, 126, 153, 155-156, 174, 185, 190
Randolf, Mrs., 173
Ranke, Leopold von, 109
Reichlin-Waldegg, Karl Alexander, 192
Remsen, Ira, 107-108, 184

197

Republican (Springfield, Mass.), 145
Retzsch, Moritz, 18
Reynolds, Heloise Marie, 180
Reynolds, James L., 101, 180
Reynolds, R., 49
Reynolds, Thomas C., 1-4, 19-20, 49, 77-83, 86, 89-92, 139, 160-161, 176-178, 180-181, 187
Rhea, Lina, 165-167
Richter, Christian Otto, 171
Richter, Jean Paul, 6, 33, 36-37, 114, 138
Riemer, Prof., Friedrich Wilhelm, 62
Risson, Johannis, 187
Ritschl, Albrecht, 106, 108, 110, 183
Ritter, Carl, 105, 106, 109
Ritter, F., 183
Rives, Alexander, 179
Rives, W. C., 83, 88
Roberts, T. N., 158
Robinson, Mrs., 81
Röth, Eduard Maximilian, Dekan, 135, 186
Roeth, Gustav, 114
Rombeau, Ernst, xii
Rose, Gustav, 150, 190
Rose, Hugh, 7
Roselius, C., 75
Rubens, Peter Paul, 2, 23
Rückert, Friedrich, 114, 122, 125
Ruppaner, Anthony, 41
Rusk, Ralph L,. 169
Russell, John, 64-65, 175

Saalfeld, Friedrich, 28, 56
Sachtleben, A., 190
Sales, Francis, 47
Santi, Comte, 63
Sartorius, Georg, 28, 48
Saunders, Romulus M., 89, 179
Savigny, Friedrich K., 16, 20, 77
Schele de Vere, Max R., 88, 179-181
Schelling, Joseph, 169
Schiller, J. F. C., 3, 10, 17, 19, 32-35, 38, 40, 53, 69f., 93, 112-114, 130, 167, 170-171
Schlegel, August Wm., 3, 10, 12-17, 19, 32, 53, 60, 70-71, 77, 90, 110, 113, 166, 174, 177
Schmidt, Oscar, 143
Schmidt, Prof., Leopold Valentin (Bonn), 106
Schneidewin, F. W., 106, 110
Schwarz, Carl, 100, 180
Schütz, Professor, Christian V. (Heidelberg), 12

Scopes, J. T., 146, 189
Scott, General Winfield, 52, 53
Sealsfield, Charles, 164
Seebach, Friedrich von, 60
Semple, J. W., 27
Sewanee Review, 184-185
Seward, William H., 97
Shakespeare, William, 3, 17, 19, 54, 69, 71
Shelby, General, 95-96
Shelly, Percy B., 169, 172
Sherman, Wm. Tecumseh, 98
Shoemaker, Floyd, C., 180
Shorey, Paul, 133
Shumway, Daniel B., 6, 191
Sidons, C. (Karl Postl, Charles Sealsfield), 74
Siegling, John, 81
Silz, Walter, 184
Simms, W. Gilmore, 81-82, 89, 91, 156, 178, 179
Simonde de Sismondi, J. C. L., 90
Simrock, Karl, 166
Smith, David W., 177
Smith, H. Joseph, 135
Smith, J. Allen, 7-8, 163
Socrates, 16
Sonnenschein, Solomon H., 101
Soret, Frédéric, 60
South Carolina Historical and Genealogical Magazine, 163, 164
Southern Literary Journal, 176
Southern Literary Messenger, 36, 38, 78-79, 82, 89, 119-120, 167, 176, 178, 180, 185
Southern Presbyterian Review, 139-141, 187-188
Southern Quarterly Review, 89, 180
Southern Review, 9, 10, 12, 21, 70, 184
Southern Review (Baltimore), 50, 119
Southwestern Presbyterian, 145
Spiegel, Karl Emil von, 62-63, 65, 81
Spohr, Louis, 59
Sprague, Caleb, 21
Sprague, Horatio, 91
Staël, Madame de, 14, 32
Stahl, Friedrich Julius, 109
Starke, Aubrey, 137, 187
Starr, Robert, C. 191
Stein, Charlotte von, 42
Stein, Luise (Mrs. James P. Parry), 60
Stevens, Walter B., 179, 182

Stieler, Joseph Karl, 176
Stier, Charles, 32
Stille, Charles J., 164
Stolberg, Countess, 42
Story, Joseph, 1, 79, 85, 177
Strauss, David, 185
Strohmeyer, Heinrich, 65
Sumner, Charles, 78, 85, 150, 177

Talmage, President, Samuel Kennedy, 143
Tanhuser, Ballad of, 115ff.
Tasso, 35
Taussig, James, 101
Taylor, Bayard, 32, 34, 40-42, 170-172, 187
Taylor, Marie Hansen, 172
Tennyson, Alfred, 137
Texas Republican, 94
Thackeray, Wm. M., 70
Theognis, 114
Thiersch, Fr. Wm., 179
Thomas, J. Wesley, 178
Thornwell, James H., 134, 143
Thucydides, 20, 110, 114
Ticknor, George, 1, 6, 9, 13, 17-19, 21, 25, 46-49, 56, 71, 90-91, 133, 165-168, 173, 186
Tidyman, Philipp, 2, 6-7, 159, 163
Tieck, Ludwig, 71, 74
Tiedeman, Dietrich T., 12, 165
Tocqueville, Alexis de, 15, 166
Tracie, M. L., 49
Trist, N. P., 49, 70, 72, 173
Tyler, John, 6

Vahlen, Johannes, 107
Van Buren, Martin, 8, 52, 74
Vedemeyer, Frau von, 24
Venable, Charles Scott, 151
Ventz, 55
Viles, Jonas, 182
Virchow, Rudolf, 142, 143
Voltaire (Arouet de), 10, 80
Vulpius, Christine, 61, 65

Wachsmuth, Wilhelm, 21
Wackerhagen, A., 168
Wadepfuhl, Walter, 162, 190
Waitz, Georg W., 105

Walker, Timothy, 71
Wallenstein, 18, 35, 64
Walsh, R., 173
Walter, W. D., 154, 191
Walz, John Albrecht, 171
Warden, D. B., 176
Warner, Augustine, 77
Warner, J. Lee, 66
Washington, George, 77, 168, 182
Watson, Seth B., 27
Weber, Georg, 105
Webster, Daniel, 46, 71
Wedemeyer, Johann Friedrich, 56, 58
Weinart, Erich, 146
Weir, William, 27
Welcker, Fr. G., 47, 106, 108-110, 183, 184
Werther, 10
Westöstlicher Divan, 112
Westliche Post, 93, 99
Wheaton, Henry, 77, 84-85, 87, 177
White, Edward D., 71, 75
White, Edward Douglas, 71
Whitter, J. G., 41
Wieland, Christian Martin, 118
Wieland, Prof. (in Leipzig), 28
Wilamowitz-Moellendorf, Ulrich, 113, 115
Wilcox, General Cadmus M., 95
Wilson, J. H., 154, 191
Wilson, Joseph, 186
Wilson, Woodrow, 2-3, 144, 186, 189
Winckelmann, Joh. Joachim, 10
Wirth, William, 71
Wöhler, Friedrich, 151
Wolf, Christian, 13
Wölfflin, Prof., Eduard, 107
Woodley, Willis H., 83, 88
Woodrow, James, 1-3, 158, 187-188, 189
Woodrow, Marion W., 142, 186
Wordsworth, William, 169
Wrisberg, Prof., Heinrich August, 6

York, Duke of, 24

Zauberlehrling, der, 112
Zelter, Dekan, 191, 192
Zobir, 122ff.

www.ingramcontent.com/pod-product-compliance
Lightning Source LLC
Chambersburg PA
CBHW020757160426
43192CB00006B/360